TARA: A SELECT BIBLIOGRAPHY

TARA

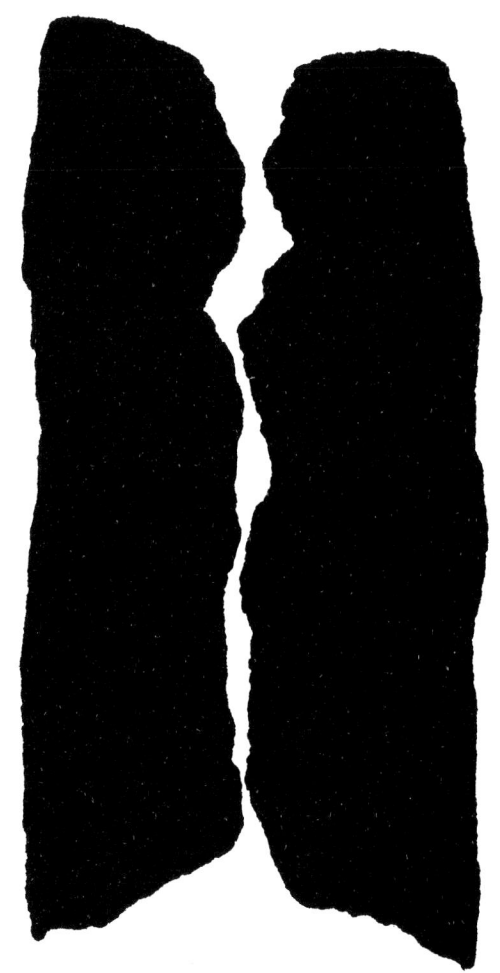

A SELECT BIBLIOGRAPHY
Edel Bhreathnach

DISCOVERY PROGRAMME MONOGRAPHS 1

First published in 1995
for the Discovery Programme
by the Royal Irish Academy,
19 Dawson Street, Dublin 2.
Copyright © Royal Irish Academy 1995.
Reprinted April 1998

All rights reserved. No part of this book may be
reprinted or reproduced or utilised in any
electronic, mechanical or other means, now
known or hereafter invented, including
photocopying and recording, or otherwise without
either the prior written consent of the publishers
or a licence permitting restricted copying in
Ireland issued by the Irish Copyright Licensing
Agency Ltd, The Writers' Centre,
19 Parnell Square, Dublin 1.

ISBN 1 874045 35 6

British Library Cataloguing-in-Publication Data.
A catalogue record for this book is available from
the British Library.

Typeset in Ireland by Wordwell Ltd
Printed by Colour Books

Cover image: Louis le Brocquy
Cover design: Geraldine Garland

THE DISCOVERY
PROGRAMME

AR THÓIR NA SEAN

**Royal Irish Academy/
Discovery Programme
Dublin 1995**

CONTENTS

Preface	vii
Acknowledgements	ix

INTRODUCTION

Kingship, mythology and sovereignty	1
High-kingship, the Uí Néill and 'synthetic historians'	10
Saints and their biographers	21
The archaeology and topography of Tara	27
The name *Temair*	34

BIBLIOGRAPHY

Notes and conventions	43
Primary sources	47
History and pseudo-history	47
A. Annals	48
B. Regnal lists	50
C. Genealogies	52
D. Law-tracts and associated texts	55
E. Hagiology and calendars	59
F. Topographical texts	67
G. Charters, deeds and papal documents	70
H. Prophecies	73
I. *Mirabilia*	74
J. Taboos	76
K. Triads	77
L. Glossaries	77
M. *Audacht Morainn*	78
N. *Lebor Gabála Érenn* and associated tales	79
Narrative literature and verse	82
O. General	83
P. Mythological Cycle	83

Q.	Ulster Cycle	85
R.	Cycle of Kings	88
S.	Fenian Cycle (*Fíanaigecht*)	102
T.	Verse	103

Literary interpretation of the sources 108

AA.	General studies	109
BB.	Kingship and sovereignty	110
CC.	Inauguration rites	114
DD.	Lug	116

Historical interpretation of the sources 117

EE.	General studies	118
FF.	The high-kingship of Ireland	118
GG.	*Feis Temro*	124
HH.	Tara and Iona	125
II.	Tara and Cashel	126
JJ.	The Gailenga and the Luigne	127

Archaeology and topography 130

KK.	General studies	131
LL.	Surveys of Tara	134
MM.	Monuments at Tara	136
NN.	Roadways	140
OO.	Excavations	140
PP.	Objects	145
QQ.	The hinterland of Tara	148
RR.	Popular descriptions and local notes	153
SS.	Tara in Ireland and Scotland	154
TT.	The characteristics of royal sites and assemblies	155

INDEXES 157

Authors	158
Sources	164
Proper names	167
Place-names and tribal names	170
Monuments at Tara	173

PREFACE

George Petrie communicated his masterly essay 'On the history and antiquities of Tara Hill' to the members of the Royal Irish Academy in 1837. He began his paper with the following comments (1839, 25):

> The locality to which this paper relates is the well-known hill of Tara, —a spot which has been celebrated by native as well as foreign writers as the chief seat of the Irish monarchs, from the earliest dawn of their history down to the middle of the sixth century, at which period it was deserted. But though its ancient splendour has been the theme of most modern Irish antiquaries and historians, their labours have thrown but little light either on its past state or existing remains, and have made but little impression on the minds of the learned.

It is ironic that over 150 years later Petrie's observations continue to describe the state of scholarship concerning Tara in the intervening period. Progress has been made in certain fields. Texts relating to Tara have been edited critically and translated. Literary analysts have tackled aspects of the mythology surrounding Tara, while historians have attempted, in recent decades in particular, to disentangle fact from the layers of fiction which form part of the literature associated with Tara. Archaeologists have also contributed by excavation and survey. Despite the labours of such experts, basic questions as to the origin, function, attributes and abandonment of the site remain unanswered. The impression left by the work of the experts to date on the minds of the learned, and more so on the popular mind, is best summed up in the acerbic words of D.A. Binchy (1982, 167) when commenting on the popular view that Saint Patrick kindled the paschal fire on the Hill of Slane in defiance of the 'high-king', Lóegaire, who was surrounded by his druids at Tara:

> Hence I underestimated the tenacity with which a 'national epic'—more particularly a politico-religious epic—can withstand all attempts to question its historical truth. We must therefore be resigned to seeing the story of the paschal fire figure side by side with the myth of the 'national monarchy' in our standard text-books. Even though an objective study may show both of them to be fictitious, this will not affect their popular appeal.

Tara, in the popular mind, continues to be associated with the high-kings of Ireland, with Saint Patrick competing with druids, and with gods and goddesses of ancient times. Much work needs to be done. It seems worthwhile, however, to review the scholarship associated with Tara since Petrie wrote his treatise and to establish the progress of experts on the topic to date.

The purpose of this publication is twofold. The Introduction is a survey of texts which are most relevant to our understanding of Tara and of the main themes which have been the focus of scholarship on Tara. These themes concentrate for the most part on concepts of kingship, mythology and sovereignty, on the high-kingship of Tara, on hagiographical connections with Tara, and on the archaeology and topography of Tara. The Introduction amounts to a general thematic survey of the published material presented in the Bibliography and may be read independently of the Bibliography itself—hence the inclusion of a separate list of references at the end. The reference system of the Introduction adheres to that used in Discovery Programme publications.

The Bibliography, which follows, is an annotated and select bibliography of the published material relating to Tara, divided between primary and secondary sources and subdivided into a series of categories. Such is the nature of the published material relating to Tara that, with the notable exception of a small number of key studies (e.g. Petrie 1839; Macalister 1931; Ó Ríordáin 1954; Binchy 1958b; Byrne 1969) which concentrate solely on Tara, most studies refer to one aspect of Tara as evidence for a specific subject. Moreover, the archaeological and topographical material is repetitive, constant reference being made to the studies by Petrie, Macalister and Ó Ríordáin. It was felt necessary, therefore, to include a wide range of material in the Bibliography to gain a good impression of scholarly conclusions concerning Tara, and in including this material some indication is given of the relevance of each entry to Tara. The Bibliography attempts to address the interests of various readers, expert and amateur, be they linguistic, literary, historical or archaeological specialists. Its primary objectives are to provide a guide to the most important publications on Tara and to attempt to establish a chronological framework for the primary texts and secondary works which are included in the Bibliography.

George Eogan

Chairman
Discovery Programme

ACKNOWLEDGEMENTS

The author acknowledges the assistance of many people in preparing this study. I am particularly grateful to Siobhán Ní Laoire, School of Celtic Studies, Dublin Institute for Advanced Studies, for her advice on bibliographical matters, to Christopher Philpott for his work in establishing the database for the Bibliography, and to Dr John Carey, School of Celtic Studies, Dublin Institute for Advanced Studies, for his thorough reading of the text and for his many valuable comments. Professor Pádraig Ó Riain, University College Cork, Dr Richard Sharpe, University of Oxford, Dr Thomas Charles-Edwards, University of Oxford, Professor Próinséas Ní Chatháin, University College Dublin, Professor Etienne Rynne, University College Galway, and Professor John Waddell, University College Galway, were most generous with their advice on the content and structure of the Bibliography, leading to many improvements in the publication. For their assistance at various times during the project I wish to thank the Director, School of Celtic Studies, Dublin Institute for Advanced Studies; Dr Marie Therese Flanagan, Queen's University, Belfast; Aideen Ireland, the National Archives; Siobhán de hÓir, Royal Society of Antiquaries of Ireland; Conor Newman, Dr Eoin Grogan and Kathleen O'Sullivan, Discovery Programme; and Siobhán O'Rafferty, Royal Irish Academy. I am most grateful to Raghnall Ó Floinn, National Museum of Ireland, for his constant encouragement and invaluable advice at all times. Without his and other contributions the work would have been less complete. Finally, I wish to thank my parents for their support and willingness to assist at all times during the past few years.

Edel Bhreathnach
June 1995

I

INTRODUCTION

KINGSHIP, MYTHOLOGY AND SOVEREIGNTY

The sacred and unusual nature of the kingship of Tara has been the theme of many scholarly works. Ritual inaugurations and assemblies, specific taboos, associations with certain goddesses who represent sovereignty, the Otherworldly nature of the kingship and its concepts of truth and justice leading to prosperity and fertility are aspects which occur frequently in the published material. These abstract concepts lead inevitably to Tara as constant reference is made to its heroic and mythological kings, Conaire Mór, Cormac mac Airt and Conn Cétchathach; its pseudo-historical kings, Níall Noígíallach and Lóegaire mac Néill; its historical king, Diarmait mac Cerbaill; its goddesses Medb (both as Medb Chrúachna and Medb Lethderg) and Eithne; the god Lug; and the ritual assembly, *Feis Temro*.

An essential introduction to all aspects of the kingship of Tara is provided in Byrne's *Irish kings and high-kings* in the chapter entitled 'The kingship of Tara' (1973, 48–69), in which the conclusion is reached that the kingship was 'cultic and probably intermittent' (*ibid.*, 57), a conclusion often repeated by the author. Binchy provided a similar introduction to the kingship of Tara in his monograph *Celtic and Anglo-Saxon kingship* (1970). He regarded the Tara monarchy as holding a special significance from earliest times, 'doubtless religious in origin' (*ibid.*, 11).

Tara and the ideology of kingship

One of the earliest studies on the kingship of Tara is Baudiš's paper 'On the antiquity of the kingship of Tara' (1916). Baudiš set out to prove that the significance assigned to Tara was not in origin a Milesian forgery 'intended to invest the seat of the parvenu conquerors with some of the splendour of antiquity' (*ibid.*, 102), but rather was chosen by the newcomers (the Milesians) because of its ancient fame. Basing his conclusions on the descriptions of taboos (*geisi*) and of the ordeals facing the heroic king of Tara, Conaire Mór, who sought to become and remain king of Tara, in the ninth-century text *Togail Bruidne Da Derga* and in the possibly earlier text *De Shíl Chonairi Móir*, Baudiš described the kingship of Tara as preserving 'in a remarkable degree the characteristics of a priest-kingship' (*ibid.*, 107). The colourful description of the ordeals awaiting Conaire Mór before he is recognised as king of Tara preserved in *De Shíl Chonairi Móir* is quoted frequently as evidence of the sacral nature of the kingship (Gwynn 1912, 134, 138–9):

> *Bai carpat ríg hi Temair nogabtais da ech oendatha nad ragabaitis riam fon carpat. Inti nad airoemath flaith Temrach, conocbath in carpat fris conachmoceth ⁊ concligtis ind hich fris. ⁊ bai casal ríg isin carbad. Intí nad aurimeth flaith Temrach ba romor do in chasal. ⁊ batar da liaic hi Temuir .i. Blocc ⁊ Bluigne; inti arfoemtis, arosilctis fris co teged in carpat etarru. ⁊ bai Fal and, Ferp Cluche, for cind oenig in charbait; inti arfemath flaith Temrach gloedad in Fal fri fonnad in charpait conidcluneth cach. Inti nad aurimeth flaith Temrach, ni airslaictis riam na da liaic .i. Bloc ⁊ Blugne. Ise mod ticed hochair lame eturru; ⁊ inti nad auremeth flaith Temrach, ni screted in Fal fria fonnad.*

There was a king's chariot at Tara. To the chariot were yoked two steeds of the same colour, which had never before been harnessed. It would tilt up before any man who was not destined to receive the kingship of Tara, so that he could not control(?) it, and the horses would spring at him. And there was a king's mantle in the chariot; whoso might not receive Tara's sovereignty the mantle was ever too big for him. And there were two flag-stones in Tara: 'Blocc' and 'Bluigne'; when they accepted a man, they would open before him until the chariot went through. And Fál was there, the 'stone penis' at the head of the chariot-course(?); when a man should have the kingship of Tara, it screeched against his chariot-axle, so that all might hear. But the two stones Blocc and Bluigne would not open before one who should not hold the sovereignty of Tara, and their usual position was such, that one's hand could only pass sideways between them; also he who was not to hold Tara's kingship, the Fál would not screech against his axle.

Wagner (1970, 17), in his constant search for comparisons with other cultures, regarded the symbol of the chariot drawn by horses as part of the symbolic array of kingship found in Iranian, Thracian, Roman(?) and Celtic traditions. He sought an explanation for the motif of the *fál*, the *ferp cluche*, which screeched against the *fonnad* of the chariot when the rightful king drove it, in the seventh-century text on kingship *Audacht Morainn* (Kelly 1976). A paragraph in this text advises the king to 'observe the driver of the old chariot' (*arid sencharpait*) who 'does not sleep' and 'looks ahead and behind' and 'defends, protects, so that he may not break(?) with neglect or violence the wheel-rims which run under him' (*na forráin fonnath fod-rethat*) (Kelly 1976, 8–9 §22, 33 §22). Wagner explains that the *fonnad* of the chariot is the *pars pro toto* term for the chariot, symbolising reality and truth (*fír flathemon*). Since *fonnad* probably means 'foundation' (derived from *fonn* 'bottom, foundation, soil, piece of land, territory'), the *fonnad* of the chariot was a symbol of the earth, 'the "female" part of the chariot looking for the *fál*, the rightful holder of the kingship' (Wagner

1970, 19). The editor of *Audacht Morainn* regards the chariot as symbolising the rule of the king, a symbol which can be compared with the classical 'ship of state' metaphor (Kelly 1976, 33).

The concept of *fír flathemon* 'the justice of a ruler', promulgated in *Audacht Morainn* (Kelly 1976, 6–11 §§12–28) as being essential to the successful rule of a king (though not specifically the king of Tara), is echoed strongly in texts associated with the kingship of Tara. The reigns of the heroic kings of Tara, Conaire Mór and Cormac mac Airt, were based on *fír flathemon*, a concept which encompassed fertility, justice, peace and truth. They became kings of Tara because they were recognised for their ability to rule justly and prosperously. Their reigns were successful for the same reason. Conaire transgressed taboos and thus the peace enjoyed during his reign came to an end. Cormac was blinded and therefore, as a blemished king, could continue to reign no longer.

The complex ideology which forms the basis of these concepts associated with kingship is explored by Ó Cathasaigh in his various works of literary analysis. He has demonstrated, for example, the relationship between the two meanings of the word *síd,* meaning both 'peace' and 'Otherworld hill or mound', on the basis of the texts associated with Conaire Mór and Cormac mac Airt (Ó Cathasaigh 1977–9). The two meanings of the word *síd* form part of the ideology of kingship. There is a clear relationship between the Otherworld and peace, a relationship which is mediated in the person of the king (*ibid.*, 147). Furthermore, 'the ideology of kingship is matched by the symbols and rituals which surround the office', and in particular by the inauguration rites of the king. Sites known as *síde* — the tumuli or hills on which inauguration rites were performed — furnish 'the physical or material correlative of the abstract connections' with the other meaning of *síd* 'peace' (*ibid.*, 148).

The terminology for the abstract concepts which are the opposite of *síd* is explored by Ó Cathasaigh in his discussion of the word *lomrad* 'shearing, melting away', a word which appears to symbolise a central theme in the ninth-century text *Cath Maige Mucrama* (O Daly 1975). *Lomrad* plays a significant part in the episode in which the false judgement made by the king of Tara, Lugaid mac Con, led to the collapse of the *Clóenfherta* (Sloping Trenches) at Tara and to the assumption by Cormac mac Airt of the kingship of Tara (Ó Cathasaigh 1980–1). *Lomrad* is an element in the Irish ideology of kingship, in which the king has a pivotal role in the determination of the fertility of the land: it conveys the negative aspect of this fertility, namely the laying waste of the land (*ibid.*, 224). The role in Irish tradition of Cormac mac Airt, the heroic king so beloved of many a commentator on Tara, is carefully analysed in Ó Cathasaigh's study *The heroic biography of Cormac mac Airt* (1977). He concludes that Cormac is a hero of kingship and that his heroic biography 'is adapted to the Irish ideology of kingship; the king is centre of the cosmos' (*ibid.*, 104). As to Cormac's historicity, he leaves it as an open question, allowing for the possibility that the 'real' Cormac may have been a creature of myth (*ibid.*, 104).

The Otherworldly patrons of Tara

While Conaire Mór and Cormac are the heroic kings most closely associated with Tara, the kingship of Tara seems also to have had its Otherworldly patrons in the god Lug and the goddesses Medb — in her manifestations as Medb Chrúachna and Medb Lethderg — and Eithne. Notice is taken in many works of Lug and Medb, but certain texts and the analysis of them are essential to our understanding of their respective roles. In general terms, it would appear that Lug is the divine manifestation of the kingship of Tara, while Medb is the female aspect of the kingship, its fertility and, ultimately, the symbol of its sovereignty. The connection between Tara and Lug reappears constantly. O'Rahilly (1946a, 277–8, 283) and Wagner (1970, 58), among others, regarded him as the progenitor or ancestor-deity of Tara, whose voice was heard through the utterances of the *Lia Fáil*. There appears to be a link between Lug and Lugaid mac Con, Cormac mac Airt's predecessor as king of Tara, although Lugaid may reflect the coalescing of various traditions centred in Munster with those located at Tara (O Daly 1975, 3–6; Ó Riain 1978, 151–3). The Luigne, a tribe settled west of Tara towards Kells, may have regarded themselves as descendants of Lug, though the linguistic evidence for this association is not as transparent as might at first appear to be the case (Ahlqvist 1974–6). It is notable that *Óenach Tailten,* 'held under the aegis of the king of Tara' (Binchy 1958b, 126), was celebrated on the festival of Lugnasad, and that Tailtiu, the goddess after whom the site of the *óenach* is named, is described in a topographical tract in *Dindshenchas Érenn* as the foster-mother of Lug. This familial connection is viewed, however, by Thurneysen (1936, 369) and by Binchy (1958b, 123) as a figment of poetic imagination.

The ninth-century text *Cath Maige Tuired* (Gray 1982), generally interpreted as reflecting the myth of the War of the Gods (Ó Cathasaigh 1983, 1), includes the well-known episode in which Lug enters Tara and assumes the kingship of Tara. Here is Ó Cathasaigh's summary of the lengthy episode (1983, 6):

> Lug arrives unannounced at Tara, 'a young warrior, fair and shapely, wearing the crown of a king', and leading a band of strangers. His name is announced to the doorkeeper, and he asks Lug what art he practises, for none without an art enters Tara. Lug says that he is a wright. The doorkeeper replies, 'We do not need you. We have a wright already, one Luchtae, son of Luachaid'. Then Lug says that he is a smith; but the doorkeeper's response is as before: they do not need him, they already have a smith. The dialogue goes on like this for a long time, Lug naming his various skills and the doorkeeper rejecting him. Finally Lug says: 'Ask the king whether he has a single man who includes all these arts, and if he has I shall not enter Tara'. Nuadu says that Lug should be admitted and he then goes into the fortress and sits in the sage's seat, for he is a sage of every art. Then Nuadu decides to change seats with Lug, and so Lug goes to the king's seat. For thirteen days, Nuadu 'rises up before' Lug in homage.

Lug is the *ildánach* or *samildánach*, the omnicompetent god. The episode is similar to the entry of Cormac mac Airt to Tara, where Lugaid mac Con relinquished the kingship of Tara to the youthful Cormac (Ó Cathasaigh 1983, 7). The importance of the term (*sam*)*ildánach*, which incorporates the term *dán* 'art' or 'craft', and the relationship between the *áes dáno* (the 'artists' or 'craftsmen') and the king and society are examined in detail by the editor of *Cath Maige Tuired* (Gray 1982–3, 17–29). She concludes elsewhere that Lug as master of all the arts is equivalent to all the *áes dáno* in Tara, who themselves represent the entire society (Gray 1989–90, 41).

Lug's association with the kingship and sovereignty of Tara is emphasised in the text *Baile in Scáil*, a text likely to have been compiled originally in the ninth century but which was added to in the early eleventh century (Meyer 1901; 1918; Herbert 1992). Conn Cétchathach, ancestor of the Dál Cuinn kings of Tara, finds himself in the Otherworld confronted by Lug, sitting on a throne and accompanied by a girl wearing a gold crown, whom Lug identifies as the sovereignty of Ireland. On Lug's instructions the girl gives Conn a drink of ale from a golden cup, and when she asks who should have the next drink, Lug names Conn's successor as king of Tara. Thus the list continues until the kings of Tara to the early eleventh century are named. This tale has been regarded as a version of the myth of sovereignty, in which the goddess of sovereignty legitimises the king's reign by means of a libation (Breatnach 1953). Lug is presented as the legitimator of the Uí Néill kings of Tara, each king being wedded to Lug's consort (the goddess of kingship), and in some sense seen as Lug's surrogate in the kingship of Tara (Ó Cathasaigh 1989, 31–2; 1983, 12). It is significant that in *Baile in Scáil* it is Lug who instructs the girl to dispense the libation. The god, Lug, is depriving the goddess of sovereignty of her right to bestow power, which is the more widely accepted understanding of the myth of sovereignty. It has been suggested that this change in emphasis from goddess to god may be due to the contemporary purpose of the text (and similarly that of the other example of the sovereignty myth, *Echtra mac nEchdach Mugmedóin*) (Herbert 1992), a matter discussed in the next section.

The theme of the relationship between the king and the goddess is one which permeates scholarship, especially in relation to its role in the legitimisation of kingship in early Ireland. It has been addressed in detail by Mac Cana in his papers 'Aspects of the theme of king and goddess in Irish literature' (1955–6; 1958–9) and by McCone in his study 'Fírinne agus torthúlacht' (1980). The goddesses who legitimised the kings of Tara were Medb — as Medb Chrúachna and Medb Lethderg — and Eithne. Medb's prowess in acquiring spouses — said to reflect her role as the goddess of sovereignty, the personification of kingship — is related in the Middle Irish text *Ferchuitred Medba* (O'Neill 1905; Meyer 1913). Medb Lethderg, Medb's manifestation in Leinster, was supposed to have ruled Tara herself in the interregnum between Art mac Cuinn and his son Cormac (Greene 1955, 31), a tradition which conflicts with that of the reign of Lugaid mac Con prior to that of Cormac mentioned in *Cath Maige Mucrama*. In an extensive study of Medb's attributes, Ó Máille (1928, 139) concluded that she was 'nothing else than the sovereignty of

Ireland'. Wagner (1975, 20–1) argued that in Celtic belief the sacral hilltop seems to have been identified with the goddess herself, pointing out that while Lug was Cú Chulainn's father, so Emer, Cú Chulainn's wife, was a representative of the hilltop-goddess *Temair* and therefore ultimately identical with Medb, whose name is another epithet of the ancestor-goddess of Tara. O'Rahilly, in his masterful discussion of aspects of the goddesses of early Ireland in their many manifestations (1946b), examined the concept of the intoxicating drink offered to the kings of Tara by Medb, a name probably associated in origin with intoxication, and by her double Etaín, whose special gift was the serving of drink in Tara. 'Receiving the cup of drink from the goddess, or winning her cup, was tantamount to winning the goddess herself' (*ibid.*, 15–16). Eithne Thóebfhota, the other goddess associated with the sovereignty of Tara (O'Rahilly 1952, 18–19), features in the Middle Irish tale *Esnada Tige Buchet* as daughter of Cathaír Mór, king of Leinster, fostered to Buchet, the hospitaller (Greene 1955, 27–44). Eithne is raped by Cormac mac Airt and begets his son, Cairpre Liphechair. In a manner similar to *Baile in Scáil* and *Echtra mac nEchdach Mugmedóin,* this tale, which is told from a Leinster viewpoint, may combine elements of the sovereignty tale with contemporary political resonances.

While the goddess could give life to the king and legitimise his reign through sexual union with him, she could also act as goddess of death and cause his downfall when he became an unjust king. Máire Bhreathnach (1982) explains this role in relation to the heroic king of Tara, Conaire Mór, and to the pseudo-historical king of Tara, Muirchertach mac Erca. Interestingly, Muirchertach mac Erca's downfall was due to Sín, who revealed that she was of the *Sentuatha Temrach* (literally the 'Old Peoples of Tara') and that she caused Muirchertach's fall to avenge her parents' deaths and the loss of her patrimony at the hands of Muirchertach and his dynasty. This admission of Sín's is not simply the utterance of a vengeful member of the Otherworld; it may also carry a contemporary political message regarding the relationship in the eleventh century between the tributary tribes of Brega and the Uí Néill.

Evidence for the physical and historical manifestation of the kingship of Tara in its ritual and sacral aspects is not immediately available. In his attempt to interpret the description of the ordeals undergone by Conaire Mór, Myles Dillon (1973, 2–3) mused:

> These are a series of ordeals which a candidate must undergo, and they cannot have much relation to fact in all their details: but one important feature emerges which was probably real, namely that the new king drove in a mock-chariot race. We can well imagine that it was important that he got safely round the course, and that this was contrived. How the scream of Fál was managed I cannot guess, if it was managed at all. Maybe the charioteer had to bring the wheel into contact with the stone as he turned for home. But this account might almost be reduced to the statement that the new king had to drive in a chariot as part of the ceremony.

Only one other account of the inauguration of the kings of Tara, apart from the Conaire Mór episode, exists, that incorporated in the twelfth-century Life of Colmán mac Lúacháin (Meyer 1911, 72.70), an account which Dillon (1973, 4) described as fanciful. He drew also on evidence from India and concluded that the chariot race, the ritual steps to the five regions (?the five provinces of Ireland) and the chanting of praise-poems by a bard were part of the ceremony and a survival of the earliest form of Indo-European kingship (*ibid.*, 8).

Tara as the centre of the cosmos

Alternative divisions of Ireland existed according to different traditions. The country could be divided into fifths based on a division between Connacht, Leinster, Ulster and Munster — separated into two parts — which met at Uisnech. In this construct Uisnech was the mid-point of Ireland, the centre of the cosmos. The alternative tradition is that the fifth province was Mide, a tradition in which Tara was the centre. The greatest exponents of the cosmological meaning of Irish literature were Alwyn and Brinley Rees, who in *Celtic heritage* sought to relate the *cóiceda* to aspects of society, drawing on the evidence of the Middle Irish text *Do Shuidigud Tellaich Themra*. Thus Connacht was learning, Ulster battle, Leinster prosperity, Munster music, and Mide, the Centre, was kingship (Rees and Rees 1961, 123, 146–72). Kingship had three divine attributes, all previously mentioned in relation to Conaire Mór and Cormac mac Airt: justice, victory and the power to give fruitfulness to the earth and health to mankind. The relationship between the centre of the cosmos and the other divisions of the universe, be they expressed geographically or as divisions in society, could be depicted in the layout of a royal fort. Alwyn and Brinley Rees regarded the *Tech Midchúarta* at Tara as the symbolic centre of the cosmos, the apartment of the gods and the 'honourable liquor house' (*ibid.*, 131–2). The possibility that there may be an associated political message in the promotion of Mide as the central *cóiced* is most likely given the nature of early medieval Irish sources. Aitchison (1994, 114–15) has suggested that it must be appraised against the background of Uí Néill ambitions for a high-kingship of Ireland:

> The Uí Néill appear to have sought legitimacy for their aspirant high kingship of Ireland by inventing the tradition, or transforming the archaic institution, of the kingship of Tara and by appropriating the monuments on the Hill of Tara as their focus of royal activities. This, therefore, is why Tara is often depicted in literary sources as the seat of an immemorial high kingship of Ireland, while the function attributed to the Centre, Mide, in *Suidigud Tellaig* is kingship, with the secondary properties of primacy (*oireochuss*), principality (*flaithemnas*), high kingship (*ardrigí*), and 'the overlordship of Ireland' ('*forbflaithius for Erind*') (ed. and trans. Best 1910: 148–51). The cosmological scheme which the *cóiceda* represents appears to be closely associated with Uí Néill aspirations of a high-kingship of Ireland.

Feis Temro

One apparent physical manifestation of the kingship of Tara was *Feis Temro*, the Feast of Tara, described in the eighth-century law-tract *Bretha Nemed* and in the later text known as *The Triads of Ireland* as one of the three things that constituted a king of overkings (*rí ruirech*) (Meyer 1906, 26.202; Binchy 1978, 2219.39–40). Many scholars have referred to *Feis Temro* since Petrie's day (e.g. O'Curry 1873, 8–23), regarding it as a national assembly held by the high-king of Ireland. O'Rahilly (1946b), followed by Carney (1955, 334–9), explained it as a symbolic wedding feast (*banfheis*) between the king and the goddess of sovereignty, the inauguration rite of the pre-Christian kings of Tara. No scholar viewed *Feis Temro* with the same critical judgement as Binchy in his paper 'The fair of Tailtiu and the feast of Tara' (1958b). Having stripped it of the traditions and falsehoods attached to it from the eleventh century to the twentieth, Binchy concluded that the historical *Feis Temro* was a 'primitive fertility rite culminating in the apotheosis of the sacred king', last held by Diarmait mac Cerbaill in 560, after which it was discarded as a relic of paganism (*ibid.*, 137–8).

The taboos of the king of Tara

Taboos or prohibitions (*geisi*) could also be viewed as a physical manifestation of the kingship of Tara. Dillon (1951–2), in his edition of a metrical and prose text described by him as 'The taboos of the kings of Ireland', attempted to illustrate the reality of a taboo by quoting the example, among others, of the king of the Ewe-speaking people of West Africa, who 'may not be seen by his subjects, so that he is permitted to leave his dwelling only at night' (*ibid.*, 1). Two sets of taboos for the king of Tara exist. The ninth-century text *Togail Bruidne Da Derga* (Knott 1936) tells of the taboos explained to Conaire Mór on his assumption of the kingship of Tara: he could not pass Tara on his right hand and Brega on his left; he could not hunt the crooked beasts (*cláenmíla*, likely to be swans) of Cernae; he could not stay away from Tara for longer than nine days; he could not spend the night in a house in which firelight was visible outside after sunset and into which a person could see from outside; three red men could not go before him into a red man's house; plunder could not be undertaken during his reign; a visiting party consisting of one man or one woman could not come into his house after sunset; he could not settle a quarrel between two of his subjects (for the original text see Knott 1936, 6.170–81).

Conaire Mór inevitably broke all his taboos and lost his kingship and his life as a result. The second text edited by Dillon, which appears to have been given its present structure in the eleventh century but which may incorporate earlier material, lists another set of taboos for the king of Tara, which do not correspond with those in *Togail Bruidne Da Derga*. The following is Dillon's text and translation (1951–2, 8–9):

Seacht n-urgarta rígh Temruch innso, adhón; turccbháil gréine fair ina lighi i mMaigh Themruch, tairléim cétaíne i mMaigh Bregh, immthecht Maighi Cuillinn iar fhuinith ngréine, slaidhe a ech hi Fán Chummair, techt dia mairt for Tethuha thuaiscirt, bruinech for Bethra issin lúan iar mBealtaine, slicht slúaigh for Áth Maighne imm mairt iar Samfhuin.

These are the seven prohibitions of the king of Tara, that is to say: that the sun should rise while he is in bed in the plain of Tara, to break a journey on Wednesday in Mag Breg, to travel over Mag Cuillinn after sunset, to strike his horses in Fán Cummair, to enter north Tethba on Tuesday, a scout(?) at Bethra on the Monday after Beltaine, the track of an army(?) on Áth Maigne on the Tuesday after Samuin.

Bleak though the taboos appear, all was not gloomy for the king of Tara according to this second text. It lists seven good things (*búada*) which brought him luck, namely the fish of the Boyne, the deer of Luibnech, the mast of Mana, the bilberries of Brí Léith, the cress of the Brosnach, water from the well of Tlachtga, and the hares of Naas (or alternatively of Maistiu) (*ibid.*, 9).

While these texts may contain a germ of an old tradition, it is not improbable that they are tainted by contemporary political realities or may even be, as Greene (1979, 11) described them, the 'mere imagining of antiquarians, for the use of the days of the week is a Christian element which cannot have been taken from the pagan past'.

Wormald (1986), in his essential reassessment of Celtic and Anglo-Saxon kingship, follows Greene in his scepticism about the archaic tradition of Irish kingship, comparing known attributes with Germanic and Scandinavian kingship. He argues that the differences between the images and power of Celtic and Anglo-Saxon kings were fewer than appears from the balance of the evidence (*ibid.*, 169). The apparent archaism of Irish kingship was due to the images portrayed in the sources which were produced 'by people whose job it was, so far as possible, to show that nothing changed in early Ireland' (*ibid.*, 170), combined with a representation of early medieval Ireland which prevailed until recently among Irish historians (*ibid.*, 171).

HIGH-KINGSHIP, THE UÍ NÉILL AND 'SYNTHETIC HISTORIANS'

Eoin MacNeill in his pioneering work *Celtic Ireland* (1921) studied the documents of the Irish 'synthetic historians', a phrase coined by him to describe those who compiled and wrote the annals, genealogies, sagas, legends and pseudo-historical works of early Ireland. He concluded (*ibid.*, 38):

> Thus the central doctrine of the historical fabric was the remotely ancient rule of the race of Mil in Tara, and the supremacy of Tara over all Ireland. Around this doctrine were grouped and dated all the traditions, mythological and heroical, of the nation, as also all its genealogical traditions. Wherever gaps existed, however large, and they existed everywhere and were as wide as might well be, they were boldly filled up. The chronological confusion of earlier efforts gave way to a settled order, for without coherence the structure could satisfy nobody.

In this work MacNeill confronted the vexed question of the authenticity of the high-kingship of Ireland, the existence of which had become (and remains) a national doctrine. MacNeill's successors in the field — O'Rahilly, Binchy, Byrne, Kelleher and Ó Corráin, to name but the chief protagonists — have continued throughout this century to argue the nature of the elusive high-kingship of Ireland.

The evolution of a high-kingship of Ireland at Tara

MacNeill (1921, 8) reached three conclusions with regard to 'the medieval history of pre-Christian Ireland', namely that the story of the monarchy before the Christian era was fictitious, that the first substantial fact was the existence of a Pentarchy (the five provinces), with no superior monarchy, about the beginning of the Christian era, and that the historical monarchy arose between this time and the time of St Patrick. In *Phases of Irish history* (1919) MacNeill suggested that the 'royal sites' of Tara and Crúachain were ruled by military kings. He continued (1919, 235):

> My first visit to Tara convinced me that what we see there is the remains of a great military encampment . . . When the booty and captives of Britain and Gaul ceased to tempt and recompense a professional soldiery, and when the old fighting castes became gradually merged in the general population, military organisation died in Ireland, not to appear until the introduction of the Galloglasses in the thirteenth century. That is one reason why Tara was deserted.

The concept of the Pentarchy was to continue as essential to the arguments surrounding the existence or otherwise of the high-kingship of Ireland. O'Rahilly, in his attempt to explain the origin of the Pentarchy, argued (1946a, 172) that prior to the 'Goidelic invasion' four provinces existed (north, south, east and west). The fifth province, the midland 'fifth' (*cóiced*), was carved out by the Goidelic invaders of the eastern midlands by Túathal Techtmar. He concluded (*ibid.*, 174):

> The Goidelic kingdom of the Midlands was at first a *cóiced*, as being one of the five territorial divisions of the country, and consequently its ruler was a *cóicedach* or provincial king. In the course of time, however, the king of Tara, as the king of the Midland kingdom was called, became by far the most powerful of Irish kings; and so in early historical times we find him claiming to be king of all Ireland and superior to the other *cóicedaig*.

Few today would agree with O'Rahilly's assessment of the evolving political scene in the late prehistoric period (for recent comments on O'Rahilly's work see McCone 1990, 57).

Binchy's contribution to the discussion is found in a number of papers, those reflecting his ideas most clearly being 'The passing of the old order' (1962b) and *Celtic and Anglo-Saxon kingship* (1970). He used his expert knowledge of the Old Irish law-tracts to support his argument concerning the evidence — or lack of it — for a supreme king at Tara. In the law-tracts three 'grades' in the hierarchy of kings are identified: the *rí* (*túaithe*) or tribal king, the *ruiri* or over-king, and the *rí ruirech* or king to whom a number of *ruirig* were bound by personal allegiance. Accepting MacNeill's theory of the Pentarchy, Binchy identified five kings who could hold the title *rí ruirech*, one for each province (*cóiced*). From the fifth century onwards, however, Tara and Cashel outweighed the other provincial kingdoms — Connacht, Leinster and what remained of the Ulaid — in power and prestige (Binchy 1962b, 124):

> Both Tara and Cashel owed their dominating position to the fact that each was the head of a group of far-flung kindred dynasties, the Uí Néill and the Eoghanacht . . . In strict law they had exactly the same status as the other provincial kings; their increased power in fact was due to the sense of family solidarity which assured to each of them the support of strong mesne kings, who in turn were themselves acknowledged as overlords by the kings of the remaining tribes.

The title *rí ruirech* is associated with another title, *ollam ríg*, which appears in the law-tracts. The Old Irish law-tract *Uraicecht Becc* includes a phrase *Ollam úas rígaib rí Muman*, which Binchy (1958a, 49) argued should be translated as 'Supreme (or 'Most transcendent') over kings is the king of Munster'. He claimed that the text implies that 'to the compiler of the *Uraicecht Becc* the king of Munster is superior to all kings' (*ibid.*, 50–1). He is not king of Ireland. 'He is simply stating what any inhabitant of Munster between the sixth and the ninth centuries would have regarded as self-evident: that the king of Cashel is the most important king in Ireland' (*ibid.*, 51). The evolution of the high-kingship is reflected in the glosses on the law-tracts. The glossators begin to gloss the title *rí ruirech* with the phrases *rí Érenn 7 rí cóicid*, thus recognising the office of the king of Ireland (Binchy 1966, 50).

Byrne (1973) asserted that the term *ard-rí* 'high-king' was not very old, an argument which Binchy (1976, 18–20) extended by claiming that had the classical jurists known the term for a more exalted grade of monarch than *ruiri*, a similar 'close' compound **airdri*, genitive **airdrech* (like *ruirech*) would have existed. This conclusion is questioned in Liam Breatnach's note (1986) on the old compound word *ardri*. Among other comments, he quotes, in response to Binchy's claim that the *rí ruirech* was the highest grade of king known to the jurists, a passage from the Old Irish law-tract on status, *Míadshlechta*. This passage speaks of the *tríath*, the first of the types of king, of whom it was said *Cóic cóicid Érenn term[i]-ætha* (MS: *tremætha*) *a mámu uile* ('the five provinces, he goes through all their submissions'). Breatnach (1986, 192–3) states: 'Clearly someone of higher standing than a king with dominion in his own province alone is indicated by this passage from the Old Irish laws'.

Whereas Binchy concentrated to a large extent on the evidence of the law-tracts and the non-recognition by Munster of the king of Tara as an over-king as proof against the existence of a high-kingship, Byrne in his numerous papers of primary importance on the subject (1969; 1971; 1973; 1974) stresses other aspects, which lead to a somewhat different conclusion. His paper *The rise of the Uí Néill and the high-kingship of Ireland* (1969), read in conjunction with the chapter entitled 'The high-kingship of Ireland' in *Irish kings and high-kings* (1973), provides a comprehensive guide to his views on the matter. The existence of a high-king of Ireland in the period prior to the ninth century is inextricably linked with the Uí Néill and their respective relations with Armagh and Iona, as expressed in the lives of Patrick by his seventh-century biographers, Muirchú and Tírechán, and in the *Vita Columbae* by Adomnán, abbot of Iona (d. 704). Of the Uí Néill, Byrne (1973, 254) states:

> Whatever the mystique that lay behind the title of king of Tara, and however vague the dominion exercised by its holder, it remains true that from their first appearance in the fifth century the Uí Néill had introduced a dynamism which disrupted the archaic hierarchy of the Five Fifths. Although tribal kingship never entirely disappeared, the new dynastic polity evolved by the Uí Néill relegated it to the position of a primitive survival. And as early as the seventh century the Uí Néill claimed to be kings of all Ireland.

While the original functions of the pagan kingship of Tara were rendered obsolete by the advent of Christianity, Armagh's victory in becoming the primatial see must have influenced the development of a high-kingship, as a national monarchy would seem to be the natural corollary to ecclesiastical unity (Byrne 1974, 149). Iona may also have played a part in promoting the idea of a high-kingship.

Enright (1985, 6) has argued that Adomnán aimed in the *Vita Columbae* to disseminate the theory of an Uí Néill right to govern the whole country while at the same time proselytising for a change in their essentially pagan sacral kingship. Binchy's evidence on the basis of the title *rí ruirech* is questioned by Byrne (1962–3, 270), in that this title could be claimed by the king of either the northern or the southern Uí Néill, as well as the Airgíalla, all of whom were subject to the king of Tara. The importance of certain texts in our understanding of the status of the high-king is reiterated on occasion by Byrne. These texts include the seventh-century regnal list *Baile Chuinn* (Murphy 1952), which seems to confirm that the kingship of Tara was no ordinary kingship that was succeeded to immediately on the death of the previous holder but rather was a prize achieved only by the most outstanding (Byrne 1967, 168), and the seventh-century law-tract on bees, *Bechbretha* (Charles-Edwards and Kelly 1983), which appears to indicate that the kingship of Tara had been held for a while by Congal Cáech (Cláen), king of the Cruithin of Ulster (d. 637, slain in the battle of Mag Rath), and therefore was not the exclusive preserve of the Uí Néill in the early historic period. (For an extensive discussion on the background to this period, and in particular the Uí Néill and the Ulaid and their relations with Iona, see Byrne 1965.)

In seeking evidence for the pre-eminence of the king of Tara in Ireland prior to the ninth century, it is interesting to note the hierarchy of eminent persons as listed in the guarantor list of the ordinance *Cáin Adomnáin,* dated to 697, a record independent of the annals (Ní Dhonnchadha 1982). Adomnán, abbot of Iona (d. 704), promulgated the law. Flann Febla, bishop-abbot of Armagh (d. 715), was the first guarantor in the list, reflecting his position as the most important ecclesiastic in the land (forty ecclesiastics in all are named). Loingsech mac Óengusso (d. 704) was accorded primary position in the list of fifty lords named as guarantors, which included Eterscél mac Maíle Umae, king of Munster. Loingsech, who was of the Cenél Conaill, is one of only two kings (the other being his grandfather, Domnall mac Áedo (d. 642)) of the Uí Néill given the title *rex Hiberniae* in the annals before the ninth century (Ní Dhonnchadha 1982, 196–7).

The career of Máel Sechnaill mac Maíle Ruanaid (Máel Sechnaill I), who succeeded to the title 'king of Tara' in 846, is marked by all commentators as being of particular importance in the evolution of the concept of high-kingship. Byrne (1973, 257) boldly states that the 'Uí Néill concept of high-kingship was first converted into political reality by Máelsechnaill mac Máele Ruanaid, styled *rí Érenn uile* "king of all Ireland" at his obit in 862'. While remarking on the successful career forged by Máel Sechnaill against other provinces, his own kinsmen and Vikings alike, Binchy (1962b, 130) concluded more cautiously that 'from about the middle of the ninth century the primacy of Tara was universally accepted, at all events in theory'. This more cautious attitude is also adopted by Ó Corráin (1977–9, 310–13) in his detailed analysis of Máel Sechnaill's career. There was a slow but steady consolidation of power in the hands of the greater kings for a century or so before the arrival of the Vikings in Ireland, and especially in the hands of the Uí Néill kings.

Máel Sechnaill, over-king of the Southern Uí Néill, who succeeded to the paramountcy of the whole of the Uí Néill (traditionally called the kingship of Tara) in 846 and ruled until his death in 862, was an able and ambitious ruler who greatly expanded his power (in favourable circumstances, let it be said) and his success lent some considerable substance to the long-standing claim of the kings of Tara to be kings of Ireland. However, his achievements were even more important historiographically than historically [quotes Binchy as above] [Ó Corráin 1978–9, 302].

The creation of 'the doctrine of an immemorial high-kingship of Ireland centred around Tara' (Byrne 1973, 269) is attributed commonly to MacNeill's synthetic historians of the eleventh and twelfth centuries. The revival of literary activity relating to Tara, however, dates to the reign of Máel Sechnaill mac Domnaill (Máel Sechnaill II), king of Tara (d. 1022) and rival of the 'usurper' Brían Bóruma, and to the work of Máel Sechnaill's poet, Cúán úa Lothcháin. It is remarkable how many scholars, from Petrie onwards, have referred to aspects of Cúán úa Lothcháin's role in the revival of interest in Tara in the late tenth and early eleventh centuries. When this corpus of scholarship is put together, it becomes clear that the background to Cúán úa Lothcháin's work is essential to our understanding of many of the better-known texts on Tara, especially the topographical texts. On the basis of a religious quatrain at the end of the poem, Ó Concheanainn (1982, 92–3) argues that Cúán composed the *dindshenchas* poem *Temair toga na tulach* (Gwynn 1903–35, vol. 1, 14–27), which lists the monuments on the Hill of Tara. So frequent are these religious quatrains at the end of *dindshenchas* poems that Ó Concheanainn (1982, 98) is led to surmise that 'Cúán, indeed, may have been the author who compiled the primary recension of Dinnshenchas C, i.e. the full version composed of prose-and-poem units, a version later added to by other eleventh-century redactors such as Eochaid Eolach Ó Céirín and the Leinster poet Fulartach'.

It is noteworthy that Tara takes precedence in the sequence of places covered by the *dindshenchas*. The metrical *dindshenchas* of Tailtiu, that site so inextricably linked to Tara, *A chóemu críche Cuind chain*, is ascribed to Cúán and was probably composed to celebrate the revival by his king, Máel Sechnaill mac Domnaill, of *Óenach Tailten* in 1006 (Binchy 1958b, 116). In addition, the metrical version of the text on the taboos of the kings of Ireland is ascribed to Cúán, an ascription which Dillon (1951–2, 2) saw no reason to question. The king of Tara, as might be expected, is accorded primary position among the kings of Ireland. The poet's opening stanza in the text dealing with the taboos of the king of Tara is equated by Cúán with the king of Ireland (Dillon 1951–2, 10–11):

A fhir áin íadas in tech
is mé Húa Locháin láeidech:
nom léicc sechat sa tech thenn
a fhuil airdrígh na Hérenn.

> Good sir who barrest the house
> I am Úa Locháin the poet:
> let me pass into the firm house
> where the high-king of Ireland is.

Ó Riain provides a *raison d'être* for Cúán's concentration on reviving the importance of Tara in his study of the contents of the Psalter of Cashel, a manuscript described by Ó Riain (1989, 110) as 'among the insignia of Brian [Bóruma]'s office as overking'. In his poem on Tara, *Temair toga na tulach*, Cúán refers to the source of his information as *Saltair Theamrach*, the Psalter of Tara (Gwynn 1903–35, vol. 1, 14–15). In the absence of any other clear independent reference to the Psalter of Tara, Ó Riain (1989, 109) surmises that there are 'strong grounds for suspecting that it was conjured up in response to the influence of the very real Psalter of Cashel'. Cúán's reason for doing this, and probably for much of his literary work, was to bolster Máel Sechnaill's claims to the kingship of Tara and to the 'overkingship of Ireland' against those of the usurper from Munster, Brían Bóruma. 'It can hardly be a coincidence that Tara's function for the Uí Néill was precisely that of Cashel for the men of Munster; it was the traditional, symbolic seat of sovereignty' (*ibid.*, 111).

Máel Sechnaill and Cúán's efforts to battle against Brían's claims to the kingship of Tara and the over-kingship are again reflected in two texts which deal with the theme of sovereignty and the kingship of Tara — the regnal list *Baile in Scáil* (Meyer 1901; 1918) and the 'sovereignty tale' *Echtra mac nEchdach Mugmedóin* (Joynt 1910). The metrical version of the *Echtra* is ascribed to Cúán úa Lothcháin, while the last identifiable king referred to in *Baile in Scáil* is none other than Máel Sechnaill II. The political significance of these texts is discussed by Máire Herbert in her paper 'Goddess and king: the sacred marriage in early Ireland' (1992). Her conclusions provide the essential background to understanding Cúán úa Lothcháin's work and his use of Tara as a constant theme. She describes *Baile in Scáil* as 'a statement of advocacy on behalf of the Uí Néill dynasty. It seeks to counter the achievements of parvenu might by proclamation of long-established right. The myth is co-opted to serve the purpose of projecting the dynasty's claim to the sovereignty of Ireland back to primordial time' (Herbert 1992, 270). Similarly, the *Echtra* reasserts the Uí Néill right to kingship 'by demonstrating its acquisition by the dynasty's eponymous ancestor [Níall Noígíallach] in an era of antiquity reaching back before Christianity' (*ibid.*, 272). Ó Corráin (1986, 146) demonstrates how at a later date the Uí Chonchobair of Connacht 'appropriated the legend of sovereignty [the story of Níall's acquisition of the kingship] which had long been the property of the Uí Néill' by composing a metrical version of the tale in which the poet declared that the era of the Uí Néill was over and that the kingship had returned to the descendants of Bríon, Níall Noígíallach's brother and ancestor of the Uí Chonchobair.

High-kingship as a national doctrine

Lebor Gabála Érenn, a text which in its most complete form appears to date from the late eleventh century, tells of the invasions of Ireland by peoples from overseas who were ultimately the ancestors of the great lineages of the country (Macalister 1938–56; Best *et al.* 1954–83, vol. 1, 1–99; Carey 1993). It reflects the efforts of medieval Irish scholars to respond to their dilemma of 'the vast blank separating Irish tradition from accepted world history' (Scowcroft 1988, 63), which they resolved by marrying native tradition with biblical chronology. A basic tenet of *Lebor Gabála* is the division of Ireland into two halves, *Leth Cuinn* (north) and *Leth Moga* (south), which equated with the overlordships of Tara and Cashel respectively. The concept of the high-kingship of Ireland, *flaithes Érenn*, is essential to the chronology of the text, a kingship embedded in time immemorial. Tara is referred to constantly in *Lebor Gabála*. The text explains, for example, that Tara is *tea-múr* 'the wall of Tea', named after Tea, the wife of Éremón, who was buried there (Best *et al.* 1954–83, vol. 1, 52). The importance of *Lebor Gabála* lies in its influence on the view adopted in later material towards Tara. The high-kingship of Ireland centred at Tara is a national doctrine from this period onwards.

Tara's appearance in sources which post-date the era of *Lebor Gabála* becomes increasingly symbolic, to the extent that it almost becomes a literary cliché. The tendency to use Tara in stock phrases is prevalent in poetry of the Middle Irish period. Tara conveys ideas of strength, nobility and legitimacy of power. The bardic poets of the post-twelfth century continued to use these stock phrases, although there is a series of bardic poems which use Tara specifically as a vehicle to legitimise the authority of native and foreign lords (O Riordan 1990). Cathal Croibhdhearg Ó Conchubhair, king of Connacht (d. 1224), had at least two poems based on this theme of Tara addressed to him. One poem composed by Muireadhach Albanach Ó Dálaigh, *Tabhrum an Cháisg ar Chathal,* proclaimed (Bergin 1970, 106, 260):

> *As é an Croibhdhearg chuirfios soir*
> *na Gulla do ghabh Theamhraigh:*
> *an duine ní diombáidh linn*
> *'ga ttiomáin uile a hÉirinn.*

> It is the Redhand that will drive eastwards the Foreigners who have seized Tara: it were no grief to me that he should banish them all from Ireland.

The 'foreigners who have seized Tara' is a reference to the Anglo-Normans. Another poem addressed to Cathal, *Táirnic in sel-sa ac Síl Néill* (Ó Cuív 1983), which retells the sovereignty tale *Echtra mac nEchdach Mugmedóin,* also uses Tara to legitimise Cathal's authority. 'The poem, for all its fine imagery and its repertoire of ancient motifs, is firmly rooted in the world of living politics' (Ó Corráin 1986, 146).

Another, less impressive, member of the Uí Chonchobhair, Aodh (d. 1309), had a remarkable poem composed about his recently erected house at Cloonfree, Co. Roscommon, by one Aonghus Ruadh Ó Dálaigh (Quiggin 1913). The poet regarded the building of Aodh's house as the transfer of Tara to Cloonfree (*ibid.*, 336–7):

1. *An tú arís, a ráith Teamhrach?*
   do-chláochláis cruth ildhealbhach;
   fúarais gnáoi 'san riocht roimhe,
   gé 'táoi ar sliocht na seanchuire . . .

3. *Do-thógbhais ceann a gClúain Fráoich*
   ar leirg uaine an fheóir fhionnmháoith,
   a ráith cheathardhruimneach Chuinn
   leathan-bhruighneach bhláith bheandchruinn.

1. Is it thou once more, Rath of Tara? thou hast changed thy various shape; thou hast found favour in thy old guise, though thou art descended from ancient hosts . . .

3. Thou hast appeared in Cloonfree above the verdant slope of the fair-smooth sward, rath of Conn of the fourfold ridge, spaciously palatial, smooth, with round pinnacles.

Gofraidh Fionn Ó Dálaigh (d. 1387) also used this device to boost the fortunes of Diarmuid 'na gCaisleán' Ó Briain, king of Thomond (d. 1364). In a eulogy to Diarmuid, *A toigh bheag tiaghar a tteagh mór* (Mac Kenna 1952), Gofraidh claimed that Diarmuid's assumption of greater power would be reflected in his change of residence from Teach Táil to Tara. By establishing his patron at Tara, the poet granted him a greater national status than he warranted in reality. Diarmuid was deposed twice, in 1343 and again in 1360.

The same poet, Gofraidh Fionn Ó Dálaigh, invoked Tara in relation to one of the Fitzgeralds of Desmond, Maurice Fitzmaurice (Muiris Óg), second earl of Desmond (d. 1358). In praising Muiris Óg, the poet likened the latter's visit to London to Lug's visit to Tara (Bergin 1913, 327, 331):

49. *Cosmhail cúairt Logha ó lios Eamhna*
    d'fhoghluim ghairggníomh
    as cúairt Muiris go lios Lonndún,
    d'fios an airdríogh.

49. Alike are the journey of Lugh from the court of Eamhain [to Tara], to learn fierce deeds, and the journey of Maurice to the court of London, to visit the high-king.

This theme of accommodating the foreign but suitable lord into the mainstream of the Gaelic tradition with reference to Tara appears in relation to other non-native lords such as the Butlers and the de Burgos (O Riordan 1990, 33–4, 36, 61). Its use in odes to native lords is regarded by Mac Cana (1985, 74–5) as a 'topos of unity' validating a rightful king. In the context of the inauguration rites associated with Irish chiefs of the later Middle Ages, it is interesting to note that the *Lia Fáil* at Tara is the only inauguration stone to be mentioned before the fifteenth century, after which references to other stones begin to appear (Simms 1987, 35–6).

The climax of the traditional, and probably the most fictitious, treatment of Tara is contained in Geoffrey Keating's *Foras Feasa ar Éirinn* ('History of Ireland'). A glance at Tara in the index of Dinneen's edition of Keating's work (Comyn and Dinneen 1901–13, vol. 4, 458–9) provides a flavour of the national institution which he described as functioning at Tara from prehistoric times. Whereas Keating (d. 1649) reflected an exaggerated view of the Tara of *Lebor Gabála*, his description of Tara, and especially of *Feis Temro*, as the centre from which a national parliament governed was prompted by contemporary political considerations. His view was undoubtedly influenced by the Old English preoccupation with a parliament (Cunningham 1986–7, 124). Similarly the Four Masters devised the structure and chronology of the annals on the doctrine of a high-kingship of Ireland embedded in time immemorial. Their use of the title *rí Teamhrach* signifies a king holding national office and not the local king the title came to signify in the late eleventh century.

A stanza attributed to Keating's contemporary, Oliver Plunkett (d. 1681), provides us with a different vision of Tara, when he lamented the sight of a rustic cutting grass on the great hill in order to feed his cattle (Murray 1912–15, 188):

> *A Theamhair na Rígh, do b'annamh leat*
> *Le linn Chormaic mhic Airt mhic Cuind*
> *Alt riabhach do bhodach bocht*
> *Bheith 'gearradh guirt air do dhruim.*

> O Tara of the kings, rarely did it happen to you in the time of Cormac son of Art son of Conn that the swarthy knuckle of a poor churl cut grass of your hill.

Early claimants to the kingship of Tara and vassal tribes of the Uí Néill

In his paper 'Historical need and literary narrative' Ó Corráin (1986) deals with another aspect of Tara's history, which, though not highlighted by scholars, appears in the margins of their commentaries about the kingship and high-kingship of Tara (*ibid.*, 147–51). This is to do with the tribes and septs other than the Uí Néill who claimed to have controlled Tara or to have assisted the Uí Néill in controlling Tara in the early historic period. Of the former, the Laigin and the Ulaid reappear frequently. The main evidence for the claim by the Laigin appears in the early poems incorporated into the Leinster genealogies (O'Brien 1962, 1–9), which have been variously dated as compositions of the fifth century to the eighth century (*ibid.*, 8–9; Carney 1971, 65–73; Byrne 1973, 137–8; Ó Corráin 1985, 57–67; Carney 1989). The poem *Nidu dír dermait* (O'Brien 1962, 8–9), for example, exhorts the Laigin not to forget that they once held power in Tara. The poet reminds them of the Leinster kings who were also kings of Tara and includes a regnal list of some of those who may have ruled Tara in the late fourth and fifth centuries (Byrne 1973, 137). Another poem seems to use the metaphor of the *Lia Fáil* either shrieking in salutation of conquests made by Labraid Loingsech, ancestor-deity of the Laigin, or weeping to signify the loss of Tara by the Laigin: *golaid Lia Fáil fri falgud fairni Faireoin* (O'Brien 1962, 3).

Carney, in his study of the early Leinster genealogical poems, describes the Laigin in the following terms (1971, 73):

> Politically they [the genealogical poems, when analysed properly] will give a picture of a dynastic group in Leinster, the Laigin or Gálióin, exercising power as far as the borders of Ulster. They are conscious of being invaders and of different ethnic origins to the rest of the country; they are given to overseas raiding, extending as far as Gaul, and are very conscious of Roman civilization; in Ireland they claim for themselves the type of superiority that is conceded to them in *Táin Bó Cuailnge*.

Ó Corráin's analysis of these poems (1985, 58, 67) demonstrates that Carney's conclusions were 'rather large claims' and that they were not as old or as unitary as suggested, but that there was no compelling linguistic or historical reason why they should not belong to the end of the seventh century or the beginning of the eighth century.

The historicity of the tribute paid by the Laigin to the Uí Néill, the *bórama Laigen*, is discussed and doubted by Mac Eoin (1968, 30) in his analysis of the versions of the death of Lóegaire mac Néill. Smyth (1974–5a; 1974–5b) approaches the question on the basis of the earliest annalistic records in his studies of what he terms the loss of the Plain of Mide (*Campus Mide*) by the Laigin to the Uí Néill in the fifth and sixth centuries. His analysis demonstrates that the Leinstermen 'carried the struggle in defence of their territory well beyond their own borders about Uisnech, and into the Huí Néill lands to the north' in the fifth and sixth centuries (1974–5a, 142). Evidence for Leinster activity in Brega can be adduced from the existence of an ogham stone from Painestown (Seneschalstown), Co. Meath (barony of Duleek), which commemorates MAQI CAIRATINI AVI INEQAGLASI 'of Mac Caírthinn grandson of Enechglas'. The Uí Enechglais were a Leinster dynastic family who lost power in the early historical period and who were pushed to the coastal margins of Leinster (around Arklow). Ó Corráin (1971, 98) suggests that the annalistic entry *AU* s.a. 446 (*prima manus*) *Bellum Femhin in quo cecidit filius Coerthin filii Coelboth. Alii dicunt de Chruithnibh fuisse* is 'a very early historical reference to a struggle waged in Brega by a leading Leinster dynast', and that later redactors (*AI* s.a. 447) confused Femen in Brega with the much better known Femen in Munster. He concludes, on the basis of this and other annalistic evidence, that 'Femen must have been an important centre of Uí Néill activity at an early period as indeed was this whole area of Brega' (*ibid.*, 99).

The possible claim by the Ulaid to the kingship of Tara, as assumed by the reference to Congal Cáech's position in the Old Irish law-tract *Bechbretha,* has been alluded to previously. The 'main sub-stratum of population under the Uí Néill dynasts of Brega' (Byrne 1966, 393) were the Cíannachta, the Gailenga and the Luigne. The geographical distribution of these tribes has caught the attention of scholars since MacNeill. Apart from their occurrence in Brega and Mide, the Gailenga and the Luigne also appear in north Connacht, while the Cíannachta had a branch among the Cenél nEógain. Their close proximity to the Uí Néill led MacNeill (1934–5) to suggest that they represented the deliberate colonisation of the midlands and border areas by the Connacht ancestors of the Uí Néill with their Connacht vassals. MacNeill's theory was questioned by O'Rahilly (1946a, 172ff) since it negated his view that the 'Midland Goidels' (ultimately the Connachta and Uí Néill) had invaded Ireland from the Meath coast inwards. Ó Corráin in his paper 'Historical need and literary narrative' (1986) makes numerous valuable comments about the relationship between the Luigne and Gailenga in his analysis of the three texts from the Cormac mac Airt 'dossier', *Geneamuin Chormaic, Scéla Eógain 7 Cormaic* and 'Nia Mór son of Lugna Fer Trí'. Of the implications of this material, he concludes (*ibid.*, 150–1) (with an interpretation which he acknowledges as being quite close to O'Rahilly's):

> Firstly, there are so many associations — including parallels of names and places — between the early Luigne material and the received prehistory of the Uí Néill that one must rule out mere coincidence. It is likely that part at least of the prehistory of the Uí Néill was built up from a common fund of historical materials shared with the progenitors of the Luigne and the Gailenga. When we come to the earliest surviving versions of the birth of Cormac [mac Airt] the legend building is already far advanced and the original relationship between the principal actors has been radically changed. Evidently the Uí Néill have distanced themselves from their original close association with, and possible origin from, the group of peoples represented by the Luigne, Gailenga and Corco'r Trí of north Connacht and it seems to me not unlikely that they began their rise to power as fellow-travellers of these very peoples. And the stages of development of the narrative parallel the changes in the political fortunes of the Uí Néill.

Byrne, in a paper of primary importance for the understanding of the history of Brega (1966), demonstrates how these tributary peoples survived the rigours of Uí Néill authority even as late as the eleventh century, and indeed how on occasion they caused not insignificant disruptions (*ibid.*, 393–5).

SAINTS AND THEIR BIOGRAPHERS

The Patrician question has been the subject of notable contention since Petrie (1839, 47ff) included in his monograph the texts describing Patrick's alleged visit to Tara. Reviews of the arguments involved appeared at regular intervals (O'Rahilly 1942; Carney 1959; Binchy 1962a; Dumville 1993), and these will not be addressed here.

Patrick, Tírechán, Muirchú and Tara

The two texts which are quoted regularly concerning Tara and Patrick are those written in the late seventh century by Bishop Tírechán and by Muirchú maccu Machtheni (Bieler 1979). Since their appearance is so frequent in works which refer to Tara, it seems appropriate to quote the passages which are most relevant (following Bieler's published edition, despite its inaccuracies).

Tírechán

> *Et intenderunt omnes magum eleuatum per tenebras nocturnales poene usque ad caelum, sed reuersus cadauer illius congluttinatum grandinibus et niuibus, commixtum scintillis igneis in terram ante faciem omnium cecidit; et est lapis illius in oris australibus orientalibusque <Temro> usque in praesentem diem, et conspexi illum oculis meis.*

> 'And all saw the druid being lifted up through the darkness of night almost to the sky, and when he came down again, his body, frozen with hailstones and snow mixed with sparks of fire, fell to the ground in the sight of all; and (the druid's) stone is in the south-eastern parts of Tara to the present day, and I have seen it with my own eyes' (Bieler 1979, 130–3 §8(6)).

The sentence referring to the druid's stone at Tara and Tírechán's comment that he saw it himself are of particular interest. It is likely to be the earliest reference to a monument at Tara, and, more importantly, is based on an eye-witness account.

> *(1) Perrexitque ad ciuitatem Temro ad Logairium filium Neill iterum, quia apud illum foedus pepigit, ut non occideretur in regno illius; sed non potuit credere, dicens: (2) 'Nam Neel pater meus non siniuit mihi credere, sed ut sepeliar in cacuminibus Temro quasi uiris consistentibus in bello' (quia utuntur gentiles in sepulcris armati promptis armis) 'facie ad faciem usque ad diem erdathe' (apud magos, id est iudicii diem Domini) 'ego filius Neill et filius Dúnlinge imMaistin in campo Liphi pro duritate odi∫u∫i ut est hoc.'*

'(1) And he proceeded again to the city of Tara to Lóiguire son of Níall, because he made a pact with him that he should not be killed within his realm; but (Lóiguire) could not accept the faith, saying: (2) "My father Niall did not allow me to accept the faith, but bade me to be buried on the ridges of Tara, I son of Niall and the sons of Dúnlang in Maistiu in Mag Liphi, face to face (with each other) in the manner of men at war" (for the pagans, armed in their tombs, have their weapons ready) "until the day of *erdathe*" (as the druids call it, that is the day of the Lord's judgement), "because of such fierceness of our (mutual) hatred" ' (Bieler 1979, 132–3 §12).

Bieler translates the phrase *in cacuminibus Temro* in this passage as 'in the ridges of Tara'. The phrase occurs elsewhere in Tírechán's work and simply means 'on the hills or heights'. It also occurs in the context of another burial, *et sepilierunt eam in cacuminibus aeclessiae desuper* ('and they buried her on the hill of the church above') (Bieler 1979, 158–9 §44(2)). Perhaps the phrase concerning Lóegaire should simply translate as 'but bade me to be buried on the Hill of Tara'?

Muirchú

Muirchú's description of Patrick's meeting with Lóegaire and his druids is longer and more dramatic (Bieler 1979, 74–99). The following passages provide an impression of Muirchú's view of Tara.

(1) In illis autem diebus quibus haec gesta sunt in praedictis regionibus fuit rex quidam magnus ferox gentilisque, imperator barbarorum regnans in Temoria, quae <tunc> erat caput <regni> Scotorum, Loiguire nomine filius Neill, origo stirpis regiae huius pene insolae.

'(1) In the days when this took place there was in those parts a great king, a fierce pagan, an emperor of non-Romans, with his royal seat at Tara, which was then the capital of the realm of the Irish, by name Lóiguire son of Níall, a scion of the family that held the kingship of almost the entire island' (Bieler 1979, 74–5 §I 10).

Muirchú's description of Tara as *caput Scotorum* has been referred to by various scholars in their attempts to unravel the existence of the high-kingship at an early period. Of this description (and of Adomnán's description of Diarmait mac Cerbaill as *totius Scotiae regnatorem deo auctore ordinatum* 'the ruler of all Ireland, ordained by God' (Anderson and Anderson 1961, 280)), Ó Corráin (1978, 8) states: 'These claims are highly tendentious and testify to ambition rather than achievement. Less explicitly, they testify, at least amongst some royal propagandists, to an awareness of the Irish as a *natio*, a wider community, rule over which, in one form or another, was a laudable ambition for an over-king of the Uí Néill in the seventh century.'

(1) Contigit uero in illo anno ut aliam idolatriae sollempnitatem, quam gentiles incantationibus multis et magicis inuentionibus nonnullisque aliis idolatriae superstitionibus, (2) congregatis etiam regibus, satrapis, ducibus, principibus et optimatibus populi, insuper et magis, incantatoribus, auruspicibus et omnis artis omnisque doni inuentoribus doctoribusque uocatis ad Loigaireum uelut quondam ad Nabucodonossor regem in Temoria istorum Babylone exercere consuerant, eadem nocte qua sanctus Patricius pasca illi illam adorarent exercerentque festiuitatem gentilem.

'(1) It so happened in that year that a feast of pagan worship was being held, which the pagans used to celebrate with many incantations and magic rites and other superstitious acts of idolatry. (2) There assembled the kings, satraps, leaders, princes, and the nobles of the people; furthermore, the druids, the fortune-tellers, and the inventors and teachers of every craft and every skill were also summoned to king Lóeguire at Tara, their Babylon, as they had been summoned at one time to Nabuchodonosor, and they held and celebrated their pagan feast on the same night on which holy Patrick celebrated Easter' (Bieler 1979, 84–5 §I 15).

The biblical imagery used in this passage has been commented upon frequently (Byrne 1973, 64–5; McCone 1990, 33–4). 'These biblical resonances help to endow Tara with an opulent imperial atmosphere highly congenial to Muirchú's political concerns . . . while simultaneously highlighting the struggle against entrenched paganism and the ability of a faithful few to triumph against huge odds with God's support' (McCone 1990, 33).

The difference between Muirchú's and Tírechán's accounts of the meeting of Patrick and Lóegaire lies in the varying purposes of their respective works. Tírechán's interests lie in establishing 'a dossier of churches and property which he considers ought to belong to Armagh' (Doherty 1991, 64), a purpose based on ecclesiastical and legal precedence. Muirchú's purpose is more political. By linking Patrick with Tara he is linking Armagh to the fortunes of the Uí Néill and, since 'only men who had risen to positions of exceptional power' were likely to attain the kingship of Tara, and in Muirchú's time they belonged to the Uí Néill, 'Armagh once more was flattering the powerful' (*ibid.*, 86). Sharpe (1982, 58) has suggested that the difference between Muirchú and Tírechán 'reflects also the extension of Uí Néill interests in Brega; the Southern Uí Néill were now allies to be cultivated'.

Tara and the Columban confederation

'The *Vita Columbae* may be seen as reflecting the view that the claim to the kingship of Ireland by the Uí Néill was divinely approved. The sixth-century Tara ruler, Diarmait mac Cerbaill, is termed *totius Scotiae regnatorem deo auctore ordinatum*, and another ancestor-figure among the Uí Néill, Áed Sláne son of Diarmait, is warned against loss of "the prerogative of monarchy over the kingdom of all Ireland, predestined for you by God" . . . His

> [Adomnán's] ideal model for Irish society would seem to have been a Christian kingship held by Uí Néill rulers, with successors of Colum Cille, their kinsman and allies, exercising a beneficent influence over them' (Herbert 1988, 52).

If this was Adomnán's ideal he does not, like his contemporary Muirchú, emphasise Tara's role in the model. Adomnán remains silent about Tara, never referring to it in his text. His silence may be to do with his propagation of a Christian kingship, viewing the kingship of Tara as pagan (Byrne 1973, 255). While Muirchú, in his dramatic account of Patrick at Tara, was creating a link between the saint and Tara, and ultimately the Uí Néill, Adomnán's link with the Uí Néill could be claimed through the fact that his patron, Columba, was a member of the Uí Néill himself. Picard (1982, 171) suggests that though Adomnán's assertion in favour of the kings of Tara is not as strong as that of Muirchú, 'it is nevertheless a clear statement of the over-kingship of Tara'. The relationship between the Columban confederation and the kings of Tara, not always one of mutual agreement, became particularly tense at one point during the reign of Áed Oirdnide (d. 819). In revenge for the killing of their *princeps*, Máel Dúin mac Cinn Fháelad, in 817, the community of Raphoe went to Tara to curse Áed (Byrne 1973, 162; Herbert 1988, 71). It is significant that although Áed belonged to the northern branch of the Uí Néill (Cenél nEógain), Tara was chosen as the location at which to curse him. The inference is that Tara's symbolic associations drew the community of Raphoe there in order to confirm their curse on the king.

The cursing of Tara by Rúadán of Lorrha

The third saint most frequently linked with Tara is Rúadán, founder of the monastery of Lorrha, Co. Tipperary. A tale possibly datable to the tenth or eleventh century tells of Rúadán's clash with the king of Tara, Diarmait mac Cerbaill. The following is Binchy's summary of the tale (1982, 172):

> Rúadán, founder and first abbot of Lorrha in north Tipperary, had given asylum to a Connacht prince who had slain one of Diarmait's officials. Diarmait, after various underlings sent by him had failed to apprehend this 'rebel' against his 'over-lordship' owing to miracles worked by the saint, went in person to Lorrha, discovered the culprit's hiding place and had him conveyed to Tara where he was thrown into prison to await execution. Rúadán followed the king and the captive, halting on the way to enlist the aid of St Brendan of Birr. Both saints on their arrival at Tara began to ring their handbells (the normal preliminary to commination) and chant 'maledictive psalms'. When these signs were ignored by the king, they began a nightly fast, which however remained quite unproductive because Diarmait warded off all its effects by himself fasting every night.

The king is finally tricked into submission by the saints, and, among other actions, Rúadán prophesies that Diarmait's descendants will not rule Tara and that Tara will be abandoned. The historicity of this tale was discussed by Binchy (1982). He regarded Diarmait mac Cerbaill as a mixture of the new and the old, acting as patron to Cíarán of Clonmacnoise while at the same time celebrating (for the last time) *Feis Temro*, marking the end of the archaic sacral monarchy. He regarded the tale as 'a fable concocted much later in order to account for the official adoption of Christianity by the kings of Tara'. He argued also that it was a doublet of the tale involving Adomnán and Írgalach úa Conaing, king of Brega (d. 701), which appears in the *Fragmentary Annals of Ireland* (Radner 1978, 46–8) and in the tenth-century Irish life of Adomnán (Herbert and Ó Riain 1988, 50–1 §5). Both versions demonstrated 'the survival of the pagan tradition of a ceremonial fast directed against secular rulers which some saints share with the Brahmins of ancient India' (Binchy 1982, 178).

The triumph of Christianity

The theme of the triumph of Christianity at the expense of Tara and other 'royal sites' is included in two earlier texts, the hymn *Genair Pátraicc* (known as Fíacc's Hymn, ascribed to a disciple of Patrick's, Fíacc of Sletty, and variously dated to between 750 and 800 (Binchy 1962a, 124–5)) and the Prologue to *Félire Óengusso*, a martyrology compiled *c*. 830 and attributed to Óengus úa Oíbléin of the monastery of Tallaght (Ó Riain 1990, 38). The author of Fíacc's Hymn tells of the arrival of a new prince (Patrick) and of the prophecy that Tara would be desolate: *bid fás tír Temrach* (Stokes and Strachan 1901–3, 2.314). The poet also introduces the theme of comparing the flourishing Christian sites (Armagh and Downpatrick) with the desolate pagan sites (Emain and Tara) (*ibid.*, 2.317), a device most forcefully used by Óengus in the Prologue (Stokes 1905, 24 §165):

> *Atbath borg tromm Temra*
> *la tairthim a flathe,*
> *col-lín corad sruithe*
> *maraid Ard mór Machae.*

> Tara's mighty burgh perished at the death of her princes: with a multitude of venerable champions the great Height of Machae (Armagh) abides.

Though this dramatic description has been quoted frequently as evidence that Tara was abandoned by the early ninth century, perhaps a note of caution should be entered in accepting Óengus's description of the total desolation of Tara. The events recorded in 817, events which took place shortly before *Félire Óengusso* was composed, when the community of Raphoe cursed Áed Oirdnide at Tara may indicate that the site's symbolic significance survived the vicissitudes of change. This possibility is reinforced by the entries in the *Annals of Ulster* and the *Annals of Inisfallen* which record that the Munster king, Feidlimid mac Crimthainn (d. 847), proved his domination of Brega and Mide in 840 by halting at Tara (*AU: conid·deisigh i Temhraigh*) and by killing a certain Indrechtach mac Maíle Dúin at Tara.

THE ARCHAEOLOGY AND TOPOGRAPHY OF TARA

Study of the topography of Tara is dominated by the monumental works of O'Donovan (1836), Petrie (1839) and Macalister (1931). O'Donovan and Petrie attempted to correlate the monuments at Tara with those known to them from the texts on Tara preserved in the corpus of place-lore known as *Dindshenchas Érenn*. Of his sources Petrie (1839, 129) states: 'The principal ancient Irish tracts written in illustration of the origin and names of Tara, and describing the localities, &c. of the hill and its monumental remains, are preserved in the ancient topographical work called the *Dinnseanchus,* a compilation of the twelfth century'. *Dindshenchas Érenn*, from which O'Donovan and Petrie culled the material for their topographical studies, consists of a group of Middle Irish legends, preserved in prose and poetry, which purport to explain the origin and background of the names of the most prominent geographical and man-made features in Ireland. The first element of the word, viz. *dind* (literally meaning 'hillock, raised ground), in the context of this body of literature, means 'landmark, eminent or notable place' (Bowen 1975–6, 114). The second element, *senchas,* is a word which embodies a fundamental part of the learned tradition in Ireland, the traditional lore of Ireland (Byrne 1974). Tara is placed in a primary position in the *dindshenchas*, being the subject of five poems and three prose accounts. O'Donovan and Petrie produced their maps mainly on the basis of the descriptions in the poem *Temair toga na tulach* (Gwynn 1903–35, vol 1, 14–27) composed by Cúán úa Lothcháin (though O'Donovan accepted the incorrect ascription in some manuscripts to an earlier Meath poet, Cináed úa hArtacáin (d. 974)) and the prose tract *Dindgnai Temrach* (Best *et al*. 1954–83, vol. 1, 120–3). This prose tract is so detailed that it is tantamount to a medieval survey of the Hill of Tara, providing information on monuments which can still be identified today and on others which have been since destroyed (Bhreathnach 1995). The medieval names of the monuments at Tara, as identified from the *dindshenchas* by O'Donovan and Petrie, became convenient terms of reference which continue to be used in archaeological and topographical descriptions. It is noteworthy that between the time that Petrie published his survey and Macalister wrote his treatise some monuments had disappeared or had been damaged, the most renowned disturbance resulting apparently from the activities of the British Israelites seeking the Ark of the Covenant there in 1899.

Macalister's survey (1931) is based primarily on the *dindshenchas* texts correlated with the monuments as he found them. In some cases he attempted to update and correct Petrie, for example incorrectly switching the identifications provided by Petrie of the *Forad* and *Tech Cormaic* (*ibid*., 25–9). The use by scholars of the *dindshenchas* texts in their attempts to identify the surviving monuments at Tara has shaped the archaeological debate concerning the site. The urge to associate monuments with those named in the *dindshenchas* has meant that the texts have not been analysed sufficiently in their own right. Surveys subsequent to Petrie's and

Macalister's have done little to add to our knowledge of the monuments, a situation which is likely to be improved by current surveys (Newman 1994; 1995).

Excavations at Tara

Further knowledge regarding the monuments has come from the scattered references to the various excavations conducted at Tara. The first 'investigations' are attributed to the British Israelites, who took it upon themselves to dig the Rath of the Synods in 1899 (Butler 1990; Lohan 1994, 110–12, 117). The most detailed published information concerning these 'investigations', apart from the justification for their actions published by the British Israelites at the time in their monthly journal *The Covenant People*, is provided by Macalister (1931, 39–43) in his survey, based on the accounts of Archdeacon Healy, rector of Kells, and Sir John Dillon, a landowner from the neighbourhood. He includes a photograph of what appears to have been the most significant discovery of the 'excavation', described by Healy (1900) as 'two circular trenches cut in the rock, the inner one about 8 feet wide, and the outer one 18 feet wide'. Information as to the objects found is scanty. Macalister, quoting Westropp as his source, refers to the discovery of human remains and Roman coins of the reign of Constantine the Great. The discovery of Roman coins may have been a hoax in that they were probably placed in the Rath of the Synods by local people during the British Israelite investigations (Dolley 1968; Bateson 1973, 71–2).

Excavations of the Mound of the Hostages were begun by Ó Ríordáin in 1955 and completed by de Valéra in 1959. The Rath of the Synods was excavated in 1953 and 1954 by Ó Ríordáin. Ó Ríordáin referred to his excavations in various publications, the most extensive of which was his pamphlet *Tara: the monuments on the hill* (1954). De Valéra added a supplementary note on the excavations completed at the Mound of the Hostages in the edition reprinted in 1961. Evans (1966, 174–7) summarised the results, providing some chronology of events at Tara as revealed by the excavations. On excavation, the Mound of the Hostages proved to be a passage tomb of Neolithic date (*c.* 2800 BC), into which were inserted burials of Early Bronze Age date (*c.* 2200–1500 BC). There was one unburnt burial of a youth laid in a flexed position, accompanied by a necklace of bronze, amber, jet and faience beads, and secondary Early Bronze Age cremations were inserted into the mound (Ó Ríordáin 1955). Excavations at the Rath of the Synods provided evidence for different phases of activity and also showed that it was surrounded by rock-cut fosses and by timber palisades. Within the enclosure burials, cremated and unburnt (O'Brien 1992, 131), were discovered, along with imported Roman glass and pottery (Bateson 1973, 71–2). A date in the first three centuries AD seems indicated by the finds. On excavation, the silted-up ditch of Ráith na Ríg was revealed as a deep, V-shaped fosse dug into solid bedrock. Traces of a trench on the inner side of this ditch which had once supported a significant palisade were also uncovered (Raftery 1994, 66). It is clear that the Hill of Tara was the focus of activity at various times from the Neolithic period onwards, although the results from archaeological excavations to date have yielded limited information as to the sequence of activity on the site. Continuous use of the Hill of Tara, whether for settlement, burial or other purposes, since early prehistoric times cannot yet be demonstrated.

Stray finds from Tara

The limited range of stray finds provenanced to Tara also reflects this occasional reuse. Two gold torcs, dating from *c.* 1200 BC (Petrie 1841; Ryan 1983, 81–2, no. 9), were found in unclear circumstances at Tara in the early nineteenth century. Later sources suggest that they may have been found near the modern church at Tara when a bank was being cleared away *c.* 1810 (Murphy and Westropp 1894, 239). Gold earrings and gold sleeve-fasteners dating from the Late Bronze Age were also found at Tara (Eogan 1983, nos 21, 22, 115). Evidence for medieval activity at Tara is scant. An annular brooch, possibly dating from the ninth century, is reputed to have been found there (Youngs 1989, 97–8, no. 77), while a block of red enamel is stated variously to have been found at Ráith Cáelchon at Tara or at Kilmessan, some distance from Tara (*ibid.*, 201, no. 196). A cresset-stone dating from the eleventh or twelfth century was reputedly found 'on the side of a well on the western slope of the [Tara] hill' (Moore 1984, 111). The annular brooch previously mentioned is not to be confused with the object most closely associated in the popular mind with Tara, the 'Tara Brooch'. Whitfield in her detailed study of its provenance (1974) has shown that this title is a misnomer. It appears that the brooch was found on the seashore at Bettystown, Co. Meath.

The characteristics of a 'royal site' in Ireland

Tara, as an example of what have become known as 'royal sites' in archaeological terminology, is regularly compared with other 'royal sites' in Ireland, the most frequently cited being Emain (Navan Fort, Co. Armagh), Crúachain (Rathcroghan, Co. Roscommon) and Dún Ailinne (Knockaulin, Co. Kildare). Published material concerning the other 'royal sites' in Ireland is not included in this bibliography, as the consideration of the detailed comparison between Tara and these other sites merits a separate study. (For a comprehensive overview of many aspects of royal sites, see the volumes of *Emania: Bulletin of the Navan Research Group*.) General studies on the identification and attributes of 'royal sites' are included in the bibliography. Wailes (1982, 7–8) sets out five 'archaeological propositions' to define a 'royal site'.

> (1) On the reasonable assumption that sites of unusual importance are likely to be unusual in appearance, we might expect unusual size, or form, or both. Such unusual features might or might not be visible on the surface.

(2) The sites might well be similar to each other in form and content . . .

(3) They should provide evidence of both ritual and residential activities (assemblies and inaugurations might well leave no trace archaeologically).

(4) At high-status residential sites of the period we might expect some residue of high-status living, such as gold, glass, or enamel . . .

(5) The sites should date from the pre-Christian Iron Age, and artefacts of La Tène character would be particularly appropriate. Continued use of the sites into the Early Christian period should not be expected . . .

Lack of archaeological evidence prevents Wailes from defining Tara, or any of the other named sites, as 'royal sites' within the terms of his own 'archaeological propositions'.

A similar attempt to define a 'royal site' is undertaken by Warner in his study of 'The archaeology of early historic Irish kingship' (1988). He suggests the following general definitions of a 'royal site' (*ibid.*, 67).

(1) Signs of ritual, such as a mound, would be strong positive evidence of royalty, but they are not necessary.

(2) The site is likely to be internally small but defensible. It might be a ringfort, crannog or stack-fort and might well be indistinguishable from others in the locality.

(3) Complexity of earthworks, unless some are of a ritual nature, is not necessary, but multivallation might be a good pointer.

(4) On excavation evidence of wealth, a very large house and mixed industrial waste would be good pointers.

A different approach in identifying the elements of a ritual site, albeit flawed in its interpretation of texts, is undertaken by Olmsted in his article on Irish 'hill-top enclosures' (1979). He has pointed to the significance of the passage in *Audacht Morainn* (Kelly 1976, 8–11 §28) which refers to the three immunities from liability for violence (*blaí*, a word which Olmsted regards as meaning 'enclosure') which protect a lord at every assembly (*óenach*). These are (1) 'the racing of horses at assemblies' (*án ech n-óenag*), (2) 'a hosting' (*dúnath*, a word also possibly meaning 'an encampment') and (3) 'the privilege of the ale-house with friends and great abundances of mead-circuit' (*búaid cuirmthige co coímaib co mannaib móraib midchórto*). Did a site on which an *óenach* was held include the essential elements respectively of a horse-racing track, an encampment and an area for eating and drinking? If so, the racing track would perhaps be the only permanent feature, and be the only one likely to leave visible traces in the form of earthworks, the others being temporary constructions built for the duration of the *óenach*.

Individual monuments at Tara

There are numerous studies of individual monuments at Tara. They tend to be confined to a limited number of monuments, such as the *Lia Fáil*, the *Clóenfherta* and the roadways which allegedly converged on Tara. It is noteworthy that some of the monuments at Tara may have had more than one name, a consideration which was missed on occasion by Hogan in his *Onomasticon Goedelicum* (Bhreathnach 1993).

The *Lia Fáil* has captured the imagination of medieval and modern scholars alike. Its capacity to cry or to weep aloud reappears throughout Old and Middle Irish texts. The introduction to *Baile in Scáil* describes its attributes most graphically (Meyer 1901, 458–9): Conn Cétchathach and his druids are ambling over the hill of Tara, when he finds a stone under his feet (*fo a chosaib*) at the mound (*dua*, presumably Duma na nGiall, the Mound of the Hostages) normally frequented by them on such occasions. Conn stands on the stone and it cries out so loudly that it could be heard not only throughout Tara but throughout Bregmag, the plain of Brega in which Tara is situated. Responding to Conn's queries about the stone, he is told that it is Fál (the glossator's popular etymology being *fo-ail .i. ail foríg*) and that the land of Fál is Tara. The land of Tailtiu will be the place where Conn's progeny (the Uí Néill) will celebrate their *óenach* 'assembly' while they hold the kingship of Tara. Every cry uttered by the Fál under Conn's foot denotes the reign of a king of his dynastic line. The two most comprehensive papers concerning the *Lia Fáil* are Guyonvarc'h's paper (1964, 436–40) on the possible etymological origins of the word *Fál* and Ó Broin's (1990) discussion of the *Lia Fáil* as a goddess and as part of the ceremony of the sacred marriage of kingship.

To the medieval mind, the strange shape of the *Clóenfherta* needed explanation. Three versions appear in the literature. The most commonly found explanation occurs in the text *Cath Maige Mucrama* (O Daly 1975), where the side of the royal house falls as a result of the unjust judgement of the king of Tara, Lugaid mac Con, who as a result has to hand over the kingship of Tara to Cormac mac Airt (*ibid.*, 58–9 §65):

> *La sain fo-cheird leth in taige for [n-]aill .i. in leth i rrucad in gúbreth. Méraid cu bráth fon inna[s]-sain .i. in Chlóenfherta Themrach.*

> With that one side of the house falls down the cliff, namely the side in which the false judgement was given. It will remain for ever like that, the Clóenfherta (crooked mound) of Tara.

A second version, also involving the motif of the false judgement, the protagonists being Lóegaire and Patrick, forms part of 'The pseudo-historical prologue to the *Senchas Már*' (Carey 1994, 31–2) and is alluded to in *Betha Cholmáin maic Luacháin* (Meyer 1911, 62–3 §58). In the final version, a Leinster tradition explains that thirty princesses of Tara were slaughtered by Dúnlang, king of Leinster, in revenge for the imposition of the tribute known as *bórama Laigen* by Túathal Techtmar, king of Tara. The slaughter is known as *Comram na Clóenfherta*, 'the Triumph of the Sloping Mound' (Ó Cuív 1976).

One of the best-known monuments on the Hill of Tara is that known as the Banqueting Hall, a name derived from the title given to it in the Middle Irish prose account, the *Tech Midchúarta*. The illustration which accompanies the Middle Irish text in the twelfth-century Book of Leinster (and in the later Yellow Book of Lecan) depicts the places accorded to various officials, from the king to the cook, in the Banqueting Hall at Tara. The concept of the *Tech Midchúarta* and the specific seating arrangements in it, arranged according to rank, appears in other texts which do not refer specifically to Tara. It is a concept which combines elements of legal status (O Daly 1962; Kelly 1986, 81–3), cosmological ideas (Rees and Rees 1961, 146–72), political rankings (Marstrander 1911, 232–5) and a literary device, describing fantastic or genuine structures (Meyer 1917, 23–4). The description which provides the most realistic view of the *Tech Midchúarta* is preserved in the law-tract on the privileges and responsibilities of poets (*ibid.*):

> *Ā̆iliu tech midchūarta*
> *milscothaib fīath fāth:*
> *fossud mainbthech a imbel ngarb n-ochrach,*
> *blāithi bith a chrann mbī,*
> *cōiri a dī ursainn*
> *irard aircsinech ar dorus,*
> *lúachid a shoillse,*
> *drongel a chomla,*
> *berrtha bir a glass,*
> *altach a airide . . .*

> I wish for a house with a mead-hall, a song of welcome with honeyed words: firm and ample its rough edged ambit, smooth the beams of its thresholds, symmetrical its two posts, lofty and conspicuous in front of the door, brilliant its light, solid and white its door valve, smooth-shaven the spit of its bolts, well-jointed its high-seat . . .

The commonly held belief that five great roadways radiated from Tara is found in Middle Irish texts such as *Airne Fíngein* (Vendryes 1953, 9–11 §vi). According to this tale, the five roads, *Slige Midlúachra*, *Slige Cúalann*, *Slige Asail*, *Slige Tola* (*Slige Dála*) and *Slige Mór*, made a magical appearance to mark the birth of Conn

Cétchathach. The reality of the existence of such roads was tested by Ó Lochlainn in his paper 'Roadways in ancient Ireland' (1940). He described the possible route of each *slige*, stating at the beginning that 'in Cormac [mac Airt]'s time Tara itself — as befitted the country's capital — was linked up by new junction roads to the main highways already for centuries in use' (*ibid.*, 470). The routes that he outlines seem to radiate as much from Dublin as they do from Tara, signifying that Dublin was far more important than Tara at the time of composition of the texts used by Ó Lochlainn in his study. In this context, it has been noted that Dublin, rather than Tara, 'whatever the poets might say, was assuming the role of the metropolis of Ireland' in the eleventh century (Byrne 1973, 271).

The hinterland of Tara

The bibliography which follows includes studies of places in the hinterland of Tara which are closely associated in the literature with Tara. Among them are Cermna, Femen, Loch nGabor, Ocha, Odba and, most importantly, Tlachtga and Tailtiu. Tara and Tailtiu (and to a lesser extent Tlachtga) are so closely connected in the literature that the alliteration between the three is used in poems throughout the Middle and Early Modern Irish period. *Óenach Tailten* is aptly described by Binchy (1958b, 115) as 'an ancient institution intimately connected with the Tara monarchy'. Binchy's study of the *óenach* should be read in conjunction with Máire MacNeill's description of the popular practices associated with Tailtiu in her important work *The Festival of Lughnasa* (1962, 311–38).

THE NAME *TEMAIR*

The text *Sanas Chormaic*, a glossary reputed to have been compiled by the king-bishop of Cashel, Cormac mac Cuilennáin (d. 908), provides two etymologies for *Temair* (Meyer 1912, 105 §212). One is derived, fictitiously, from *tea-múr*, 'the wall (*múr*) of Tea', wife of Eirimón, who expired on the Hill of Tara and whose sepulchral monument (*múr*) was raised on the hill. The second definition, possibly equally fictitious though gaining more acceptance by modern scholars (Byrne 1973, 56), is *teomoro .i. conspicio*, the idea of a height (of a house or a hill) from which there is a fine view.

Despite the importance of the site, the origins of the name *Temair* have attracted little notice from linguistic scholars. Wagner, in footnotes and asides in his series of papers on Celtic religion, suggested that the word could be related to Old Irish *temel* 'darkness' and was cognate with Latin *tenebrae* (Wagner 1975, 21, n. 39). Accepting Thurneysen's (1936) etymology of *Tailtiu*, meaning 'the Beautiful One', Wagner (1979, 26) felt that the contrast between *Tailtiu* and *Temair* ('the Dark One') reflected the same dual function of the goddess of life and death that could be found in connection with some river names.

In identifying Eochaid Feidlech, father of Medb, as the god of death, Borgeaud (1971) emphasises the associations with death by suggesting also that the etymology of *Temair* lay in a meaning of 'darkness' or 'twilight'. Noting the number of other places named *Temair* in Ireland, he draws the parallel with the use of *Pylos* 'the Gate of the Dead' in place-names of the Peloponnese (*ibid.*, 42).

Temair as a personal name occurs, an example being Temair, daughter of Áed Builc, king of the Déssi, and wife of the seventh-century king of Tara, Diarmait mac Áedo Sláine (Bhreathnach 1984, 61, n. 10). Evidence that the personal name Temair may be imbued with connotations of sovereignty is implied in the reference in the genealogies of the Uí Bairrche, a Leinster tribe, to *Temair ingen Meic Dara* (O'Brien 1962, 48).

Tara was accorded a series of alternative literary names, among them *Druim Léith* (alias *Liathdruim*), *Druim Caín*, *Cathair Chrófhind*, *Fordruim*, *Tulach in Trír* and *Carn in Áenfhir* (Gwynn 1903–35, I, 2–5; McCaughey 1960, 173). Hogan (1910, 630) in his *Onomasticon Goedelicum* lists ten places elsewhere in Ireland named *Temair,* while Ó Ceallaigh (1950, 179–80) noted that the long table-top mountain in the Glens of Antrim known as 'the Three Taghmores' was explained locally as the 'three Temairs'. Similarly Watson (1904–5; 1926, 505) noted examples of the place-name Tara in Scotland: they include Dale of Taras (*Dail Teamhair*) in Glencasley, Sutherland, and *Druim Teamhra*, north of Loch Gorm in Islay.

(References to *Temair Lúachra*, also known as *Temair Érenn*, have been included in the bibliography for a number of reasons. It is sometimes confused in the literature with *Temair Breg* (Tara, Co. Meath) (Watson 1941, xxxvi–xxxix), and whenever discussed in the archaeological literature is assumed to consist of a complex of monuments, not unlike Tara (Doyle 1927; Westropp 1918). It has been suggested that it is part of the series of monuments located in the Ballyhoura Hills on the borders of counties Cork and Limerick (Westropp 1918), that area being the subject of an archaeological project being undertaken under the aegis of the Discovery Programme (Doody 1993, 20–30).)

The origin of the Anglicised version of *Temair*, Tara, appears to lie in the variants of the place-name which are used in Anglo-Norman documents. A medieval charter of the Hospitallers of St John, *c.* 1285, describes a road going from Skreen to Tara as going *versus Taueragh* (Brooks 1936, 175 §254), which must represent the equivalent of the Irish *co Te(a)mraig* (accusative singular of *Temair*). Another text lists churches which are a subject of dispute in the diocese of Meath *c.* 1231–3 and states *et quidam alii religiosi Midensi diocesi in [ecclesiis] de Scrin et Tauerach* (Brooks 1953, 40 §37), a phrase which seems to translate into Latin the later genitive of the word in Irish, *Temra(ch)* (*DIL* T, 141–2).

Tara appears on occasion in Anglo-Norman charters and deeds of the late twelfth and thirteenth centuries. The secular lords who were granted the lands of Tara at that time were the de Repenteni family, who also held lands in County Louth (Curtis 1932–43, vol. 1, 43 §98, 359 §852). The ecclesiastical landowners at Tara were the Hospitallers of St John, who were based at Kilmainham, Co. Dublin, and in whose charters Tara appears as one of their churches in Meath (Brooks 1936, 175; McNeill 1932, 35). It is interesting to note that these Anglo-Norman texts contain the first references to the location of a church at Tara. The Hospitallers' possessions, including the church at Tara, were confirmed to them by Pope Innocent III in 1212 (Sheehy 1962–5, I, 148–52 §72).

REFERENCES

Ahlqvist, A. 1974–6 Two ethnic names in Ptolemy. *Bulletin of the Board of Celtic Studies* **26**, 143–6.

Aitchison, N.B. 1994 *Armagh and the royal centres in early medieval Ireland. Monuments, cosmology and the past*. Suffolk.

Anderson, A.O. and Anderson, M.O. (eds) 1961 *Adomnán's Life of Columba*. London.

Bateson, J.D. 1973 Roman material from Ireland: a re-consideration. *Proceedings of the Royal Irish Academy* **73**C, 21–97.

Baudiš, J. 1916 On the antiquity of the kingship of Tara. *Ériu* **8**, 101–7.

Bergin, O. 1913 A poem by Gofraidh Fionn Ó Dálaigh. In E.C. Quiggin (ed.), *Essays and studies presented to William Ridgeway*, 323–32. Cambridge.

Bergin, O. 1970 *Irish bardic poetry*. Dublin.

Best, R.I. 1910 The settling of the manor of Tara. *Ériu* **4**, 121–72.

Best, R.I., Bergin, O., O'Brien, M.A. and O'Sullivan, A. 1954–83 *The Book of Leinster, formerly Lebar na Núachongbála* (6 vols). Dublin.

Bhreathnach, E. 1993 Tara: the literary and historical perspective. *Discovery Programme Reports* **1**, 98–103. Dublin.

Bhreathnach, E. 1995 The topography of Tara: the documentary evidence. *Discovery Programme Reports* **2**, 68–76. Dublin.

Bhreathnach, M. 1982 The sovereignty goddess as goddess of death? *Zeitschrift für celtische Philologie* **39**, 243–60.

Bhreathnach, M. 1984 A new edition of *Tochmarc Becfhola*. *Ériu* **35**, 59–91.

Bieler, L. 1979 *The Patrician texts in the Book of Armagh*. Scriptores Latini Hiberniae, 10. Dublin.

Binchy, D.A. 1958a The date and provenance of *Uraicecht Becc*. *Ériu* **18**, 44–54.

Binchy, D.A. 1958b The fair of Tailtiu and the feast of Tara. *Ériu* **18**, 113–38.

Binchy, D.A. 1962a Patrick and his biographers: ancient and modern. *Studia Hibernica* **2**, 7–173.

Binchy, D.A. 1962b The passing of the old order. In B. Ó Cuív (ed.), *The impact of the Scandinavian invasions on the Celtic-speaking peoples c. 800–1100 A.D.*, 119–32. Dublin.

Binchy, D.A. 1966 Bretha Déin Chécht. *Ériu* **20**, 1–66.

Binchy, D.A. 1970 *Celtic and Anglo-Saxon kingship*. Oxford.

Binchy, D.A. 1976 Irish history and Irish law: II. *Studia Hibernica* **16**, 7–45.

Binchy, D.A. 1978 *Corpus iuris Hibernici ad fidem codicum manuscriptorum recognovit* (6 vols). Dublin.

Binchy, D.A. 1982 A pre-Christian survival in mediaeval Irish hagiography. In D. Dumville, R. McKitterick and D. Whitelock (eds), *Ireland in early mediaeval Europe*, 165–78. Cambridge.

Borgeaud, W.A. 1971 Hibernica: Echu–Echoch, Echoid–Echdach, Temair. *Beiträge* zur Namenforschung **6**, 40–4.

Bowen, C. 1975–6 A historical inventory of the *Dindshenchas*. *Studia Celtica* **10–11**, 113–37.

Breatnach, L. 1986 Varia VI: 3. *Ardrí* as an old compound. *Ériu* **37**, 192–3.

Breatnach, R.A. 1953 The lady and the king: a theme of Irish literature. *Studies* **42**, 321–36.

Brooks, E. St John 1936 *Register of the Hospital of S. John the Baptist (without the New Gate, Dublin)*. Dublin.

Brooks, E. St John 1953 *The Irish Cartularies of Llanthony Prima and Secunda*. Dublin.

Butler, H. 1990 The British Israelites at Tara. In R.F. Foster (ed.), *The sub-prefect should have held his tongue and other essays*, 68–70. London.

Byrne, F.J. 1962–3 Review of B. Ó Cuív (ed.), *The impact of the Scandinavian invasions on the Celtic-speaking peoples c. 800–1100 A.D.* (Dublin 1962). *Irish Historical Studies* **13**, 269–71.

Byrne, F.J. 1965 The Ireland of St Columba. *Historical Studies* **5**, 37–58.

Byrne, F.J. 1966 Historical note on Cnogba (Knowth). Appendix to G. Eogan, 'Excavations at Knowth, Co. Meath, 1962–1965'. *Proceedings of the Royal Irish Academy* **66**C, 383–400.

Byrne, F.J. 1967 Seventh century documents. *Irish Ecclesiastical Record* **108**, 164–82.

Byrne, F.J. 1969 *The rise of the Uí Néill and the high-kingship of Ireland*. Dublin. O'Donnell Lecture Series.

Byrne, F.J. 1971 Tribes and tribalism in early Ireland. *Ériu* **22**, 128–66.

Byrne, F.J. 1973 *Irish kings and high-kings*. London.

Byrne, F.J. 1974 *Senchas*: the nature of Gaelic historical tradition. *Historical Studies* **9**, 137–59.

Carey, J. 1993 *A new introduction to Lebor Gabála Érenn*. Dublin. Irish Texts Society.

Carey, J. 1994 An edition of the pseudo-historical prologue to the *Senchas Már*. *Ériu* **45**, 1–32.

Carney, J. 1955 *Studies in Irish literature and history*. Dublin.

Carney, J. 1959 Comments on the present state of the Patrician problem. *Irish Ecclesiastical Record* **92**, 1–28.

Carney, J. 1971 Three Old Irish accentual poems. *Ériu* **22**, 23–80.

Carney, J. 1989 The dating of archaic Irish verse. In S. Tranter and H. Tristram (eds), *Early Irish literature — media and communication. Mündlichkeit und Schriftlichkeit in der frühen irischen Literatur*, 39–55. Tübingen.

Charles-Edwards, T. and Kelly, F. 1983 *Bechbretha: An Old Irish law-tract on bee-keeping*. Dublin.

Comyn, D. and Dinneen, P.S. 1901–13 *Foras Feasa ar Éirinn. The History of Ireland by Geoffrey Keating D.D.* (4 vols). Irish Texts Society, 4, 8, 9, 15. London.

Cunningham, B. 1986–7 Seventeenth-century interpretations of the past: the case of Geoffrey Keating. *Irish Historical Studies* **25**, 116–28.

Curtis, E. 1932–43 *Calendar of Ormond deeds 1172–1350 A.D.* (6 vols). Dublin.

DIL 1913–76 *Dictionary of the Irish language*. Dublin. Royal Irish Academy.

Dillon, M. 1951–2 The taboos of the kings of Ireland. *Proceedings of the Royal Irish Academy* **54**C, 1–36.

Dillon, M. 1973 The consecration of Irish kings. *Celtica* **10**, 1–8.

Doherty, C. 1991 The cult of St Patrick and the politics of Armagh in the seventh century. In J.-M. Picard (ed.), *Ireland and northern France AD 600–850*, 53–94. Dublin.

Dolley, M. 1968 Two numismatic notes: II. The mythical Roman coin-hoard from Tara. *Journal of the Royal Society of Antiquaries of Ireland* **98**, 62–5.

Doody, M. 1993 Ballyhoura Hills project: interim report. *Discovery Programme Reports* **1**, 20–30. Dublin.

Doyle, J.J. 1927 Teamhair Luachra (Tara-Luachra). *Journal of the Royal Society of Antiquaries of Ireland* **57**, 59–63.

Dumville, D.N. (ed.) 1993 *St Patrick A.D. 493–1993*. Suffolk.

Enright, M.J. 1985 *Iona, Tara and Soissons; the origin of the royal anointing ritual*. Berlin and New York.

Eogan, G. 1983 *The hoards of the Irish Later Bronze Age*. Dublin.

Evans, E. E. 1966 *Prehistoric and Early Christian Ireland: a guide*. London.

Gray, E.A. 1982 *Cath Maige Tuired*. Irish Texts Society, 52. Naas.

Gray, E.A. 1982–3 *Cath Maige Tuired*: myth and structure (24–120). *Éigse* **19**, 1–35.

Gray, E.A. 1989–90 Lug and Cú Chulainn: king and warrior, god and man. *Studia Celtica* **24–5**, 38–52.

Greene, D. 1955 *Fingal Rónáin and other stories*. Mediaeval and Modern Irish Series, 16. Dublin.

Greene, D. 1979 Tabu in early Irish narrative. In H. Bekker-Nielsen *et al.* (eds), *Medieval narrative: a symposium*, 9–19. Odense.

Guyonvarc'h, C.J. 1964 Notes d'etymologie gauloises et celtiques xx. *Ogam* **16**, 427–46.

Gwynn, E. 1903–35 *The Metrical Dindshenchas* (5 vols). Dublin. (Todd Lecture Series; reprinted in 1991 by the Dublin Institute for Advanced Studies.)

Gwynn, L. 1912 De Shíl Chonairi Móir. *Ériu* **6**, 130–43.

Healy, J. 1900 Miscellanea: Tara. *Journal of the Royal Society of Antiquaries of Ireland* **30**, 176.

Herbert, M. 1988 *Iona, Kells, and Derry: the history and hagiography of the monastic familia of Columba*. Oxford.

Herbert, M. 1992 Goddess and king: the sacred marriage in early Ireland. In L.O. Fradenburg (ed.), *Women and sovereignty*, 264–75. Edinburgh.

Herbert, M. and Ó Riain, P. 1988 *Betha Adamnáin: The Irish life of Adamnán*. Irish Texts Society, 54. Cork.

Hogan, E. 1910 *Onomasticon Goedelicum*. Dublin.

Joynt, M. 1910 Echtra maic Echdach Mugmedóin. *Ériu* **4**, 91–111.

Kelleher, J.V. 1968–9 The pre-Norman Irish genealogies. *Irish Historical Studies* **16**, 138–53.

Kelly, F. 1976 *Audacht Morainn*. Dublin.

Kelly, F. 1986 An Old-Irish text on court procedure. *Peritia* **5**, 74–106.

Knott, E. 1936 *Togail Bruidne Da Derga*. Mediaeval and Modern Irish Series, 8. Dublin.

Lohan, R. 1994 *Guide to the archives of the Office of Public Works*. Dublin.

Macalister, R.A.S. 1931 *Tara: a pagan sanctuary of ancient Ireland*. London.

Macalister, R.A.S. 1938–56 *Lebor Gabála Érenn* (5 vols). Irish Texts Society, 34–5, 39, 41, 44. Dublin.

Mac Cana, P. 1955–6 Aspects of the theme of king and goddess in Irish literature. *Études Celtiques* **7**, 76–114, 356–413.

Mac Cana, P. 1958–9 Aspects of the theme of king and goddess in Irish literature. *Études Celtiques* **8**, 59–65.

Mac Cana, P. 1985 Early Irish ideology and the concept of unity. In R. Kearney (ed.), *The Irish mind,* 56–78. Dublin.

McCaughey, T.P. 1960 Tract on the chief places of Meath. *Celtica* **5**, 172–6.

McCone, K.R. 1980 Fírinne agus torthúlacht. *Léachtaí Cholm Cille* **11**, 136–73. Maigh Nuad.

McCone, K. 1990 *Pagan past and Christian present in early Irish literature*. Maynooth.

Mac Eoin, G.S. 1968 The mysterious death of Loegaire mac Néill. *Studia Hibernica* **8**, 21–48.

MacKenna, L. 1952 A poem by Gofraidh Fionn Ó Dálaigh. *Ériu* **16**, 132–9.

McNeill, C. 1932 *Registrum de Kilmainham. Register of chapter acts of the Hospital of St John of Jerusalem in Ireland, 1326–1339*. Dublin.

MacNeill, E. 1919 *Phases of Irish history*. Dublin.

MacNeill, E. 1921 *Celtic Ireland*. Dublin.

MacNeill, E. 1934–5 Colonisation under early kings of Tara. *Journal of the Galway Archaeological and Historical Society* **16**, 101–24.

MacNeill, M. 1962 *The Festival of Lughnasa*. Oxford.

Marstrander, C. 1911 A new version of the Battle of Mag Rath. *Ériu* **5**, 226–47.

Meyer, K. 1901 Baile in Scáil. *Zeitschrift für celtische Philologie* **3**, 457–66.

Meyer, K. 1906 *The triads of Ireland*. Todd Lecture Series, 13. Dublin.

Meyer, K. 1911 *Betha Colmáin maic Lúacháin: Life of Colmán son of Lúachán*. Todd Lecture Series, 17. Dublin/London.

Meyer, K. 1912 *Sanas Cormaic* : an Old-Irish glossary compiled by Cormac úa Cuilennáin. *Anecdota from Irish Manuscripts* **4**. Dublin.

Meyer, K. 1913 Ferchuitred Medba. *Anecdota from Irish Manuscripts* **5**, 17–22. Dublin.

Meyer, K. 1917 *Miscellanea Hibernica*. University of Illinois Studies in Language and Literature vol. 2, no. 4. Urbana, Illinois.

Meyer, K. 1918 Das ende von *Baile in Scáil*. *Zeitschrift für celtische Philologie* **12**, 232–8.

Moore, M. 1984 Irish cresset-stones. *Journal of the Royal Society of Antiquaries of Ireland* **114**, 98–116.

Murphy, D. and Westropp, T.J. 1894 Notes on the antiquities of Tara (*Teamhair* na Rígh). *Journal of the Royal Society of Antiquaries of Ireland* **24**, 232–42.

Murphy, G. 1952 On the dates of two sources in Thurneysen's *Heldensage*. *Ériu* **16**, 145–56.

Murray, L. 1912–15 Old times in Dundalk and its neighbourhood. *Louth Archaeological Journal* **3**, 181–8.

Newman, C. 1993 The Tara survey. Interim report. *Discovery Programme Reports* **1**, 70–89. Dublin.

Newman, C. 1995 The Tara survey. Interim report. *Discovery Programme Reports* **2**, 62–7. Dublin.

Ní Dhonnchadha, M. 1982 The guarantor list of *Cáin Adomnáin*, 697. *Peritia* **1**, 178–215.

O'Brien, E. 1992 Pagan and Christian burial in Ireland during the first millennium AD: continuity and change. In N. Edwards and A. Lane (eds), *The early church in Wales and the West*, 130–7. Oxford.

O'Brien, M.A. 1962 *Corpus genealogiarum Hiberniae*, vol. 1. Dublin.

Ó Broin, T. 1990 *Lia Fáil*: fact and fiction in the tradition. *Celtica* **21**, 393–401.

Ó Cathasaigh, T. 1977 *The heroic biography of Cormac mac Airt*. Dublin.

Ó Cathasaigh, T. 1977–9 The semantics of *síd*. *Éigse* **17**, 137–55.

Ó Cathasaigh, T. 1980–1 The theme of *lommrad* in *Cath Maige Mucrama*. *Éigse* **18**, 211–24.

Ó Cathasaigh, T. 1983 *Cath Maige Tuired* as exemplary myth. In P. de Brún, S. Ó Coileáin and P. Ó Riain (eds), *Folia Gadelica. Essays presented by former students to R.A. Breatnach*, 1–19. Cork.

Ó Cathasaigh, T. 1989 The eponym of Cnogba. *Éigse* **23**, 27–38.

Ó Ceallaigh, S. 1950 Old lights on place-names: new lights on maps. *Journal of the Royal Society of Antiquaries of Ireland* **80**, 172–86.

Ó Concheanainn, T. 1982 A pious redactor of *Dinnshenchas Érenn*. *Ériu* **33**, 85–98.

Ó Corráin, D. 1971 Topographical notes — II: *Mag Femin, Femen*, and some early annals. *Ériu* **22**, 97–9.

Ó Corráin, D. 1978 Nationality and kingship in pre-Norman Ireland. *Historical Studies* **11**, 1–35.

Ó Corráin, D. 1977–9 High-kings, Vikings and other kings. *Historical Studies* **21**, 282–323.

Ó Corráin, D. 1985 Irish origin legends and genealogy: recurrent aetiologies. In T. Nyberg *et al.* (eds), *History and heroic tale: a symposium*, 51–96. Odense.

Ó Corráin, D. 1986 Historical need and literary narrative. In D. Ellis Evans, J.G. Griffith and E.M. Jope (eds), *Proceedings of the 7th International Congress of Celtic Studies, Oxford 1983*, 141–58. Oxford.

Ó Cuív, B. 1976 Comram na Clóenfherta. *Celtica* **11**, 168–79.

Ó Cuív, B. 1983 A poem composed for Cathal Croibhdhearg Ó Conchubair. *Ériu* **34**, 157–74.

O'Curry, E. 1873 *On the manners and customs of the ancient Irish* (3 vols). Dublin.

O Daly, M. 1962 Lānellach Tigi Rīch 7 Ruirech. *Ériu* **19**, 81–6.

O Daly, M. 1975 *Cath Maige Mucrama*. Irish Texts Society, 50. Dublin.

O'Donovan, J. 1836 Ordnance Survey Letters: Meath, 1836.

Olmsted, G.S. 1979 A contemporary view on Irish 'hill-top enclosures'. *Études Celtiques* **16**, 171–85.

Ó Lochlainn, C. 1940 Roadways in ancient Ireland. In J. Ryan (ed.), *Féilsgríbhinn Eoin mhic Néill*, 465–74. Dublin.

Ó Máille, T. 1928 Medb Chruachna. *Zeitschrift für celtische Philologie* **17**, 129–46.

O'Neill, J. 1905 Cath Bóinde. *Ériu* **2**, 173–85.

O'Rahilly, T.F. 1942 *The two Patricks*. Dublin.

O'Rahilly, T.F. 1946a *Early Irish history and mythology*. Dublin.

O'Rahilly, T.F. 1946b On the origin of the names *Érainn* and *Ériu*. *Ériu* **14**, 7–28.

O'Rahilly, T.F. 1952 Buchet the herdsman. *Ériu* **16**, 7–20.

Ó Riain, P. 1978 Traces of Lug in early Irish hagiographical tradition. *Zeitschrift für celtische Philologie* **36**, 138–56.

Ó Riain, P. 1989 The Psalter of Cashel: a provisional list of contents. *Éigse* **23**, 107–30.

Ó Riain, P. 1990 The Tallaght martyrologies, re-dated. *Cambridge Medieval Celtic Studies* **20**, 21–38.

Ó Ríordáin, S.P. 1954 *Tara: the monuments on the hill*. Dundalk.

Ó Ríordáin, S.P. 1955 A burial with faience beads at Tara. *Proceedings of the Prehistoric Society* **21**, 163–73.

O Riordan, M. 1990 *The Gaelic mind and the collapse of the Gaelic world*. Cork.

Petrie, G. 1839 On the history and antiquities of Tara Hill. *Transactions of the Royal Irish Academy* **18**, 25–232.

Petrie, G. 1841 On two gold torcs found at Tara. *Proceedings of the Royal Irish Academy* **1**, 274–6.

Picard, J.-M. 1982 The purpose of Adomnán's *Vita Columbae*. *Peritia* **1**, 160–77.

Quiggin, E.C. 1913 O'Conor's house at Cloonfree. In E.C. Quiggin (ed.), *Essays and studies presented to William Ridgeway*, 333–52. Cambridge.

Radner, J.N. 1978 *Fragmentary annals of Ireland*. Dublin.

Raftery, B. 1994 *Pagan Celtic Ireland. The enigma of the Irish Iron Age*. London.

Rees, A. and Rees, B. 1961 *Celtic heritage: ancient tradition in Ireland and Wales*. London.

Ryan, M. (ed.) 1983 *Treasures of Ireland: Irish art 3000 BC–1500 AD*. Dublin.

Scowcroft, M. 1987 *Leabhar Gabhála* — Part I: the growth of the text. *Ériu* **38**, 80–142.

Scowcroft, M. 1988 *Leabhar Gabhála* — Part II: the growth of the tradition. *Ériu* **39**, 1–66.

Sharpe, R. 1982 St Patrick and the see of Armagh. *Cambridge Medieval Celtic Studies* **4**, 33–59.

Sheehy, M.P. 1962–5 *Pontifica Hibernica: medieval papal chancery documents concerning Ireland 640–1261* (2 vols). Dublin.

Simms, K. 1987 *From kings to warlords: the changing political structure of Gaelic Ireland in the later Middle Ages.* Studies in Celtic History VII. Woodbridge, Suffolk.

Smyth, A.P. 1972 The earliest Irish annals: their first contemporary entries, and the earliest centres of recording. *Proceedings of the Royal Irish Academy* **72**C, 1–48.

Smyth, A.P. 1974–5a The Húi Néill and the Leinstermen in the Annals of Ulster, 431–516 A.D. *Études Celtiques* **14**, 121–43.

Smyth, A.P. 1974–5b Húi Failgi relations with the Húi Néill in the century after the loss of the Plain of Mide. *Études Celtiques* **14**, 503–23.

Stokes, W. 1905 *Félire Óengusso Céli Dé: The Martyrology of Oengus the Culdee.* London. Henry Bradshaw Society.

Stokes, W. and Strachan, J. 1901–3 *Thesaurus Palaeohibernicus* (2 vols). Dublin.

Thurneysen, R. 1936 Allerlei Keltisches: 2. Tailtiu. *Zeitschrift für celtische Philologie* **20**, 368–9.

Vendryes, J. 1953 *Airne Fíngein.* Mediaeval and Modern Irish Series, 15. Dublin.

Wagner, H. 1970 Studies in the origins of early Celtic civilisation. *Zeitschrift für celtische Philologie* **31**, 1–58.

Wagner, H. 1975 Studies in the origins of early Celtic traditions. *Ériu* **26**, 1–26.

Wagner, H. 1979 Origins of pagan Irish religion and the study of names. *Bulletin of the Ulster Place-names Society,* ser. 2, no. 2, 24–40.

Wailes, B. 1982 The Irish 'royal sites' in history and archaeology. *Cambridge Medieval Celtic Studies* **3**, 1–29.

Warner, R. 1988 The archaeology of early historic Irish kingship. In S.T. Driscoll and M.R. Nieke (eds), *Power and politics in early medieval Britain and Ireland,* 47–68. Edinburgh.

Watson, J.C. 1941 *Mesca Ulad.* Mediaeval and Modern Irish Series, 13. Dublin.

Watson, W.J. 1904–5 Notes: Tara. *The Celtic Review* **1**, 286.

Watson, W.J. 1926 *The history of the Celtic place-names of Scotland.* Edinburgh and London.

Westropp, T.J. 1918 Temair Erann, an ancient cemetery of the Ernai on Slievereagh, County Limerick. *Journal of the Royal Society of Antiquaries of Ireland* **48**, 111–20.

Whitfield, N. 1974 The finding of the Tara brooch. *Journal of the Royal Society of Antiquaries of Ireland* **104**, 120–42.

Wormald, P. 1986 Celtic and Anglo-Saxon kingship: some further thoughts. In P.E. Szarmach (ed.), *Sources of Anglo-Saxon culture,* 151–83. Studies in Medieval Culture, 20. Kalamazoo.

Youngs, S. (ed.) 1989 *'The work of angels': masterpieces of Celtic metalwork, 6th to 9th centuries AD.* London.

II

BIBLIOGRAPHY

NOTES AND CONVENTIONS

There are two objectives to this select and annotated bibliography of the published material relating to Tara. The first is to provide a comprehensive guide to the most important publications on the subject with the interests of archaeologists, historians and literary critics in mind. The bibliography is based on a search through the American, British, Continental and Irish journals which in any way concern Celtic studies (language, literature, history and archaeology), through series of texts (e.g. the Mediaeval and Modern Irish Series published by the Dublin Institute for Advanced Studies), and through a wide range of other miscellaneous works. Since Tara is referred to so frequently (e.g. as part of stock alliterative phrases in Irish early medieval and bardic poetry) it was not feasible (nor indeed desirable) to include every individual reference, but all references of substance encountered have been incorporated. While the objective was to cover as much material as possible in order to provide a complete assessment of published works on Tara, the nature of the subject is such that the bibliography cannot be exhaustive. Some material of less import than other works is included since it is important not to pass over or ignore any item which is capable of furnishing clues to a wider and more complete interpretation of the overall subject. The bibliography is a selection, therefore, of the published primary texts and secondary works which are most relevant to an understanding of the archaeological, historical, symbolic and topographical significance of Tara.

The bibliography concentrates in its choice of primary published texts on those of the early medieval period, as many texts which post-date that period are derivative, add little to our knowledge of Tara and are explained in their own contemporary contexts. Primary texts which date from *c.* 1600 onwards (e.g. Geoffrey Keating's *Foras Feasa ar Éirinn*) are among those excluded and are intended to form part of another Discovery Programme publication on the political and symbolic significance of Tara from the late medieval period to modern times.

The second objective of the bibliography is to provide a chronological framework for the primary texts and for the secondary works which are included.

To that end, a date, in some cases more specific than in others, has been attributed to each primary text. Since editors of Old and Middle Irish texts in particular have been loath to assign texts to a very specific period other than using phrases such as 'Old Irish', 'Middle Irish', or 'Middle Irish with Old Irish usage', this is reflected in the variety of date ranges assigned to the texts in the bibliography. Where an editor assigns a specific date to a text, that is noted in the entry. Where the text has been analysed elsewhere and dated more accurately or specifically, that date is the one noted in the entry. In cases in which the text has only been assigned a general date bracket or none at all, one of the following date ranges is entered: (i) Old Irish, AD 600–900; (ii) Middle Irish, AD 900–1200; (iii) Early Modern Irish, AD 1200–1650.

Structure of the bibliography

There are four main parts to the bibliography: (i) the primary sources, (ii) literary interpretation of the sources, (iii) historical interpretation of the sources, and (iv) the archaeology and topography of Tara. The primary sources are categorised as historical and pseudo-historical sources (a category in which, owing to the nature of the material, it is not always easy to distinguish one from the other), narrative literature and verse. Each category begins with a brief explanatory paragraph, the aim of which is to indicate the relevance of that category to the understanding of Tara. A text is described according to its title (or first line in the case of verse), followed by a list of the manuscripts in which the text is preserved, editions of the text (with reference to translations), an indication of dating, a general summary of the content, and a specific explanation of its relevance to Tara. Owing to the lack of standardised orthography in Old, Middle and Early Modern Irish, the most commonly used titles of texts have been preferred. The manuscript citations are general and are to be regarded as a guide only. The full citations will be found in the editions referred to in the entries. In cases in which editors do not give manuscript citations, the editors' methods are followed. Manuscripts with a popular title (e.g. the Book of Leinster, the Book of Ballymote) are accorded that title. The citations of the manuscripts of the Royal Irish Academy (RIA) also include the numbers assigned to them in the list in K. Mulchrone, E. Fitzpatrick and A.I. Pearson's *Catalogue of Irish manuscripts in the Royal Irish Academy, Index 1* (Dublin, 1948), 1–32. Manuscripts kept at Trinity College Dublin (TCD) include the numbers assigned to them in T. K. Abbott's *Catalogue of the Irish manuscripts in the Library of Trinity College, Dublin* (Dublin, 1921). The editions included are selective. An emphasis is placed on more recent editions, on more comprehensive editions or on editions of one text which are based on different versions of a text. Accessibility was also a factor in the choice of editions. Secondary works which refer to a specific text and its relevance to Tara are included with the different categories of primary texts in chronological sequence. This format provides some idea as to how the contents of the texts are seen as contributing to an understanding of Tara. (Note that BL = British Library (British Museum); Bod =

Bodleian Library, Oxford; NLI = National Library of Ireland; and UCD = University College Dublin.)

The three remaining parts of the bibliography contain secondary works only. Within their subcategories the works follow a chronological sequence. The interpretation of the sources as literature and mythology deals primarily with concepts of kingship and sovereignty perceived to be closely associated with the kingship of Tara. The interpretation of sources from a historical perspective concentrates on the existence or otherwise of the high-kingship of Tara. The section on the archaeology and topography of Tara represents an attempt to gather together as many references as possible to the published sources on the material culture and topographical features of the monument and its hinterland, with the exception of accounts of the activities of the British Israelites from 1898 to 1903. This subject will form part of the forthcoming study on the modern significance of Tara referred to above.

In certain instances, entries are relevant to more than one category. The full entry is included in one category and is referred to by number at the end of any other section of relevance, introduced by the phrase 'See also no.'. Quotation from a specific page of a work is indicated by the page number in brackets (e.g. (515)). Quotations from original texts and non-English words and phrases are italicised.

Any bibliography of Tara could easily become a bibliography of the sources for early medieval Ireland, such is the importance of the subject for the period. Those prompted by this bibliography into other, wider fields will find ample material in works such as J.F. Kenney's *The sources for the early history of Ireland: Ecclesiastical* (3rd edn; Dublin, 1979), R.I. Best's *Bibliography of Irish philology and of printed Irish literature to 1912* (Dublin, 1913) and his *Bibliography of Irish philology and manuscript literature 1913–41* (Dublin, 1942), and R. Baumgarten's *Bibliography of Irish linguistics and literature 1942–71* (Dublin, 1986).

PRIMARY SOURCES

HISTORY AND PSEUDO-HISTORY

A.	Annals	1–9
B.	Regnal lists	10–17
C.	Genealogies	18–25
D.	Law-tracts	26–37
E.	Hagiology	38–64
F.	Topographical texts	65–72
G.	Charters, deeds and papal documents	73–80
H.	Prophecies	81–3
I.	*Mirabilia*	84–9
J.	Taboos	90–1
K.	Triads	92
L.	Glossaries	93–4
M.	*Audacht Morainn*	95–7
N.	*Lebor Gabála Érenn* and associated tales	98–105

TARA: A SELECT BIBLIOGRAPHY

A. Annals

The most frequent entry concerning Tara in the annals is the use of the title *rí Temra(ch)* 'king of Tara'. The title refers in certain instances to the king of Brega, while elsewhere, most particularly in the *Annals of the Four Masters*, it is synonymous with the title '[high]-king of Ireland'. Records of historic events which took place at Tara are rare and are common to all major annalistic collections. The most notable are *c*. 560 (the last celebration of *Feis Temro* by Diarmait mac Cerbaill), 780 (a synod held at Tara), 817 (the cursing of the king of Tara by the *familia* of Colum Cille), 840 (Feidlimid mac Crimthainn, king of Munster, halts at Tara), 980 (the Battle of Tara) and 1104 (Domnall úa Lochlainn at Tara). The annals listed below include a number of the most important collections of Irish annalistic records and are essential tools in understanding the historical significance of Tara in the medieval period.

1. *The Annals of Ulster*

    MSS: TCD H 1 8 (no. 1282); Bod Rawlinson B 489.

    EDITIONS: Hennessy, W.M. and Mac Carthy, B. 1887–1901 *Annala Uladh, Annals of Ulster. Otherwise, Annala Senait, Annals of Senat; A chronicle of Irish affairs from A.D. 431, to A.D. 1540* (4 vols). Dublin.
    Mac Airt, S. and Mac Niocaill, G. 1983 *The Annals of Ulster (to A.D. 1131)*. Dublin.

    DATE RANGE: Prehistory to 1588.

2. *The Annals of Inisfallen*

    MS: Bod Rawlinson B 503.

    EDITION: Mac Airt, S. 1951 *The Annals of Inisfallen*. Dublin.

    DATE RANGE: Prehistory to 1450.

3. *The Annals of Tigernach*

    MS: Bod Rawlinson B 488; B 502; TCD H 1 8 (no. 1282).

    EDITION: Stokes, W. 1895–7 The Annals of Tigernach. *Revue Celtique* **16**, 374–419; **17**, 6–33, 119–263, 337–420; **18**, 9–59, 150–97, 267–303, 374–91. (Reprinted 1993, Felinfach reprint, 2 vols. Llanerch Publishers.)

    DATE RANGE: Prehistory to 1178.

4. *Chronicum Scotorum*

    MS: TCD H 1 18 (no. 1292).

    EDITION: Hennessy, W.M. 1866 *Chronicum Scotorum. A chronicle of Irish affairs from the earliest times to A.D. 1135; with a supplement, containing the events from 1141–1150*. Rolls Series. London. (Reprinted 1964, Wiesbaden reprint. Kraus Reprint Ltd.)

    DATE RANGE: Prehistory to 1150.

5. *The Annals of the Four Masters*

    MSS: RIA 23 P 6 (no. 687) and 7 (no. 688); C iii 3 (no. 1220); TCD H 2 9–10 (no. 1300); H 2 11 (no.1301); Franciscan Library Killiney A 13.

EDITION: O'Donovan, J. 1848–51 *Annala Rioghachta Éireann. Annals of the Kingdom of Ireland by the Four Masters from the earliest period to the year 1616* (7 vols). Dublin. (Reprinted 1990, De Búrca Rare Books, Dublin, with a new introduction by K. Nicholls.)

DATE RANGE: Prehistory to 1616.

6. Kelleher, J.V. 1971 The *Táin* and the annals. *Ériu* **22**, 107–27.

   A discussion on the synchronisms and sources of the annals from the earliest entries. The author attempts to associate the composition and 'rediscovery' of the *Táin* with Cuanu, abbot of the monastery of Louth (d. 825). He links its transmission with the ecclesiastical family, the Uí Gormáin, who originated in Louth and who moved later to Clonmacnoise.

   TARA: 113–15. The deletion of non-Dál Cuinn, and subsequently Uí Néill, kings of Tara from the annalistic records of the fifth and sixth centuries, and from other sources dating to a period before the eighth century, may indicate a revision of the sources, possibly during the reigns of two kings of Tara, Domnall Midi (d. 763) and Donnchad Midi (d. 797). (Kelleher's theories are questioned by D.N. Dumville, 'Ulster heroes in the early Irish annals: a caveat', *Éigse* **17** (1977–9), 47–54.)

7. Smyth, A.P. 1972 The earliest Irish annals: their first contemporary entries, and the earliest centres of recording. *Proceedings of the Royal Irish Academy* **72**C, 1–48.

   An analysis of the earliest annalistic entries and theories regarding their origin. The author attempts to locate and to date the earliest annalistic collections.

   TARA: 6–12; 45. The author notes that the first notice of the beginning of the reign of an Uí Néill 'over-king' (the entry recording the beginning of the reign of Diarmait mac Cerbaill in 544) corresponds exactly with the period in the middle of the sixth century at which there is evidence for the beginnings of contemporaneity of entry in the *Annals of Ulster*. An understanding of how the chronology of early Uí Néill dynasts who claimed to hold the kingship of Tara was devised is crucial to supporting the authenticity of the first contemporary annalistic entries.

8. Smyth, A.P. 1974–5 The Húi Néill and the Leinstermen in the Annals of Ulster, 431–516 A.D. *Études Celtiques* **14**, 121–43.

   A discussion on the fifth and sixth centuries in the area known as *Campus Mide*, the Plain of Meath. The author demonstrates how the Leinstermen lost the *Campus Mide* during that period to the Uí Néill, following bitter conflict between the two. There is also a detailed analysis of the historical authenticity of the reigns of the early historical Uí Néill kings of Tara from Lóegaire mac Néill to Muirchertach mac Erca (?d. 543).

9. Smyth, A.P. 1974–5 Húi Failgi relations with the Húi Néill in the century after the loss of the Plain of Mide. *Études Celtiques* **14**, 503–23.

   An article which explains the state of the Leinster dynasties following the loss of the *Campus Mide*. Particular reference is made to relations between the dominant, but ailing, dynasty of Uí Failgi and the Uí Néill in the sixth and seventh centuries. The following comment by the author regarding Tara (515) is noteworthy:

> The attention of archaeologists which has so often been concentrated on the royal site of Tara (Co. Meath) could in future be directed with greater profit to this confined area in Westmeath [a small area of land hemmed in between the lakes of Owel, Drin and Deravaragh]. A detailed survey of the many forts in this area, followed by systematic excavation by those competent in the period, should yield a cross-section of material from the proto-historic period up to 800 A.D., and indeed beyond.

B. Regnal lists

The lists of the kings of Tara, and by extension the kings of Ireland, reflect the gradual and all-embracing nature of the domination of Tara by the Uí Néill from the seventh century onwards. The earliest list, *Baile Chuinn*, a document likely to date from the late seventh century, is biased towards the southern Uí Néill and contains references to Uí Néill dynasts who are later excised from the official lists (e.g. Coirpre mac Néill) or who were total outsiders (e.g. Féachno, possibly Fiachnae mac Báetain of the Dál nAraidi). *Baile in Scáil* and the later lists reflect the official version of the kingship of Tara according to the doctrine of the Uí Néill.

10. *Baile Chuinn Chétchathaig*

    MSS: RIA 23 N 10 (no. 967); BL Egerton 88.

    EDITIONS: Thurneysen, R. 1912 *Zu irischen Handschriften und Litteraturdenkmälern*, 48–52. Berlin.
    Murphy, G. 1952 On the dates of two sources used in Thurneysen's *Heldensage*. *Ériu* **16**, 145–56: 145–51 (with translation).

    DATE: Seventh century.

    A text which purports to foretell the (southern Uí Néill) kings destined to reign at Tara from the time of the legendary Art mac Cuinn Chétchathaig onwards. The last identifiable king referred to in the text is Fínnachta Fledach (d. 695). Whereas Thurneysen eventually assigned the text to the tenth century, on the basis that it included an allusion to Níall Glúndub (d. 919), Murphy concluded that the king-list was a seventh-century text. He suggested that the text may have been composed at a time when Fínnachta Fledach had not yet assumed the kingship of Tara but was merely an heir-apparent, *rígdamna* (*c.* 675).

11. *Baile in Scáil*

    MSS: Bod Rawlinson B 512; BL Harley 5280.

    EDITIONS: Meyer, K. 1901 Baile in Scáil. *Zeitschrift für celtische Philologie* **3**, 457–66.
    Meyer, K. 1918 Das Ende von *Baile in Scáil*. *Zeitschrift für celtische Philologie* **12**, 232–8.
    Meyer, K. 1921 Der Anfang von *Baile in Scáil*. *Zeitschrift für celtische Philologie* **13**, 371–82.
    Thurneysen, R. 1936 Baile in Scáil. *Zeitschrift für celtische Philologie* **20**, 213–27.

    DATE: Ninth or tenth century with eleventh-century additions.

    A prophetic king-list which enumerates the kings of Tara from Conn Cétchathach to Donnchad mac Flainn (d. 944), later extended as far as Máel Sechnaill II (d. 1022).

The list is one of the most important texts concerning the kingship of Tara, both in its political and its symbolic manifestations. It is the 'official' list of the kings of Tara, as perceived by Uí Néill propagandists, whose ancestor, Conn Cétchathach, is granted the sovereignty of Tara (and implicitly the sovereignty of Ireland) by the god Lug in the preface to the king-list.

12. Ó Cathasaigh, T. 1989 The eponym of Cnogba. *Éigse* **23**, 27–38.

    A discussion of associations between the place-name Cnogba (Knowth, Co. Meath), the god Lug, and the goddess of sovereignty, Buí.

    TARA: 30–3. The author notes Lug's part in *Baile in Scáil*, where he is presented as legitimator of the Dál Cuinn (and hence also of the Uí Néill) kings of Tara. Each of the kings named in the text is wedded to Lug's consort (the goddess of kingship), and they replace Lug as king to act as his surrogate in the kingship of Tara.

13. Herbert, M. 1992 Goddess and king: the sacred marriage in early Ireland. In L.O. Fradenburg (ed.), *Women and sovereignty*, 264–75. Edinburgh.

    An important study of the concept of sovereignty, which is conceived of as female, in its literary and historical manifestations. The author argues that the role of the goddess is diminished and is appropriated by the king in the texts *Baile in Scáil* and *Echtra mac nEchdach Mugmedóin* for a contemporary political purpose. Both texts are statements on behalf of the Uí Néill and are regarded as a reassertion of their right to kingship, and in particular to the kingship of Tara, which was threatened by the Munster dynasty of Dál Cais in the guise of Brían Bóruma. This interpretation suggests a final date of composition in the early eleventh century for *Baile in Scáil*.

14. Ó Buachalla, B. 1989 Aodh Eanghach and the Irish king-hero. In D. Ó Corráin, L. Breatnach and K. McCone (eds), *Sages, saints and storytellers. Celtic studies in honour of Professor James Carney*, 200–32. Maynooth.

    A discussion of the prophetic figure Áed Eangach, who from the tenth century onwards plays a role in Irish political literature.

    TARA: 209–11. Áed Eangach is especially associated with Tara. He appears first in *Baile in Scáil* and the consistent theme in literature from then on is that Tara will recognise him, the *Lia Fáil* will proclaim him, and he will restore Tara.

15. Berchán

    FIRST LINE: *Airis bic, a mheic b[h]ic bháin*.

    MSS: Book of Uí Máine; RIA 23 G 4 (no. 679); 23 H 22 (no. 667); 23 N 12 (no. 488); 23 E 16 (no. 491).

    EDITION: Anderson, A.O. 1930 The prophecy of Berchan. *Zeitschrift für celtische Philologie* **18**, 1–56.

    DATE: A composite poem, the last Irish king referred to being Toirdelbach mac Diarmata, king of Thomond (d. 1167), and the last Scottish king Domnall Bán (d. 1097).

    A prophecy in verse foretelling the kings of Ireland and Scotland ascribed to Berchán, a sixth-century saint to whom later prophetic texts are attributed. While the text does not relate as directly to the kingship of Tara as do *Baile Chuinn* and *Baile in Scáil*, it provides details on kings associated with Tara which occasionally diverge from those found in the annals. For example, Máel Mithig mac Flannacáin, *flaithrí Temrach* (d. 919) (or his son Congalach Cnogba — see editor's note 23 §47), is described as dying at Clonmacnoise (49c *attigh Ciaráin ad-bhéla*), whereas the annals list him among the dead with Níall Glúndub at the Battle of Dublin.

16. Flann Mainistrech (d. 1056)

    FIRST LINES:
    I *Cia triallaid nech aisnis senchais /Ailig eltaig.*
    II *Cind cethri ndíni iar Frigrind /forraig gleogal.*
    III *Ascnam ní seol sadal /iarsain slicht cen breobail.*
    IV *Aní do ronsat do chalmu /clanna Eogain.*
    V *A ngluind a n-ēchta a n-orgni /batar infhir.*
    VI *Mide magen clainne Cuind/forod clainne Néill nertluind.*
    VII *Síl Aeda Sláne na sleg/dia sásar mór ríg ragel.*

    MS: Book of Leinster.

    EDITIONS: MacNeill, J. [alias E.] 1913 Poems by Flann Mainistrech on the dynasties of Ailech, Mide and Brega. *Archivium Hibernicum* **2**, 37–99. (Poem I not included in edition; rest with translation.)
    Best, R.I. and O'Brien, M.A. 1965 *The Book of Leinster, formerly Lebar na Núachongbála,* vol. 4, 782–814 (diplomatic edition). Dublin.

    DATE: Eleventh century.

    Poems ascribed to Flann Mainistrech, *fer léigind* of Monasterboice (d. 1056), concerning kings of the Uí Néill dynasties of Ailech, Mide and Brega (see F.J. Byrne, 'Historical note on Cnogba (Knowth)', *Proceedings of the Royal Irish Academy* **66**C (1967–8), 391–2, on the ascriptions to Flann Mainistrech). The last kings referred to are Níall mac Máil Shechnaill, king of Ailech (d. 1061), Murchad mac Flainn, king of Mide (d. 1076) (in an interpolated quatrain), and Muirchertach mac Congalaig, king of Brega (d. 995).

17. Miscellaneous (associated with *Lebor Gabála*, see no. 98).

    MSS: RIA D iv 3 (no. 1224); Book of Lecan; Bod Rawlinson B 512.

    EDITION: Thurneysen, R. 1933 Synchronismen der irischen Könige. *Zeitschrift für celtische Philologie* **19**, 81–99.

    DATE: Primarily eleventh century with twelfth-century additions.

    A regnal list of high-kings of Ireland, kings of Irish provinces and of Scotland. The text is useful for comparison of its details with other regnal lists and with information on the kings of Tara contained in annalistic references.

C. Genealogies

The extensive corpus of Irish genealogies contains many references to Tara, some of which may be the earliest allusions to survive. The most notable early references to Tara are preserved in the poems on the genealogies of the Leinstermen, variously dated from the fifth to the eighth century and preserved in the twelfth-century codex Rawlinson B 502. They reflect a period prior to total domination of Tara by the Uí Néill, when the Leinstermen (*Laigin*) appear to have held the kingship of Tara. Annalistic entries suggest that this control may not have been wrested from them finally until the early eighth century. Genealogical material emanating from Munster, such as that found in the text *Conall Corc and the Corcu Loígde*, depicts an ambiguous attitude towards the supremacy of Tara.

18. MSS: Bod Rawlinson B 502; Book of Leinster (with variants from Book of Lecan, Book of Ballymote and Laud Miscellany 610).

    EDITION: O'Brien, M.A. 1962 *Corpus genealogiarum Hiberniae*, vol. 1. Dublin. (Reprinted 1976 with an introduction by J.V. Kelleher.)

    DATE: Early twelfth century. This is the date of the final compilation of the genealogical collections. Earlier strata can be identified, most notably dating from the tenth century.

    A volume containing pre-Norman genealogies from the twelfth-century codices Rawlinson B 502 and the Book of Leinster.

    TARA: See index, 764. The Rawlinson genealogies contain possibly very early (pre-800) references to Tara in the series of poems known as the early Leinster genealogical poems (1–9). These include a reference to the *Lia Fáil* (3, 115b23) and the poem *Nidu dír dermait dála cach ríg rómdae* (8–9), which exhorts the Leinstermen not to forget that the kingship of Tara once belonged to them. A regnal list of the Leinster kings of Tara is embedded in this poem, possibly dating from the fourth and fifth centuries. Among the other noteworthy allusions to Tara in the Rawlinson genealogies is the reference to Cathaír Mór, progenitor of the Leinstermen, residing at Tara as king, while Conn Cétchathach, progenitor of the Uí Néill, resided at Kells (70, 124a24–5). It is claimed that Cathaír Mór was killed by the Luigne Temrach (70, 124a31). (For valuable comments on this volume, see review by F.J. Byrne, *Zeitschrift für celtische Philologie* **29** (1962–4), 381–5.)

19. MS: TCD H 2 7 (no. 1298).

    EDITION: Dobbs, M.E. 1940 Miscellany from H.2.7 (T.C.D.). *Zeitschrift für celtische Philologie* **21**, 307–18.

    DATE: Prior to the year 800.

    A miscellany of early genealogical details of the Eóganacht Chaisil and the Corcu Loígde of Munster, as well as Leinster families.

    TARA: 310 §5; 312 §11. These are two references which allude to septs who may have had early associations with Tara: the Caíltrige, descended from Caílte mac Liatháin Cherddae, and the Cosgrig (*sic*) Temrach, descended from Lugaid Coscrach. The latter are described as living in the territory of the Déssi in the Rawlinson B 502 genealogies (O'Brien: 257, 155a12).

20. MS: Bod Laud Miscellany 610.

    EDITIONS: Meyer, K. 1912 The Laud genealogies and tribal histories. *Zeitschrift für celtische Philologie* **8**, 291–338.
    MacNeill, J. 1912 Notes on the Laud genealogies (including corrections by Kuno Meyer to his text). *Zeitschrift für celtische Philologie* **8**, 411–19.

DATE: Includes early material, possibly dating from the eighth century.

Extensive genealogical material from the fifteenth-century manuscript Laud Miscellany 610, which includes some very early Munster genealogies.

TARA: There are three passages of particular reference to Tara. The first (309–12) is a version of *Scéla Eógain 7 Cormaic*, from the Cormac mac Airt cycle. The second (313.16–18, 26–30) tells of the three sons of Búan mac Lóegairi Birn, from whom the Osraige descended, that they first took possession of Tara (*ciatarochlan[n]sat cletha hi Temuir* 'that they had first fixed stakes/wooden posts in Tara'). They were replaced at Tara by 'the second' Míl Espáine, who left the soil (*úr*) of Thebes (?; MS *Themis*) there. The name *Temair* is described as soil of the soil of Thebes (*úr dind húir a Themis*). Reference (325.21–2) is also made to the claim that Tara was first built by Ollam Fótla, after whom the wall *múr n-ollaman* was named.

21. *Conall Corc and the Corco Loígde*

    MS: Bod Laud Miscellany 610.

    EDITIONS: Meyer, K. 1910 Conall Corc and the Corco Luigde. *Anecdota from Irish Manuscripts* **3**, 57–63.
    Hull, V. 1947 Conall Corc and the Corco Luigde. *Publications of the Modern Language Association of America* **62**, 887–909 (translation only).

    DATE: Seventh or eighth century.

    Primarily a genealogical tract relating to Conall Corc, progenitor of the various branches of the Eóganacht dynasty in Munster.

    TARA: The text appears to reveal the attitudes of the Eóganachta to Tara and its supremacy in Ireland. Of note is the passage 58.18–25, where reference is made to *Angubai Már oc Temair* ('a great lamentation at Tara') which was caused by the death of Níall Noígíallach's son at the hands of Níall's hostages, the Corco Daulai. Corc ransomed the hostages from Níall (*Crecsus Corc di Niall*) and made them (and their descendants) pay direct tribute to the king of Cashel. An inference is also made in the text (59.16–17) that Corc was regarded — by Munster propagandists at least — as having claimed the kingship of Ireland (*Iadais rige nEirenn imbi intan donanic Femen*). (For the significance of this inference and other possible imitations of Uí Néill propaganda, see no. 257.)

22. FIRST LINE: *Fidbaid cubra clanna Neill*.

    MS: TCD H 2 7 (no. 1298).

    EDITION: Ní C. Dobs, M. [alias Dobbs, M.E.] 1940 Cenél Fiachach m. Néill. *Zeitschrift für celtische Philologie* **21**, 1–23.

    DATE: The prose form dates possibly from the eleventh century. The metrical tract is ascribed to Seaán Ó Dubhagáin (d. 1372).

    Genealogies of the southern Uí Néill sept, Cenél Fiachach, whose territory stretched north of Birr to Uisnech.

    TARA: The prose introduction (2–3) describes the divisions of land among the sons of Níall Noígíallach, with the 'sovereignty of Tara' (*follomnas Temrach*) being assigned to Lóegaire. Reference is made in the verse to Luigne mac Érimóin seizing Tara (15.331 *Luigní mac Eirimoin uill/ do gab go laecda Liathdruim*). Luigne's descendants at the time of composition were the Meic Gilli Martain family (15.335–6).

23. Kelleher, J.V. 1968–9 The pre-Norman Irish genealogies. *Irish Historical Studies* **16**, 138–53.

An assessment of M.A. O'Brien's *Corpus genealogiarum Hiberniae,* including further theories on the structure and development of the Irish genealogies. Throughout this study, the author asserts that the main schema reflected in the pre-Norman genealogies was devised at a time when the Uí Néill dominated the kingship of Tara. This domination, the author suggests, happened at or not long before the middle of the eighth century, when the Uí Néill kingship of Tara was, to some degree, an over-kingship of Ireland.

24. Carney, J. 1971 Three old Irish accentual poems. *Ériu* **22**, 23–80.

A discussion of the dating and context of the earliest fragments of Irish poetry, with particular reference to the types of metres employed. The author discusses, among others, the poems of the Munster ecclesiastic Colmán mac Lénéni, the series of poems known as the Leinster poems preserved in the Leinster genealogies, and the poems of Luccreth moccu Chíara.

TARA: 65–73. The author's discussion concerning the dating of the Leinster texts is important insofar as these possibly contain some of the earliest references to Tara. The Leinstermen, according to Carney, are seen as exercising power as far as the borders of Ulster, are of different ethnic origin to the rest of Ireland, are given to overseas raiding, and are very conscious of Roman civilisation. (For an extension of Carney's view on the Leinster poems, see his paper 'The dating of archaic Irish verse', in S. Tranter and H. Tristram (eds), *Early Irish literature — media and communication. Mündlichkeit und Schriftlichkeit in der frühen irischen Literatur* (Tübingen, 1989), 39-55.)

25. Ó Corráin, D. 1985 Irish origin legends and genealogy: recurrent aetiologies. In T. Nyberg *et al.* (eds), *History and heroic tale: a symposium*, 51–96. Odense.

An analysis of the earliest Irish genealogical material viewed with regard to their structure, dating and the influences — especially scriptural — which can be identified. Particular reference is made to the early Leinster genealogical material.

TARA: 58–60. Linguistic and historical evidence indicates that the poem *Nidu dír dermait*, which formally is a list of kings of Leinster who ruled from Tara, dates from the early decades of the seventh century. The king-list is highly edited in that it includes only kings who descended from Cathaír Mór.

D. Law-tracts and associated texts

The law-tracts do not contain many references to kings of Tara. Two references, however, are noteworthy. The tract on bee-keeping, *Bechbretha*, appears to refer to Congal Cáech of the Cruithne of Ulster holding the kingship of Tara. Congal Cáech was killed at the Battle of Mag Rath in 637. The tract on the status of poets, *Bretha Nemed*, refers to *Feis Temro* as one of three elements which constitute a king of over-kings (*rí ruirech*).The law-tracts are valuable also insofar as the tract on status, *Críth Gablach*, and other associated texts provide the source for the depiction of the *tech midchúarta*, which appears in its most florid form in the tract and accompanying illustration of the *Tech Midchúarta* at Tara preserved in the twelfth-century Book of Leinster.

26. *Críth Gablach*

MS: TCD H 3 18 (no. 1337).

EDITIONS: MacNeill, E. 1921–4 Ancient Irish law. The law of status or franchise. *Proceedings of the Royal Irish Academy* **36**C, 281–306 (with translation).
Binchy, D.A. 1941 *Críth Gablach*. Mediaeval and Modern Irish Series, 11. Dublin.

DATE: Early eighth century.

A law-tract, *Críth Gablach,* which deals with matters of rank and status.

TARA: (Binchy's edn) 18 §32.462–5; 23 §46. The text refers to a *rí midchúarta* (possibly a king presiding over a banqueting hall). According to Binchy (n. 36, 462f.), the quatrain in which the term is found is corrupt and difficult to interpret. The longer passage (§46) describes the arrangements at a king's house (*tech ríg*) according to rank. Allusion is made to strife at the ale-house (*cuirmthech*). The author of *Críth Gablach* glosses one type of law (*rechtge*) enforced by a king, *rechtge do indarbbu echtarchiníuil* 'a *rechtge* for the expulsion of a foreign race', *.i. fri Saxanu* 'against the Saxons' (522–3). This may be an allusion to the raid by Egfrid, king of Northumbria, on Brega in 684 (see editor's note, p. xiv).

27. FIRST LINE: *Áiliu tech midchúarta*.

MSS: TCD H 2 15B (no. 1317); Bod. Laud Miscellany 610; Book of Ballymote.

EDITIONS: Thurneysen, R. 1891 Mittelirische Verslehren. *Irische Texte* (3rd ser.) **1**, 51 §94. Leipzig.
Meyer, K. 1917 *Miscellanea Hibernica,* 23–4 (with translation). Urbana, Illinois.
Gwynn, E.J. 1942 An Old-Irish tract on the privileges and responsibilities of poets. *Ériu* **13**, 1–60, 220–36: 40.13–19.

DATE: Possibly the eighth century.

The poem, *Áiliu tech midchúarta*, which describes a *tech midchúarta*, is a structural description not associated with any specific location. The text includes references to features such as the beams (*a chrann*) of its thresholds, its two posts (*a di ursainn*), its door valve (*a chomla*), its bolt (*a glass*), and its high seat (*a airide*).

28. FIRST LINE: [A]*rsiasar coimhdhi Temrae sceo Tailten suidhi coimhdemhair*.

MS: NLI G 7.

EDITION: O Daly, M. 1952 A poem on the Airgialla. *Ériu* **16**, 179–88 (with translation).

DATE: Possibly the eighth century.

A poem which concerns the status and rights of the northern vassal tribe, the Airgíalla, in the context of their relationship with the Uí Néill. It is noteworthy that the kings of the Uí Néill are not described as kings of Tara (31c *dlegar do ríg hUe Neill*).

TARA: 179–80 §§1–5. The opening part of the poem describes the seating arrangements of the provincial kings around the king of Tara. As significant as the formal seating arrangements are the designations assigned to the seated kings — *ri Mumhen* (king of Munster), *ri Loigen* (king of Leinster), *righ Connacht* (king of Connacht), *clanda… Choirpre Lifechair* (?Airgíalla), and the Uí Néill. The Airgíalla and the Uí Néill are regarded as equal in nobility (10a *Comshaire ceneuil do Uip Néill fri Oirgialda*).

29. MS: NLI G 7.

    EDITION: O Daly, M. 1962 Lānellach Tigi Rīch 7 Ruirech. *Ériu* **19**, 81–6 (with translation).

    DATE: Eighth or ninth century.

    An Old Irish text which describes the full complement of the house of a king (*rí*) and overking (*ruire*). The text describes the seating arrangements around a king according to status (smith, seer, judge, spearmen, sureties, queen, hospitallers, leeches, leather-bottle makers, jesters, horn-blowers, charioteers, flute-players, hunters, fishermen, trappers and fence-makers). The importance of the text for Tara is that it is an earlier version of the seating arrangements described in the *Tech Midchúarta* text preserved in the Book of Leinster. The editor comments that this text is closer in date and content to that in the law-tract *Críth Gablach* than to that in the Book of Leinster.

30. MS: TCD H 3 18 (no. 1337).

    EDITION: Kelly, F. 1986 An Old-Irish text on court procedure. *Peritia* **5**, 74–106 (with translation).

    DATE: Eighth or ninth century.

    A bipartite Old Irish text which deals with court procedure.

    TARA: 81–3. The first part of the text describes the seating arrangements of the court. In his discussion of the physical attributes of the building housing an assembly of king and judges, the editor draws on parallels such as the *Tech Midchúarta*.

31. FIRST LINE: *Temair, saer in sossadh.*

    MS: BL Harley 5280.

    EDITION: Meyer, K. 1912 Mitteilungen aus irischen Handschriften: Rangordnung der Könige in Tara. *Zeitschrift für celtische Philologie* **8**, 108.

    DATE: Possibly the tenth or eleventh century.

    A Middle Irish poem describing the seating arrangements of provincial kings (Caisel, Laigin, Ulaid, Fochla (the northern Uí Néill) and Connacht) around the king of Tara.

32. MSS: Book of Leinster; Yellow Book of Lecan; Book of Ballymote; RIA B iii 1 (no. 742); B iv 2 (no. 1080); D ii 2 (no. 1222); D ii 1 (no. 1225); TCD H 1 12 (no. 1286); Rennes Irish MS. (Note: the full range of texts preserved in the Book of Leinster appears only in some of these MSS. The Yellow Book of Lecan is the only other MS to include the illustration of the *Tech Midchúarta* at Tara.)

    EDITION: Best, R.I., Bergin, O. and O'Brien, M.A. 1954 *The Book of Leinster, formerly Lebar na Núachongbála,* vol. 1, 112–20. Dublin.

    DATE: Eleventh century.

    This section of the Book of Leinster describes by illustration, prose and metrical account the seating arrangements at the *Tech Midchúarta* at Tara. The prose account explains that all kings of Tara of note (e.g. Art mac Cuinn, Níall Noígíallach, Lóegaire mac Néill) had a *tech midchúarta* at Tara, but none could surpass that of Cormac mac Airt in size or in numbers attending.

33. Wagner, H. 1974 Der königliche Palast in keltischer Tradition. *Zeitschrift für celtische Philologie* **33**, 6–14.

   A note on the associations of the royal palace sometimes referred to as *in tech mór* (*midchúarta*).

   TARA: 7–8; 11. The author alludes to the use of the 'magic number' fifty in the description of Tara's *tech midchúarta* in the Middle Irish text *Turim Tigi Temrach* (see no. 32).

34. Charles-Edwards, T.M. 1994 A contract between king and people in early medieval Ireland? *Críth Gablach* on kingship. *Peritia* **8**, 107–19.

   A discussion of the passage in the law-tract on status, *Críth Gablach*, dealing with kingship, with particular reference to the relationship between king and people as a contract, and by extension between under-kings and over-kings and between church and laity.

   TARA: 113; 116–17. The part of the text in *Críth Gablach* dealing with the arrangement of the king's household (§46) forms one element of the *córus ríg*, 'what is appropriate for a king'. The author notes that the poem on the status and rights of the Airgíalla (see no. 28) 'uses legal terminology on a very large scale'. The relationship between the Airgíalla and the Uí Néill is perceived as a series of rights and obligations, established by a contract guaranteed by named sureties (116–17).

35. *Bechbretha*

   MSS: TCD H 2 15A (no. 1316) (only complete copy). Various fragments and glosses are listed by the editors, 4–12.

   EDITION: Charles-Edwards, T. and Kelly, F. 1983 *Bechbretha. An Old Irish law-tract on bee-keeping* [with translation]. Dublin.

   DATE: Middle of the seventh century.

   TARA: 68–70 §§30–3; nn 123–34. An Old Irish law-tract on bee-keeping incorporates one of the most significant references in the early Irish law-tracts to a king of Tara. The king referred to is Congal Cáech, who was known to have been the king of the Cruithne, killed in 637 at the Battle of Mag Rath.

36. *Bretha Nemed*

   MS: BL Nero A 7.

   EDITION: Binchy, D.A. 1978 *Corpus iuris Hibernici ad fidem codicum manuscriptorum recognovit*, vol. 6, 2211–32. Dublin.
   (See also E.J. Gwynn, 'An Old-Irish tract on the privileges and responsibilities of poets', *Ériu* **13** (1942), 1–60; F. Kelly, *A guide to early Irish law* (Dublin, 1988), 268–9; L. Breatnach, 'The first third of *Bretha Nemed Toísech*', *Ériu* **40** (1989), 1–40.)

   DATE: Eighth century.

   A law-tract on the status of clerics, poets and other professionals.

   TARA: 2219.39–40. A significant passage which defines the status of a *rí ruirech*. That which constitutes a *rí ruirech* is *roimse, feis temruch, fonaidm ríg ruirech* (Binchy proposed that *ruirech* be omitted from the text), 'abundance, *Feis Temro*, binding of kings'. Since the law-tract is likely to be of Munster origin (Breatnach), it reveals that some form of supremacy was associated with Tara, in that to gain the status of a *rí ruirech* a king had to be able to celebrate *Feis Temro* (see nos 40 and 92).

37. *Córus Béscnai*

    MS: TCD H 2 15A (no. 1316); TCD H 3 17 (no. 1336); TCD H 3 18 (no. 1337).

    EDITION: Binchy, D.A. 1978 *Corpus iuris Hibernici as fidem codicum manuscriptorum recognovit*, vol. 2, 520–36. Dublin. (See translation (often inaccurate) in *Ancient laws of Ireland*, vol. 3, 3–79.)

    DATE: Eighth century.

    TARA: 527.14–528.6. A summarised version of the encounter between Lóegaire and Patrick, significantly inserted into the law-tracts to demonstrate the concept of authority. Note (527.26) the inference that Corc, progenitor of the Eóganacht dynasty in Munster, was at Lóegaire's court as a hostage (*Corc mac Luigdech cetaroslecht do bai side a ngiall la Laegaire*). (Note also that 'The pseudo-historical prologue to the *Senchas Már*' draws on *Córus Béscnai* and presents Lóegaire's court as the place where the entire legal system was codified (see no. 51).)

E. Hagiology and calendars

The most renowned episodes relating to Tara are found in the lives of saints. They are dramatic incidents, usually with an element of ecclesiastical or political propaganda, and they have influenced greatly subsequent views of the early history of Tara. Most notable among these incidents is the account of the confrontation between Patrick and Lóegaire, king of Tara, and his druids. This is contained in its earliest form in the seventh-century account of the saint's *itinerarium* and his biography, compiled by Bishop Tírechán and Muirchú maccu Machtheni respectively. Later versions occur in the *Vita Tripartita* and in other Latin lives. (These Latin lives are not included here; for the most recent edition see L. Bieler, *Four Latin lives of St Patrick* (Dublin, 1971) (Scriptores Latini Hiberniae, 8).) Another episode is the cursing of Tara by Rúadán as a result of conflict with the king of Tara, Diarmait mac Cerbaill, an incident created by hagiographers in the tenth or eleventh centuries for their own purposes, not least to explain the Christianisation of the kingship of Tara. The abandonment of Tara in favour of ecclesiastical centres like Armagh is proclaimed by the author of the Prologue to *Félire Óengusso*, which was compiled *c*. 830 by someone at the monastery of Tallaght conscious of the affairs of the Leinster dynasty, the Uí Dúnlainge, and of the southern Uí Néill dynasty, Clann Cholmáin Móir. Both had an interest in the mon-astery. It lay in border lands which were a source of contention between the two dynasties.

Patrick

38. Tírechán

    MS: Book of Armagh.

    EDITION: Bieler, L. 1979 *The Patrician texts in the Book of Armagh*, 122–67 (with translation). Scriptores Latini Hiberniae, 10. Dublin. (Earlier editions and discussions of the texts are listed in Bieler's edition, 57–8.)

    DATE: Late seventh century.

Some of the earliest descriptions of Tara are contained in Bishop Tírechán's *Collectanea*, an itinerary of churches with Patrician associations. (For an interpretation of the motives behind Tírechán's work see C. Swift, 'Tírechán's motives in compiling the *Collectanea*: an alternative interpretation', *Ériu* **45** (1994), 53–82.) Tírechán, though not as dramatic in his account of the contest between Patrick and the king and his druids as Patrick's other seventh-century biographer, Muirchú, includes what must be the first eye-witness account of a monument at Tara. He describes how a druid came to an unedifying end at the hands of Patrick by falling from the sky to the ground frozen with hailstones and snow, 'and (the druid's) stone is in the south-eastern parts of Tara to the present day, and I have seen it with my own eyes' (*et est lapis illius in oris australibus orientalibusque <Temro> usque in praesentem diem, et conspexi illum oculis meis*) (130–3 §8 (6)). Lóegaire tells of how his father, Níall Noígíallach, bade that he should not accept the new faith, but that he should be buried in the ridges or ramparts of Tara (*in cacuminibus Temro*) facing his enemies, the Leinstermen (132–3 §12 (2)).

39. Muirchú

   MSS: The Book of Armagh; Brussels Bibliothèque Royale 64; Vienna Nationalbibliothek Ser. nov. 3642 (fragments).

   EDITION: Bieler, L. 1979 *The Patrician texts in the Book of Armagh*, 62–123 (with translation). Scriptores Latini Hiberniae, 10. Dublin. (Earlier editions and discussions of the texts are listed in Bieler's edition, 57–8.)

   DATE: Late seventh century.

   TARA: 74–99. The seventh-century biography of Saint Patrick written by Muirchú maccu Machtheni includes the dramatic description of the contest between Patrick and the king of Tara, Lóegaire, and his druids at Easter. The episode moves between Tara and Slane. Muirchú's opening passage describes Tara as the capital of the Irish ruled over by the fierce pagan, Lóegaire, the emperor of the barbarians (*imperator barbarorum regnans in Temoria, quae <tunc> erat caput <regni> Scotorum*) (74 I 10 (1)). He compares Tara (84 I 15 (2)) with Babylon (*in Temoria istorum Babylone*); he tells (92 I 19 (1), (3)) of Lóegaire and his guests eating and drinking in the palace of Tara (*in palatio Temoriae*), and of Patrick entering the banqueting hall of Tara (*in caenacolum Temoriae*); he recounts the tale (96 I 20 (11)–(15)) of the building of a house of green and of dry wood to test God's choice between a druid and Benignus, a boy who had followed Patrick. This house reappears in later descriptions of the topography of Tara as *tech Benén*.

40. *Cáin Fhuithirbe*

   MSS: Editor lists (36–7) the glossed extracts as found in D.A. Binchy's *Corpus iuris Hibernici* (Dublin, 1978).

   EDITION: Breatnach, L. 1986 The ecclesiastical element in the Old-Irish legal tract *Cáin Fhuithirbe*. *Peritia* **5**, 36–52.

   DATE: *c.* 680.

   An examination of the fragments of the Old Irish legal tract *Cáin Fhuithirbe*, which is dated to *c.* 680.

   TARA: 49–51. The text incorporates early references to the contest between Patrick and Lóegaire and the king's conversion, though no reference is made to Tara. There is an allusion, however, to a high-king (*ardrech*), which in the context of the fragmentary text seems to describe Lóegaire. This is important as *Cáin Fhuithirbe* is a Munster text and provides a valuable piece of evidence for the spread of the Patrician cult in the seventh century.

41. FIRST LINE: *Génair Patraicc i nNemthur* (Fíacc's Hymn).

    MS: Liber Hymnorum.

    EDITION: Stokes, W. and Strachan, J. 1903 *Thesaurus Paleohibernicus*, vol. 2, 307–21 (with translation). Dublin.

    DATE: *c*. 750–800.

    TARA: 314.19–20, 317.43–4. The Old Irish hymn known as *Génair Pátraic* (also called 'Fíacc's Hymn' on account of its ascription to Fíacc of Sletty, one of Patrick's disciples) incorporates sentiments similar to those in the Prologue to *Félire Óengusso* (see no. 64), the desolation of Tara and the triumph of Christianity (*bid fás tír Temrach túae*) (314.20). *I nArdmachae fil ríge, is cían doréracht Emain./ is cell mór Dún Lethglasse nímdil cid díthrub Temair* ('In Armagh is the Kingdom; long since has Emain been forsaken;/ Downpatrick is a great church; it is not dear to me that Tara should be desolate') (317.43–4).

42. *Vita Tripartita*

    MSS: BL Egerton 93; Bod Rawlinson B 512; TCD H 3 18 (no. 1337).

    EDITIONS: Stokes, W. 1887 *The Tripartite Life of Patrick with other documents related to the saint* (2 vols) (with translation). London.
    Mulchrone, K. 1939 *Bethu Phátraic. The Tripartite Life of Patrick, vol. 1 (text and sources)*. Dublin and London.

    DATE: Ninth to eleventh centuries.

    The text known as the Tripartite Life of Patrick, so-called because it consists of three homilies which portray the all-conquering saint processing triumphantly through the country. (On the dating of the text see, among the many studies, K. Jackson, 'The date of the Tripartite Life of St Patrick', *Zeitschrift für celtische Philologie* **41** (1986), 5–45.)

    TARA: Mulchrone, 26–37, 47. The life recounts in a manner similar to Muirchú, but in a somewhat more dramatic fashion, Patrick's encounter with Lóegaire and his druids at Tara. The text provides no physical description of Tara but is merely the setting for the dramatic encounter. It loses its symbolic importance when Patrick conquers the druids and converts Lóegaire. Tailtiu, unlike Tara, is blessed by the saint (*Is ann sin dano bennachais blae [oí]naig Tailten, cona bérthar marb di co bráth*) (47).

43. MacNeill, E. 1929 The origin of the Tripartite Life of Saint Patrick. *Journal of the Royal Society of Antiquaries of Ireland* **59**, 1–15.

    An analysis of the *Vita Tripartita*, about which the author concludes that the text embodies an older life of St Patrick written in Irish by a contemporary of his seventh-century biographer, Tírechán. He also concludes that the order of narration was topographical, not chronological, and that it incorporates much of the material in the *Notulae* preserved in the Book of Armagh which support the claims of the Patrician *paruchia*.

TARA: 4. On the basis of references incorporated in the lives of St Patrick and of regnal lists preserved in the manuscript Laud Miscellany 610, the author suggested that it was quite probable that the kingships of Crúachain and Tara were held simultaneously by the same kings until the death of Ailill Molt (d. 483).

44. MacNeill, E. 1932 The *Vita Tripartita* of St Patrick. *Ériu* **11**, 1–41.

A detailed discussion of the *Vita Tripartita*. In it the author deals with later accretions to the *Vita Tripartita* which are identified on the basis of language and historical references, and with the importance of the topographical sequence in the life.

TARA: 9–13. The topographical sequence followed by the *Vita Tripartita* is, according to the author, a historic statement of very great importance, in that it reflects the political geography of Ireland in the latter part of the seventh century. Thus the circuit begins with Brega, with Tara and Tailtiu, centres of political importance of the time. His observations concerning the various Uí Néill dynasties of the region are important in attempting to understand the early political development of the hinterland of Tara.

45. MacNeill, E. 1940–1 The hymn of St Secundinus in honour of St Patrick. *Irish Historical Studies* **2**, 129–53.

A discussion on the date, attribution, content, language and historical background to the poem *Audite Omnes* in praise of St Patrick ascribed to Secundinus, referred to in the annals as one of Patrick's assistants.

TARA: 130. The author notes the proximity of Dunshaughlin (Domnach Sechnaill, named after Secundinus) to Tara, and surmises that the fact that Dunshaughlin became one of the first bishoprics in Ireland is of great historical significance. It shows, according to MacNeill, that King Lóegaire, if he remained a heathen, was not at all hostile to the new religion and its organisation. It must also have given Secundinus a position second only to Patrick, at least in the minds of the people.

46. Carney, J. 1955 *Studies in Irish literature and history*. Dublin.

A series of essays on aspects of early Irish literature and history.

TARA: 324–73 ('Patrick and the kings'). In examining the dates associated with St Patrick and their influence on the compilation of the early Irish annals, the author reassesses the dates for the reigns of early kings of Tara, Níall Noígíallach, Nath Í (d. 445) and Lóegaire (floruit *c.* 454). The nature of *Feis Temro* is assessed; it is viewed by the author as the symbolic wedding feast of a king and sovereignty, personified by a goddess. The historicity of the annalistic records of *Feis Temro* tend to be found acceptable, and it is suggested that in the early period a king of Tara, before his solemn inauguration, exacted the recognition of the Laigin, whom Tara regarded as being under its tribute (see also nos 7 and 247–8).

47. Binchy, D.A. 1961 The background of early Irish literature. *Studia Hibernica* **1**, 7–18.

A discussion of the background to the introduction of writing into Ireland, the oral tradition and the Christianisation of Ireland.

TARA: 14–17. The author comments on the evolution of the kingship of Tara (and Ireland) and on Patrick's associations with Tara, ideas which he repeats in many other works. He argues against the existence of a high-kingship of Ireland on the basis that there is no trace in the laws of a king of Ireland and that it was manufactured by 'synthetic historians' who tried to rewrite the history of Ireland on the basis of Latin histories, which dealt exclusively with Great Kings. The stories associating Patrick with the Tara dynasty and the midlands are later accretions, linked to the rise of the Uí Néill.

48. Binchy, D.A. 1962 Patrick and his biographers: ancient and modern. *Studia Hibernica* **2**, 7–173.

    An essential guide to Patrician studies, particularly those of the twentieth century.

    TARA: There are many references to Tara, the most significant of which are: 61 (the similarity between Armagh's claim to hegemony over all churches throughout Ireland and that put forward about the same time by the head of the Uí Néill dynasties, the king of Tara); 63 (the further similarity between Armagh's claims to the primacy and the idea of the immemorial 'high-kingship' of Tara: neither is given such powers or status in the law-tracts); 68ff (Lóegaire and Patrick); 100–3 (the veracity of dates relating to the reign of Lóegaire mac Néill); 105, 149, 162 (the proximity of Dunshaughlin to Tara and the use of the personal name Máel Sechnaill among the southern Uí Néill); 105, 149–50 (the paschal fire episode and Patrick at Tara).

49. Binchy, D.A. 1968 St Patrick's 'First Synod'. *Studia Hibernica* **8**, 49–59.

    A discussion of the text of a canon known as the First Synod of Patrick.

    TARA: 56. The author suggests that since *Feis Temro* was not celebrated after the reign of Diarmait mac Cerbaill (d. ?565), the kings of Tara who followed Diarmait were Christian.

50. de Paor, L. 1971 The aggrandisement of Armagh. *Historical Studies* **8**, 95–110.

    A discussion of the rise of Armagh, Patrick's cult and early Patrician churches (as opposed to the 'new' monastic establishments), Tírechán and Muirchú.

    TARA: 103–4. The author concludes, as do many historians, that the description of the confrontation between Lóegaire and Patrick at Tara is just as likely to have been borrowed from biblical and early Christian story-telling as from historical fact (see also no. 188).

51. Binchy, D.A. 1975–6 The pseudo-historical prologue to the *Senchas Már*. *Studia Celtica* **10–11**, 15–28.

    A discussion of the origin, historicity and purpose of the text known as the Prologue to the *Senchas Már*, a collection of law-tracts. (See also J. Carey, 'An edition of the pseudo-historical prologue to the *Senchas Már*', *Ériu* **45** (1994), 1–32.)

    TARA: 18; 20. The author alludes to one of the versions explaining the *Clóenfherta*, whereby Patrick's anger at Lóegaire and his followers causes an earthquake which in turn causes the Hill of Tara to slant. He reiterates that the confrontation between the king of Tara and Patrick was a fiction invented by those who were engaged in joint propaganda for the primacy of Armagh and the claim of the Uí Néill to the kingship of Ireland.

52. Sharpe, R. 1982 St Patrick and the See of Armagh. *Cambridge Medieval Celtic Studies* **4**, 33–59.

A discussion of the lack of evidence for the foundation of Armagh as a see by Patrick, with particular reference to the assumed connection between Armagh and Emain Macha.

TARA: 53; 57–8. The author notes that findings at Tara suggest that, like Emain, occupation in the proto-historic period was very limited, and that the idea of the kingship of Tara recalls a significance attached to the site from the prehistoric past, not a royal capital. With regard to the more favourable attitude to the Tara monarchy in Muirchú's version of the conversion of Lóegaire as opposed to Tírechán's brief account of the king's refusal to believe, the author explains this as part of the closer alliance which developed between Armagh and the southern Uí Néill in the late seventh century.

53. Moisl, H. 1987 The church and the native tradition of learning in early medieval Ireland. In P. Ní Chatháin and M. Richter (eds), *Irland und die Christenheit/ Ireland and Christendom. Bibelstudien und Mission/ The Bible and the Missions*, 258–71. Stuttgart.

A detailed discussion of the extent to which the Irish churchmen — accustomed to the secular learned order and its functions — used native traditional learning as a vehicle for the furtherance of their own interests. The author bases his argument primarily on the evidence of the 'Tara episode' in Muirchú's biography of Patrick. He argues that the vernacular Tara tradition has to be considered alongside the scriptural material as a possible model, such is the correspondence between the depictions by Patrick's hagiographers and the vernacular accounts. Since the title 'king of Tara' had by the seventh century become the prerogative of the Uí Néill and the basis of their political ambitions, the body of historical traditions attaching to Tara became in effect the Uí Néill dynastic tradition, and was therefore available as a means of legitimising the Uí Néill position.

54. Doherty, C. 1991 The cult of St Patrick and the politics of Armagh in the seventh century. In J.-M. Picard (ed.), *Ireland and northern France AD 600–850*, 53–94. Dublin.

An extensive discussion on the rise of Armagh to pre-eminence and the early development of the cult of Patrick in Ireland and on the Continent.

TARA: 86. The author discusses the purposes and background to the writings of Muirchú and Tírechán, and explains the significance of the setting in relation to Muirchú's dramatic account of Patrick's meeting with Lóegaire at Tara. Tara was not a capital in the sense of a city, but was 'an inauguration site of no mere local significance'.

55. de Paor, L. 1993 *St Patrick's world. The Christian culture of Ireland's apostolic age*. Dublin.

A popular introduction to the history of the Patrician period in Ireland and to the texts which provide information on Patrick and his era. Translations of the primary Patrician texts are provided.

TARA: 31–3; 36. The political structure of fifth-century Ireland is covered. With regard to Tara, the author suggests that the fosse encircling the hilltop was not built to provide defence against any earthly power. It was a symbolic or ritual defensive work, protecting the outside world against the powerful mana within the enclosure.

56. Dumville, D.N. (ed.) 1993 *St Patrick A.D. 493–1993*. Suffolk.

    A series of papers commemorating the 1500th anniversary of the death of Patrick. The study covers aspects of the historiography of Patrick.

    TARA: 45–50 ('St Patrick and fifth-century Irish chronology: the kings') follows the ideas propounded by James Carney about the chronology of the early kings of Tara as evinced from the annals, as opposed to the chronology postulated by Tírechán and Muirchú; 98 (Secundinus, Domnach Sechnaill and the use of the name Máel Sechnaill by the southern Uí Néill dynasty, Clann Cholmáin).

Adomnán

57. *Cáin Adomnáin*

    MSS: Bod Rawlinson B 512: Brussels Bibliothèque Royale 2324–40.

    EDITION: Ní Dhonnchadha, M. 1982 The guarantor list of *Cáin Adomnáin*, 697. *Peritia* **1**, 178–215 (guarantor list only).

    DATE: *c.* 697.

    A study of the guarantor list appended to the ecclesiastical law *Cáin Adomnáin*, the 'Lex Innocentium', which was proclaimed by the abbot of Iona, Adomnán (d. 704). (For an edition of the full text, see K. Meyer, 'Cáin Adamnáin', *Anecdota Oxoniensa*, Medieval and Modern Series 12 (Oxford, 1905).) The *Cáin* assured the protection of all non-combatants, women, clerics and children, and of church property. Ninety-one ecclesiastical and secular figures are set forth as guarantors of the legislation. The editor argues that the date of *c.* 697 is genuine on the basis of the evidence provided by this list.

    TARA: The list includes a number of kings who would have had familial ties with Tara or whose territories would be in the hinterland of Tara. The titles assigned to all individuals are unlikely to be contemporary: §41 (Loingsech mac Oenghusa, *rí Erenn*); §70 (Mainei mac Neill [*tánaise* to the kingship of Brega]); §82 (Fócortach [*tánaise* to the kingship of Brega]); §83 (Garban Mide, *rí*); §86 (Conall Grant, *rii deiscirt Breg*: see editor's note); §88 (Toicthech mac Cinnfaelad, *rí Lugne*); §89 (Bodbhchath, *rí Luighne*); §90 (Irgalach ua Conaing, *rí Ciannachtae* [king of Brega]).

Rúadán

58. MSS: Marsh's Library Dublin Z 3.1.5 (Codex Kilkenniensis); TCD E 3 11 (no. 175).

    EDITION: Plummer, C. 1910 *Vitae sanctorum Hiberniae* (2 vols). Oxford.

    DATE: Possibly the eleventh century or later.

    TARA: Vol. 2, 245–9 §§15–19. The Life of Rúadán, which provides the late but dramatic account of the cursing of Tara by Rúadán as a result of the misdemeanours of its king, Diarmait mac Cerbaill.

59. MSS: Brussels Bibliothèque Royale 2324–40, 4190–200 (O'Clery MSS); RIA A iv 1 (no. 968) (Stowe MS).

    EDITION: Plummer, C. 1922 *Bethada náem nÉrenn: Lives of Irish saints* (2 vols) (with translation). Oxford.

DATE: Possibly the twelfth century or later.

TARA: Vol. 1, 88–90 §§186–91. The Life of Brendan of Clonfert includes a version of the cursing of Diarmait mac Cerbaill and of Tara by Rúadán, the latter in this case being assisted by Brendan. 323–5 §§35–43. The Life of Rúadán tells of the saint's fast against the king of Tara, Diarmait mac Cerbaill (d. ?565), and of his cursing of Tara.

60. MS: Codex Salmanticensis (Brussels Bibliothèque Royale MS 7672–4).

    EDITION: Heist, W.W. 1965 *Vitae sanctorum Hiberniae ex codice olim Salmanticensi nunc Bruxellensi*. Brussels.

    DATE: Eleventh century or earlier.

    Latin lives of Irish saints preserved in the fourteenth-century manuscript, the Codex Salmanticensis.

    TARA: 163–5. A version of Rúadán's clash with the king of Tara, Diarmait mac Cerbaill, and the saint's cursing of Tara, which led to its final abandonment.

61. Binchy, D.A. 1982 A pre-Christian survival in mediaeval Irish hagiography. In D. Dumville, R. McKitterick and D. Whitelock (eds), *Ireland in early mediaeval Europe*, 165–78. Cambridge.

    A discussion of the background to the tale of the cursing of Tara by Rúadán. The author argues that the tale was concocted (perhaps as late as the eleventh century) to account for the official adoption of Christianity by the kings of Tara in the sixth century.

Colmán mac Lúacháin

62. MS: Rennes Irish MS.

    EDITION: Meyer, K. 1911 *Betha Colmáin maic Lúacháin. Life of Colmán son of Luachán* (with translation). Todd Lecture Series, 17. Dublin and London.

    DATE: Twelfth century.

    The twelfth-century Life of Colmán of Lann (Lynn, Co. Westmeath).

    TARA: 62 §58; 72 §70. The Life of Colmán alludes to the explanation from 'The pseudo-historical prologue to the *Senchas Már*' (see no. 51) for the collapse of the *Clóenḟerta* at Tara (described in this instance as *Cláenráith Temrach*), which claims that the house fell during the reign of Lóegaire mac Néill when Patrick proclaimed a judgement in it against the king. It also preserves a description of an inauguration ceremony of the king of Tara, in which the king is inaugurated at *Cart[h]i na nGiall* ('the pillar-stone of the hostages'), with one of the Uí Fhorannáin standing at a flagstone beneath, holding a horsewhip.

Ciarán

63. MSS: Liber Flavus Fergusiorum; Book of Leinster.

EDITION: Fraser, J. 1912 The miracle of Ciaran's hand. *Ériu* **6**, 159–60.

DATE: Possibly the twelfth century.

A late Middle Irish tale which relates how Ciarán of Clonmacnoise attended *Óenach Tailten* in the company of Diarmait mac Cerbaill (d. ?565) and his working of a strange miracle on the hand of an unfaithful man.

64. *Félire Óengusso*

MSS: Leabhar Breac; Bod Rawlinson B 505; Bod Laud Miscellany 610; RIA 23 P 3 (no. 1242); Franciscan Library Killiney A 7; Bod Rawlinson B 512; Brussels Bibliothèque Royale 5100–4; BL Egerton 88; TCD H 3 18 (no. 1337).

EDITION: Stokes, W. 1905 *Félire Óengusso Céli Dé: The Martyrology of Oengus the Culdee* (with translation). London. Henry Bradshaw Society. (Reprinted Dublin, 1984.)

DATE: *c*. 830.

The calendar of saints known as *Félire Óengusso*, which probably dates from *c*. 830 (see P. Ó Riain, 'The Tallaght martyrologies, redated', *Cambridge Medieval Celtic Studies* **20** (1990), 21–38).

TARA: 24.165–8. This verse forms part of a number of oft-quoted verses in the Prologue proclaiming the flourishing state of Christianity in Ireland and the abandonment of Tara, Crúachain, Dún Ailinne and Emain. *Atbath borg tromm Temra/ la tairthim a flathe; /col-lín corad sruithe /maraid Ard mór Machae*. ('Tara's mighty burgh perished at the death of her princes: with a multitude of venerable champions the great Height of Machae [Armagh] abides') (Stokes 1905, 24 §165).

F. Topographical texts

Early medieval prose and metrical topographical accounts of the Hill of Tara have influenced our image of the site to this day. Two accounts in particular have provided the basis for recent studies of Tara and its monuments. They are the prose account *Dindgnai Temrach* 'Tara's Remarkable Places' and the poem *Temair toga na tulach*, ascribed to the poet Cúán úa Lothcháin (d. 1024). The latter forms part of a series of poems on Tara contained in the early medieval corpus known as *Dindshenchas Érenn*. The interest generated in Tara and its monuments in the late tenth and early eleventh century, mirrored especially in the compositions of Cúán úa Lothcháin, may reflect as much propaganda on behalf of Máel Sechnaill II, king of Tara (d. 1022), as it does antiquarian enthusiasm.

Dindshenchas Érenn

65. FIRST LINES: Tara: *Temair Breg, cid ní diatá* (I. 2–5).
Ní cheil maissi dona mnáib (I. 6–13).
Temair toga na tulach (I. 14–27).
Domun duthain a lainde (I. 28–37).
Temair, Tailtiu, tír n-óenaig (I. 38–45).
Skreen: *Achall araicci Temair* (I. 46–53).
Tailtiu: *A chóemu críche Cuind chain* (IV. 146–63).

MSS: Book of Leinster; Rennes Irish MS; Book of Ballymote; Yellow Book of Lecan. These are the primary manuscripts in which *Dindshenchas Érenn* survives. For a list of the other recensions and detailed citations, see Gwynn's notes to the individual poems.

EDITION: Gwynn, E.J. 1903–35 *The Metrical Dindshenchas* (5 vols) (with translation). Todd Lecture Series. Dublin.

DATE: Eleventh century.

Five volumes incorporating texts, translations and commentary on the body of Middle Irish topographical material known as *Dindshenchas Érenn*. Part I consists of the five poems on Tara preserved in the *dindshenchas* and of one poem on Achall, the Hill of Skreen. The poem *Temair toga na tulach*, probably composed by the poet Cúán úa Lothcháin (d. 1024), lists the monuments on the hill and is to be compared with the prose account, *Dindgnai Temrach* (no. 66). Part IV, 146–63. The *dindshenchas* of Tailtiu, *A chóemu críche Cuind chain*, is likely also to have been composed by Cúán úa Lothcháin, when *Óenach Tailten* was revived in 1006 by his patron, Máel Sechnaill II.

66. MSS: Book of Leinster; Book of Ballymote; Rennes Irish MS; Bod Rawlinson B 506; Edinburgh MS XVI Kilbride no. 12.

EDITIONS: Stokes, W. 1892 The Bodleian *Dinnshenchas*. *Folklore* **3**, 467–516: 469–70.
Stokes, W. 1894 The prose tales in the Rennes *Dindshenchas*. *Revue Celtique* **15**, 272–336: 277–89 (with translation).
Best, R.I., Bergin, O. and O'Brien, M.A. (eds) 1954 *The Book of Leinster, formerly Lebar na Núachongbála,* vol. 1, 120–3. Dublin.

DATE: Eleventh century.

Versions of the prose account of the monuments at Tara, entitled *Dindgnai Temrach*. This account enumerates in detail the monuments on the hill and labels them with names, most of which were used by George Petrie in his identification of the existing monuments as part of his study for the Ordnance Survey in 1836.

67. Ó Concheanainn, T. 1982 A pious redactor of *Dinnshenchas Érenn*. *Ériu* **33**, 85–98.

Discussion of 'pious' insertions into *dindshenchas* texts, and, through this, evidence of the development of *Dindshenchas Érenn*. Important *vis-à-vis* structures and development of *dindshenchas* in that the author suggests that these pious insertions are the hallmark of compositions by the poet Cúán úa Lothcháin (d. 1024).

TARA: 92–3 §5 (v). The author surmises that the inclusion of a religious quatrain at the end of the poem *Temair toga na tulach*, which, among other things, describes the monuments at Tara, is evidence of composition by Cúán úa Lothcháin.

68. Ó Riain, P. 1989 The Psalter of Cashel: a provisional list of contents. *Éigse* **23**, 107–30.

On the origin, history and contents of the Psalter of Cashel, described by the author as the first miscellaneous manuscript ever produced in Ireland and as belonging to the insignia of Brían Bóruma's office as over-king.

TARA: 108–12. The author discusses the authenticity of the so-called Psalter of Tara, referred to in the *dindshenchas* poem on Tara attributed to Cúán úa Lothcháin (d. 1024). He concludes that this psalter never existed but was invented by the poet to promote the cause of Brían's rival, Máel Sechnaill II, king of Tara (d. 1022). This invention formed only part of Cúán's promotion of Máel Sechnaill's cause. The author cites other works of his, including the main surviving recension of the Tara *dindshenchas*, and of the text on the taboos of the kings of Ireland, where Cúán begins with the prohibitions of the kings of Tara. He may also have been the author of a poem of celebration when *Óenach Tailten* was revived in 1006.

69. Bhreathnach, E. 1995 The topography of Tara: the documentary evidence. *Discovery Programme Reports* **2**, 68–76. Dublin.

   A survey of the medieval topographical texts concerning Tara and the context in which they were composed. Specific reference is made to the prose account, *Dindgnai Temrach*.

Miscellaneous topographical texts

70. FIRST LINE: *Ind fhilid ra fetatar*.

    MS: NLI G 7.

    EDITION: O Daly, M. 1960 On the origins of Tara. *Celtica* **5**, 186–91 (with translation).

    DATE: *c*. 900.

    A fragmentary text in Old Irish on the origins of the name Tara. The prose introduction describes how Érimón, son of Míl of Spain, took a wife from among the Thebans and brought her to Ireland. He built her a *dún* on the loveliest hill in Ireland. This *dún* was Tara, the author's imaginative etymology for *Temair* being *Tebe-múr* 'wall of Thebes'. Apart from providing an early *dindshenchas* text on Tara, which does not tally fully with the other better-known *dindshenchas* texts, its importance lies also in its reference to structures at Tara. Reference is made in the prose introduction to the poem to three walls on the upper part of the hill (*trí múir eutha inna hóchtar*). The poem itself includes a reference to an earthen rampart (*múr talman*). The incomplete §4, translated by the editor as 'He saw the outer trench(?) (*in* [*n-*]*aurthuili*) which closed in against the height; vaster still was the encircling rampart (*in borg*) . . .', is intriguing.

71. FIRST LINE: *A fhir thall tríallus in scél*.

    MS: BL Egerton 1782.

    EDITION: Meyer, K. 1921 Mitteilungen aus irischen Handschriften: Fíngin macc Flaind .cc. *Zeitschrift für celtische Philologie* **13**, 3–7.

    DATE: Possibly the eleventh or twelfth century.

    A poem containing material similar to that included in *Lebor Gabála* on the original inhabitants and place-names of Ireland.

    TARA: 5 §15. The poet asks what are the three names for Tara. The answer: *Líathdruimm, Druimm Cáin, Temair*.

72. MS: TCD H 3 17 (no. 1336).

EDITION: McCaughey, T.P. 1960 Tract on the chief places of Meath. *Celtica* **5**, 172–6 (with translation).

DATE: Early Modern Irish (possibly thirteenth-century).

A tract which describes the prominent places of Meath, namely Tara, Tailtiu, Tlachtga and Uisnech, and the relationship between the kings of Meath and the kings of other provinces. While the text is later than *Dindshenchas Érenn*, it is important for topographical details concerning Tara (including alternative names for Tara: *Tulach in Trír, Carnd in Aenfhir* and *Druim C(h)aín*) and its hinterland.

G. Charters, deeds and papal documents

Documents which date to the period of the Anglo-Norman arrival in Ireland are significant in relation to Tara for a number of reasons. They include the earliest references to a church being located on the hill. They indicate the rivalry between ecclesiastical organisations for control of this church. The disputes among the Anglo-Normans, and in particular between King John and the de Lacy family in the early thirteenth century, are also reflected in these documents. Finally, they provide us with the earliest evidence for the form of the Anglicised version of the place-name Tara in forms such as *Taueragh, Tauerac(h)*, probably derived from the genitive or locative of Irish *Temair, Temra(ch)*.

73. Book of Kells Charters

    MSS: Book of Kells; TCD E 3 8 (no. 58); BL Add. 4791; RIA A v 3 (no. 934).

    EDITIONS: Mac Niocaill, G. 1961 *Notitiae as Leabhar Cheanannais 1033–1161*. Gaillimh.
    Mac Niocaill, G. 1990 The Irish 'charters'. In P. Fox (ed.), *The Book of Kells, MS 58, Trinity College Library Dublin*, 153–65. Luzern.

    DATE: 1033–1161.

    The mid-eleventh- and twelfth-century charters preserved in the Book of Kells relating to the church of Kells, Co. Meath.

    TARA: (From Mac Niocaill 1961 edition) I.20–7; II.1; III.23–4; IV.7. The references to Tara in the charters are primarily to kings of Tara who witnessed the charters or who made grants of land to the church of Kells. What emerges from these documents is that the title 'king of Tara' by this period was accorded to local kings subject to the greater provincial lords of Mide, Connacht, Munster, etc. Despite this relative insignificance, however, the mystique of the title continued to linger, as evidenced in one charter (I.25–7, date 1033–49) where kings are warned not to insult (*sárugud*) Colum Cille, 'for though dangerous (*gúasacht*) for every king to do so, it is of greater danger for the king of Tara, as he is a brother of Colum Cille's (*ocus gid gúasacht do cach ríg is gúas(ach)tachu do ríg Temrach, úair is bráthair hé do Colum Cille*). (For a recent reassessment of the Kells charters see M. Herbert, 'Charter material from the Book of Kells', in F. O'Mahony (ed.), *The Book of Kells. Proceedings of a conference at Trinity College Dublin, 6–9 September 1992* (Aldershot, 1994), 60–77.)

74. The Irish Pipe Roll of 14 John, 1211–12

    MS: Armagh Public Library H II 16 (with an additional fragment E 6 9).

    EDITION: Davies, O. and Quinn, D.B. 1941 The Irish Pipe Roll of 14 John, 1211–12. *Ulster Journal of Archaeology* **4** (supplement), 1–76.

DATE: 1211–12.

The earliest extant pipe roll (or financial account) of the Anglo-Norman exchequer in Ireland, dating from the reign of King John.

TARA: 30–1 ('Fines made with the king'). William Petit, steward of Mide, accounts for a payment rendered from Richard de Feypo for having two cases brought under jurisdiction of the royal judges (writs of praecipe) in relation to two landholdings, one knight's fee for '*Ataneracht* (read *Tauerach*), which he claims against Randulph de Repentiny' (see nos 75–6).

75. Chartularies of St Mary's Abbey

MSS: Bod Rawlinson B 495; BL Cotton Tiberius A xi.

EDITION: Gilbert, J.T. 1884 *Chartularies of St Mary's Abbey, Dublin with the register of its house at Dunbrody and annals of Ireland* (2 vols). Rolls Series. London.

DATE: Late twelfth to early thirteenth century.

The medieval charters of the Cistercian monastery of St Mary's Abbey, Dublin, and of its daughter-house at Dunbrody, Co. Wexford. While it is known from the context of the contents of these charters that they date from the late twelfth and early thirteenth centuries, the individual charters are not dated precisely by year.

TARA: The charters include some notable details about Anglo-Norman and ecclesiastical activity associated with Tara, details which are supported by other documentation such as the Ormond Deeds (no. 76) or the charters relating to the Hospitallers (nos 77–8). Vol. 1, 37–8 §12. Ralph de Repenteni (see no. 76) confirms a mark of silver, to be handed over annually by his tenant Jordanus Molendinarius de Tauerach and his descendants (see no. 78), to the monks of St Mary's Abbey. The inference is that the sum of money was part of the profit gained during the year from de Repenteni's *villa* at Tara (*marcam unam mei redditus in villa de Tauerach*). This is confirmed by the affirmation of his father's donation by Peter de Repenteni (43–4 §19) from the annual profit (*annuatim percipiendam*) from his holding at Tara (*in tenemento meo de Tauerach*). Holders of the title 'chaplain of Tara' appear on occasion as witnesses to the charters (*Hiis testibus . . . capellano de Tauerach*). Of particular note are the following. 36 §10. *Henrico de Tauerach,* who witnessed a charter relating to lands at Glencullen, Co. Dublin, between the abbot of St Mary's Abbey and John, son of Diarmait mac Gilla Mocholmóc. This charter was witnessed also by Richard de la Corner, bishop of Meath (1230–50) (see no. 77). 38–44 §§12–14. Chaplains of Tara, notably a certain William, witnessed a series of grants made to St Mary's Abbey by the de Repenteni family. 165 §141. A settlement made concerning certain churches in Meath, including Tara, in 1233 at the behest of the pope (see no. 80).

76. Ormond Deeds

MSS: NLI D 141; D 957.

EDITION: Curtis, E. 1932 *Calendar of Ormond Deeds 1172–1350 A.D.* Dublin. Irish Manuscripts Commission.

DATE: 1194–1210; *c.* 1241.

The earliest deeds of the Marquess of Ormond, dating from the twelfth century onwards.

TARA: 43 §98; 359 §852. The first deed (regarded by the editor as 'pre-1241', see no. 75) is from Walter de Lacy to Peter de Repenteni 'to be intentive to his sister, the Lady Alice Pipard, he having granted to her the service which Peter de Repenteni owes for Taueragh, according to the charter made to her'. The second deed, which is earlier (dated between 1194 and 1210), infers that one Ralph de Repenteni held land at *Tauerac* (Tara).

77. Charters of the Hospitallers of St John of Jerusalem, Kilmainham

    MS: Bod Rawlinson B 501.

    EDITION: McNeill, C. 1932 *Registrum de Kilmainham: Register of Chapter Acts of the Hospital of St John of Jerusalem in Ireland, 1326–1339*. Dublin. Irish Manuscripts Commission.

    DATE: Thirteenth and fourteenth centuries.

    Medieval charters detailing lands held by the Hospitallers of St John of Jerusalem, whose chief house was at Kilmainham, Co. Dublin.

    TARA: 35. A grant by the Hospitallers to one William, son of Richard Mowere of Cardomiston, Tara. The grant was part of rival claims between Richard de la Corner, bishop of Meath (1232–50), and the Hospitallers as to the tithes of a church at Tara (*in tenemento de Taueraght*) and others in County Meath. The Register indicates that the Hospitallers retained for their own use a hospice at Cardomiston in the fourteenth century. The church was dedicated to St Patrick. 138–44. A confirmation by Pope Innocent III of the Hospitallers' possessions (see no. 80).

78. Charters of the Hospitallers of St John the Baptist, New Gate

    MS: Bod Rawlinson B 498.

    EDITION: Brooks, E. St John 1936 *Register of the Hospital of S. John the Baptist (without the New Gate, Dublin)*. Dublin. Irish Manuscripts Commission.

    DATE: *c.* 1285.

    Medieval charters relating to the Hospital of Saint John the Baptist in Dublin.

    TARA: 175 §254. A grant made by Robert Molendinarius of Skreen to the Hospitallers which refers to a royal road (*iuxta regalem viam*) which runs from Skreen to Tara (*qua itur de villa de Scryn versus Taueragh*).

79. Chartularies of Llanthony Prima and Secunda

    MSS: London PRO C 115 A/8 and C 115 A/2.

    EDITION: Brooks, E. St John 1953 *The Irish Cartularies of Llanthony Prima and Secunda*. Dublin. Irish Manuscripts Commission.

    DATE: *c.* 1231.

    Medieval charters relating to extensive lands held in Meath by the Welsh monasteries of Llanthony, which had daughter-houses at Colp and Duleek, Co. Meath.

    TARA: 40–6 §37. This document deals with a dispute between St Mary's Abbey, Dublin, and the Hospitallers concerning certain churches in Meath, including the church at Tara (*et quidam alii religiosi Midensi diocesi in [ecclesiis] de Scrin et Tauerach*).

80. Papal chancery documents

   MSS: No. 72: Vatican Registers RV 8; Bod Rawlinson B 495; London PRO C115–A8; London PRO C115–A2.

   EDITION: Sheehy, M.P. 1962–5 *Pontificia Hibernica: medieval papal chancery documents concerning Ireland 640–1261* (2 vols). Dublin.

   DATE: 1212 and 1231.

   A collection of papal documents (in Latin) relating to Ireland in the early medieval period.

   TARA: Vol. 1, 149–52, no. 72. Dated 1212. Pope Innocent III takes the Brothers of the Hospital of St John of Jerusalem in Kilmainham under the protection of the Apostolic See and confirms their possessions to them, including the church at Tara (see no. 77). Vol. 2, 40, no. 203. Dated 1231. In correspondence addressed to the bishop of Leighlin and the dean and *magister scolarum* of Drogheda, Pope Gregory IX appoints them as judges in the dispute between the bishop-elect of Meath and certain religious orders concerning the right of presentation to the church of Tara (see nos 75 and 79).

H. Prophecies

A poetic genre of early medieval Irish literature is that of the prophecy, many of which are fictitiously ascribed to Colum Cille. Tara does not escape the attention of the prophets, one of whom — in the poem *Temair Bregh, gidh línmair libh lín a fer*, echoing the sentiments of the Prologue to *Félire Óengusso* (see no. 64) — predicts the downfall of Tara and the rise of the monastery of Duleek.

81. FIRST LINE: *Longas Inbir Domnann Sacsain gaibthe murthr̄ācht.*

   MS: Bod Laud 615.

   EDITION: Meyer, K. 1915 Mitteilungen aus irischen Handschriften: Colum Cille cecinit. *Zeitschrift für celtische Philologie* **10**, 343–4.

   DATE: Middle Irish.

   A Middle Irish poem hailing the reign of the prophetic king Flann Cinach, who is mentioned also in *Baile in Scáil*.

   TARA: 343 §§1–2. The poem makes an oblique reference to the arrival of Saxons on the east coast (*Inbir Domnann*) and possibly to Saxons gaining booty at Tara (*Saxain mnā co ndremna, meldai būar im Temhrai*).

82. FIRST LINE: *Temair Bregh, gidh línmair libh līn a fer.*

   MS: Bod Laud 615.

   EDITION: Meyer, K. 1921 Mitteilungen aus irischen Handschriften: Tara's Untergang. *Zeitschrift für celtische Philologie* **13**, 9.

   DATE: Middle Irish.

   A Middle Irish poem ascribed to Colum Cille predicting the downfall of Tara. It follows a theme similar to the Prologue in *Félire Óengusso*, where the downfall of Tara (and other royal sites) is attributed to their non-Christian associations. In this case the counter to the deserted site at Tara is the flourishing monastery of Duleek.

83. FIRST LINE: *Ailech cen gíall. Temair hi tráig.*

    MS: Brussels Bibliothèque Royale 5100–4.

    EDITION: Thurneysen, R. 1915 Allerlei irisches: 1. Bec mac Dé. *Zeitschrift für celtische Philologie* **10**, 421–2.

    DATE: Middle Irish.

    A version of the prophecies ascribed to the prophet Bec mac Dé.

    TARA: 421.1. Among the prophecies of doom described is that Tara will decline (*Temair hi tráig*) and that the Loígis will reign above all (*Laígis ós cháich*).

See also no. 14.

I. *Mirabilia*

Descriptions of Irish wonders (*mirabilia*) appear to be a phenomenon of the eleventh and twelfth centuries. The most renowned of these texts about Ireland, which includes a list of *mirabilia*, is Giraldus Cambrensis's *Topographia Hibernica*. Tara is not mentioned by Giraldus, but does appear in native Irish and in Norse wonder-tracts. It is likely that the *dindshenchas* is the source for the wonders at Tara. The 'dwarf's grave' is undoubtedly *Lecht in Abaicc* of the *dindshenchas*, while the description of the *Lia Fáil* also coincides with that in the *dindshenchas*.

84. Bishop Patrick of Dublin

    FIRST LINE: *Plurima mira malum signantia signa futurum.*

    MSS: BL Cotton MS Titus D.XXIV; Paris Bibliothèque Nationale MSS Lat. 4126 and 11108.

    EDITION: Gwynn, A. 1955 *The writings of Bishop Patrick 1074–1084*. Scriptores Latini Hiberniae 1. Dublin.

    DATE: Late eleventh century.

    A poem on the wonders of Ireland, *Versus sancti Patricii episcopi de mirabilibus Hibernie*, composed by Bishop Patrick, who ruled the small diocese of the Norse–Irish city of Dublin from 1074 to 1084.

    TARA: 60 §11. The three wonders of Tara (*tres res maxime mire*) are enumerated: 'a stone, a small boy and a dwarf's tomb'. The stone is the *Lia Fáil*, *Nam lapis, ut fertur, calcatus rege sonabat/ Iam rugiens* ('For they tell that the stone, when trod by a king's foot, roared loudly').

85. *De Ingantaib Érenn*

    MS: Book of Ballymote.

    EDITION: Todd, J. Henthorn 1848 Appendix to *Leabhar Breathnach annso sis. The Irish version of the Historia Brittonum of Nennius*, 192–219. Dublin.

DATE: Twelfth century.

The Irish prose version of the text known as *De Ingantaib Érenn*, the 'Wonders of Ireland', from the fifteenth-century manuscript Book of Ballymote, which cites the twelfth-century Book of Glendalough as its source.

TARA: 198–201. The same three wonders are associated with Tara as described in Bishop Patrick's poem (no. 84). (Passages from another version preserved in TCD H 3 17 (no. 1336) are included in the footnotes. Tara: 199–200, note k.)

86. FIRST LINE: *Inganta Éirend uili eter tráigh ocus tuili*.

    MS: Book of Uí Maine.

    EDITION: Meyer, K. 1905 Mitteilungen aus irischen Handschriften: irische Mirabilia. *Zeitschrift für celtische Philologie* **5**, 23–4.

    DATE: Possibly the eleventh or twelfth century.

    A Middle Irish poem on the wonders of Ireland.

    TARA: 23 §2. One of the wonders of Ireland is the *loigi inn abaic* (the dwarf's grave) at Tara, which is described as measuring three feet (*trí troithi and go fáilidh/ d'fir mór is do maethnáidhin*).

87. Meyer, K. 1910 The Irish *mirabilia* in the Norse '*Speculum Regale*'. *Ériu* **4**, 1–16.

    A discussion of a Norse text known as *Konungs Skuggsjá* (Meyer *Kongs Skuggsjo*), which was drawn up at the request of Hakon Hakonarson, king of Norway (1217–63). The Norse title is equivalent to the Latin *Speculum Regale,* and the text takes the form of advice given by a father to his son. Part of the text involves the son asking for information about Ireland.

    TARA: 10 §16. Among the wonders of Ireland is *Themer* (Tara), 'the chief seat and king's castle'. The text describes how the king of Tara gave a false judgement and as a consequence 'the tribunal, the palace and castle, and the whole place, were overthrown and collapsed. And thus it has remained ever since.' This tale is not included in Giraldus Cambrensis's *Topographia Hibernica* nor in the text known as *De Ingantaib Érenn* (no. 85). It appears to be a jumbled version of the tale about the collapse of the *Clóenfherta* and the desertion of Tara as a result of Rúadán's curse.

88. Young, J. 1938 Two of the Irish *Mirabilia* in the 'King's Mirror'. *Études Celtiques* **3**, 21–6.

    A further discussion of the sources for the Irish material found in the *Konungs Skuggsjá*.

    TARA: 23–4. The author links the wonder at Tara with the story about the origin of the *Clóenfherta*. He supports Meyer's belief that contemporary oral sources were used for the Irish wonders.

89. Sayers, W. 1989 Portraits of the ruler: Óláfr Pái Hoskuldsson and Cormac mac Airt. *Journal of Indo-European Studies* **17**, 77–97.

    A discussion of similarities between the main character of the Icelandic *Laxdaela* saga and the Cormac mac Airt cycle.

TARA: 89–90. The author surmises that the episode in the *Konungs Skuggsjá* about the overthrow of Tara derives from the early portion of the Cormac mac Airt biography. Its inclusion illustrates that conceptions of Irish kingship were not unknown in the north.

See also no. 168.

J. Taboos

The taboos associated with the kingship of Tara are listed in the text *Togail Bruidne Da Derga*, possibly dating from the ninth century, and in a later tract which describes the taboos of the kings of Tara — regarded as kings of Ireland — and the provinces. While an aura of pagan custom emanates from these taboos, they are more likely to combine both Christian and non-Christian concepts of kingship, which are ultimately bound up with the idea of the just ruler.

90. MSS: Book of Lecan; Book of Ballymote; Book of Lismore; Liber Flavus Fergusiorum; RIA 23 M 18 (no. 156); 23 D 5 (no. 154); BL Egerton 1782.

    EDITION: Dillon, M. 1951–2 The taboos of the kings of Ireland. *Proceedings of the Royal Irish Academy* **54**C, 1–36 (with translation).

    DATE: Possibly Old Irish (prose); eleventh-century (verse).

    Prose and verse texts describing the prohibitions (*urgarta*) and prescriptions (*ada*) of the kings of Tara, Leinster, Munster, Connacht and Ulster. The verse is ascribed to Cúan úa Lothcháin (d. 1024).

    TARA: 8–11; 22–5; 27; 29–30. Seven taboos and seven prescriptions are accorded the king of Tara. The dissimilarity between them and the taboos listed in the text *Togail Bruidne Da Derga* (no. 127) is noteworthy.

91. Greene, D. 1979 Tabu in early Irish narrative. In H. Bekker-Nielsen *et al.* (eds), *Medieval narrative: a symposium*, 9–19. Odense.

    A discussion of the development of the concept of *geis* (taboo) in early Irish literature and the influence of that development on the art of the narrative.

    TARA: 11–14. The author comments that the text on the taboos of the kings of Ireland (no. 90) is a compilation which can hardly be older than the ninth century and which is of no historical value. He surmises that the prohibitions are the mere imagining of antiquarians, for the use of the days of the week is a Christian element which cannot have been taken over from the pagan past. What is retained is the tradition that Irish kings of the pagan past had taboos as part of their sacral function. The taboos in *Togail Bruidne Da Derga*, which in their present form are presented as quasi-magical but which replace a much more profound reflection of the duties of kingship, are linked to the concept of *fír flathemon*, the justice of the ruler.

K. Triads

A form of gnomic literature favoured by the early Irish is the triad, placing pieces of information together in groups of three. Tara appears twice in the collection known as the *Triads of Ireland*.

92. MSS: Yellow Book of Lecan; Book of Ballymote; Book of Uí Maine; Book of Lecan; RIA 23 N 10; TCD H 1 15 (no. 1289).

    EDITION: Meyer, K. 1906 *The Triads of Ireland*. Todd Lecture Series, 13. Dublin.

    DATE: Second half of the ninth century.

    A list of triads grouping topographical features of Ireland and gnomic beliefs.

    TARA: 6 §54; 26 §202. Tara, along with Cashel and Crúachain, is reckoned as one of the three households (*tellaich*) of Ireland. The holding of *Feis Temro* is one of the three things that constitutes a king (see no. 36).

L. Glossaries

The influence of Isidore of Seville's *Etymologiae*, a medieval encyclopaedia, manifests itself in numerous genres of ecclesiastical learning in Ireland, including the genre known as glossaries. The Irish glossaries, an example of which is attributed to Cormac mac Cuilennáin, king of Munster (d. 908), are lists of definitions and derivations of words. The origin of the name *Temair* is listed in Cormac's glossary as meaning 'a height', an explanation that has yet to be fully refuted.

93. *Sanas Cormaic*

    MSS: Yellow Book of Lecan; Leabhar Breac; TCD H 2 15. (Complete copies only; see Russell (no. 94), 2–5.)

    EDITIONS: Stokes, W. 1862 *Three Irish glossaries*, 1–46. London and Edinburgh.
    Meyer, K. 1912 *Sanas Cormaic*. An Old-Irish glossary compiled by Cormac úa Cuilennáin. *Anecdota from Irish manuscripts* **4**. Dublin. (Reprinted 1994, Felinfach reprint, Llanerch Publishers.)

    DATE: Late ninth or early tenth century.

    Sanas Cormaic is a glossary reputedly compiled by Cormac mac Cuilennáin, king of Cashel (d. 908).

    TARA: Stokes, 42; Meyer, 105 §1212. The glossary provides two explanations for the word *Temair*. The first is *tea-múr*, the wall of Tea, daughter of Lugaid mac Íthae. The alternative is *temair*, meaning a height from which there is a fine view, be it a geographical or a structural feature (*unde dicitur temair na túaithe 7 temair in tighe*).

94. Russell, P. 1988 The sounds of silence: the growth of Cormac's Glossary. *Cambridge Medieval Celtic Studies* **15**, 1–30.

    A survey of Irish glossaries, with particular reference to the evolution of *Sanas Cormaic*.

    TARA: 10–11. The author cites, as evidence for the genuineness of the ascription to Cormac mac Cuilennáin, the inclusion as a marginal gloss in the Book of Leinster version of the *dindshenchas* of Tara of a reference to Cormac as the source for the explanation of the name *Temair*.

M. *Audacht Morainn*

Audacht Morainn 'The Testament of Morann' is a text in archaic Old Irish, possibly dating from *c.* 700. It is an example of the literary genre known as the *Speculum Principum* 'Mirror of Princes', which contains advice to a king on how to rule with justice and truth. Tara is not mentioned in *Audacht Morainn*, but the text includes a curious passage on the assembly (*óenach*) held by a king.

95. MSS: RIA 23 N 10 (no. 967); 23 N 27 (no. 966); National Library of Scotland 72.1.42; BL Egerton 88. (Recension B. See editor's introductory remarks concerning the different recensions and manuscript traditions of the text, xiii–xxix.)

    EDITION: Kelly, F. 1976 *Audacht Morainn*. Dublin.

    DATE: *c.* 700.

    Audacht Morainn is an early example of the *Speculum Principum*, a tract providing advice to a king. It sheds light on the institution of kingship in early Irish society and on aspects of early Irish law.

    TARA: 8–10 §28. This passage lists the three exemptions from liability for violence (*blaí búraig*) at every assembly (*óenach*) which protect every lord (? *comdeth*). He is not liable for injuries incurred during horse-races (*án ech*), a hosting or encampment (*dúnath*), or the privilege of the ale-house with friends and great abundances of mead-circuit (*búaid cuirmthige co coímaib co mannaib móraib midchórto*). This list implies that the horse-race, the encampment and the ale-house were the essential components of the *óenach*, three activities which might leave little or no trace of permanent structures at a site such as Tara.

96. MSS: Book of Ballymote; Book of Fermoy; Book of Lecan; TCD H 3 18 (no. 1337); Book of Lismore. (These citations refer to the Middle Irish introduction to *Audacht Morainn*.)

    EDITION: Thurneysen, R. 1917 Morands Fürstenspiegel. *Zeitschrift für celtische Philologie* **11**, 56–106 (with German translation).

    DATE: Possibly the tenth century.

    One recension of *Audacht Morainn* and a Middle Irish introduction which was attached to the text.

    TARA: 64–5 §14. The Middle Irish prose preface attempts to explain the conflict between *sóerchlanda Érenn* (the noble classes) and the *aithechthúatha* (the subject peoples), and how Feradach Finn Fechtnach, to whom Morann, the judge, gives advice, came to hold the kingship of Tara. This conflict may have a historical connotation in that it may reflect the conflict between the southern Uí Néill and a vassal tribe, the Gailenga, during the ninth and tenth centuries.

97. Olmsted, G.S. 1979 A contemporary view on Irish 'hill-top enclosures'. *Études Celtiques* **16**, 171–85.

    A discussion of the passage in *Audacht Morainn* which describes the three immunities (*blaí*, which Olmsted takes to mean 'enclosure', but see no. 95) of an assembly. The author views the passage as important in that it may provide the earliest description of the uses of Irish 'royal sites'.

N. *Lebor Gabála Érenn* and associated tales

Lebor Gabála Érenn, a text which in its most complete form appears to date from the late eleventh century, tells of the invasion of Ireland by peoples from overseas, who were ultimately the ancestors of the great lineages of the country. The *Lebor Gabála* is a marriage of much native tradition and biblical and medieval classical references, used to place the Irish within the biblical chronology. A basic tenet of the text is the division of Ireland into two halves, *Leth Cuinn* (north) and *Leth Moga* (south), which are associated with the overlordships of Tara and Cashel respectively. Of the associated tales, the most interesting is *Do Shuidigud Tellaich Themra* 'The Settling of the Manor of Tara', which describes Tara and Uisnech as 'the kidneys of Ireland'.

Lebor Gabála Érenn

98. MSS: See list of manuscripts and recensions in the introduction, vol. 1, vi–viii.

    EDITION: Macalister, R.A.S. 1938–56 *Lebor Gabála Érenn. The book of the taking of Ireland* (5 vols) (with translation). Irish Texts Society, 34–5, 39, 41, 44. Dublin.

    DATE: Eleventh to twelfth century.

    TARA: Vol. 4, 244.2093–6. This verse, attributed to the poet Cináed úa hArtacáin (d. 974), describes the *Lia Fáil* as *in cloch for stáit mo di sáil* ('the stone upon which my heels are standing'). For further descriptions of the *Lia Fáil*, see vol. 4, 106–7, 110–13, 142–5, 168–9 and 174–5. Vol. 5. The text in this volume is entitled the 'Roll of Kings' and incorporates the 'official version' of who held the kingship of Tara from time immemorial. For the establishment of Tara, see vol. 5, 39–41, 62–3 and 82–3.

99. Dillon, M. 1956 *Lebor Gabála Érenn*. *Journal of the Royal Society of Antiquaries of Ireland* **86**, 62–72.

    An analysis of the *Lebor Gabála*, which provides a description of the text and its sources, and discusses its use as a historical document and as a source for mythology.

100. Scowcroft, R.M. 1987 *Leabhar Gabhála* — Part I: the growth of the text. *Ériu* **38**, 81–142.
     Scowcroft, R.M. 1988 *Leabhar Gabhála* — Part II: the growth of the tradition. *Ériu* **39**, 1–66.
     A detailed analysis of the textual, structural and historical background to the growth and compilation of the *Lebor Gabála*, which is described as the foundation and canon of early Irish historiography and, because it deals with prehistory, of mythography as well. As such, though unreliable as a source for the study of ancient history or pagan religion, it sheds great light on the political and cultural mythology of its authors. The author's analysis concludes that the *Lebor Gabála* grew up in response to a medieval problem — the vast blank separating Irish tradition from accepted world history — which it solved in a medieval way, allowing Christian universalism to multiply its patterns across an Irish stage.

101. Carey, J. 1993 *A new introduction to Lebor Gabála Érenn*. Dublin. Irish Texts Society.

     An introduction to Macalister's edition of the *Lebor Gabála* which provides a background to the publication of his edition. There is also an overview of the tradition of historical fabrication or 'pseudo-history' on which the *Lebor Gabála* is so dependent. This tradition drew on classical, medieval Latin and biblical learning as well as on native origin legends. The author concludes that, whatever one's views may be as to the relative importance of clerical and secular learning in early Ireland, the reality and pivotal importance of the process of accommodation between the two cannot be questioned. The *Lebor Gabála* is the most important representative of Irish pseudo-historic writings.

102. Carey, J. 1994 *The Irish national origin-legend: synthetic pseudohistory*. Quiggin Pamphlets on the Sources of Mediaeval Gaelic History 1. Cambridge.

A detailed analysis of the sources for the origin legend of the Irish as provided in the *Lebor Gabála*. The importance of the *Historia Brittonum* and of work by medieval scholars such as Orosius and Isidore of Seville is underlined. It is suggested that a proto-*Lebor Gabála* existed in the ninth century, but that the text developed to its most complete form in the hands of poets such as Eochaid úa Flainn (d. 1004) and Flann Mainistrech (d. 1056).

Associated tales

103. *Do Shuidigud Tellaich Themra*

    MSS: Yellow Book of Lecan; Book of Lismore.

    EDITION: Best, R.I. 1910 The settling of the manor of Tara. *Ériu* **4**, 121–72 (with translation).

    DATE: Possibly the tenth or eleventh century.

    A Middle Irish text which recounts how the nobles of Ireland during the reign of Diarmait mac Cerbaill (d. ?565) complained at the extent of the royal domain (*tellach, aurland*) of Tara. They refused to attend *Feis Temro* until an arrangement defining its limitations was made. This is done through the judgement of Fintan mac Bóchrai, with the assistance of the mysterious Tréfuilngid Tré-eochair. The text is informative in its collection of lore associated with Tara, for example the description of *Feis Temro* (§2, compare with other *tech midchúarta*-type arrangements), and its description of Tara and Uisnech as two kidneys from which the five provinces of Ireland radiate (§32 . . . *Ocus dobert drumain de fri cech cóiced in-nHérind, ar is amlaid atá Temair 7 hUisnech i nHerind amail bit a di áraind a mmíl indile*). (For a discussion of the significance of the term *tellach*, see T.M. Charles-Edwards, *Early Irish and Welsh kinship* (Oxford, 1993), 259–73.)

104. Rees, B. 1975–6 Ailsefydlu'r traddodiad. *Studia Celtica* **10–11**, 110–12.

    An explanation, including parallels in the Welsh tradition, for the Middle Irish tale *Do Shuidigud Tellaich Themra*. The author refers to parallels from Africa and from Wales, mainly based on folk-motifs.

See also nos 186, 212 and 405.

105. *Cath Tailten*

MS: TCD H 4 22 (no. 1363).

EDITION: Dobs, M. Ní C. [alias Dobbs, M.E.] 1937 Tochomlad mac Miledh a hEspain i nErind: no Cath Taillten? *Études Celtiques* **2**, 50–91 (with translation).

DATE: Possibly the twelfth century.

A late Middle Irish tale on the progress of the sons of Míl from Spain to Ireland.

TARA: 53; 58. In the text an alternative name for Tara is referred to, which appears as both *Cathair Crobinni* and *Cathair Cronidi*.

NARRATIVE LITERATURE AND VERSE

O. General	106–7
P. Mythological Cycle	108–15
Q. Ulster Cycle	116–24
R. Cycle of Kings	125–66
S. Fenian Cycle (*Fíanaigecht*)	167–70
T. Verse	171–83

O. General

106. O'Grady, S.H. 1892 *Silva Gadelica* (2 vols). London.

    A miscellaneous collection of texts with translations.

    TARA: 72–82 (*Aided Dhiarmada*); 82–4 (*Genemain Áeda Sláine*); 85–7 (*Tochmarc Becfhola*); 89–92 (*Teasmolad Cormaic*); 94–233 (*Agallamh na Senórach*); 253–6 (*Coimpert Cormaic meic Airt*); 310–18 (*Fotha Chath Mhucrama*); 319–26 (*Cath Chrionna*); 326–30 (*Echtra mac nEchach Muigmedoin*); 330–6 (*Aided Crimthainn*). References are to the texts in vol. 1.

107. Dillon, M. 1946 *The cycles of the kings*. London.

    Useful synopses and notes on tales, many of which are important to Tara.

    TARA: 11–14: The cycle of Conn of the Hundred Battles and Eogan Mór (including *Baile in Scáil*). 15–29: The cycle of Lugaid mac Con and Cormac mac Airt, AD 227. 30–7: The cycle of Crimthann son of Fidach, AD 366. 38–41: The cycle of Niall of the Nine Hostages, AD 379. 56–74: The cycle of Domnall son of Aed son of Ainmire, AD 628–42. 75–98: The cycle of Diarmait son of Aed Sláine and Guaire Aidne, AD 643.

P. Mythological Cycle

The text *Cath Maige Tuired* recounts the War of the Gods in which the Túatha Dé Danann conquer the Fomoiri. Central to the tale is the omnicompetent Lug, whose entry to Núadu's court at Tara demonstrates that he is master of all crafts (*samildánach*) and marks the beginning of his accession to his rightful place as king of Tara.

108. MS: TCD H 2 17 (no. 1319).

    EDITION: Fraser, J. 1916 The First Battle of Moytura. *Ériu* **8**, 1–63 (with translation).

    DATE: Middle Irish.

    A Middle Irish text on the first battle of Moytura (*Cath Maige Tuired*) which deals with the wanderings of the Fir Bolg and their battle with the Túatha Dé Danann, the arrival of the latter and the great Battle of Moytura fought between them.

    TARA: 14 §16; 24 §26; 26 §29. The references to Tara are to monuments, including Ráith na Ríg, where *Feis Temro* is held and which is described as *imlican urgna na hErenn* ('the illustrious navel (*umbilicus*) of Ireland'). Tara is also described as *Cnoc Gabála na nGiall* ('the hill of the holding of hostages') and *Tulach techtairechta na tromslúagh* ('the hill of the summoning of the hosts').

109. MSS: Yellow Book of Lecan; Book of Ballymote; BL Egerton 105.

    EDITION: Hull, V. 1930 The four jewels of the Tuatha Dé Danann. *Zeitschrift für celtische Philologie* **18**, 73–89 (with translation).

    DATE: Possibly the twelfth or thirteenth century.

A late Middle Irish tract relating to the four treasures brought to Ireland by the Túatha Dé Danann, namely the *Lia Fáil, claideb Nuadat* (the sword of Núadu), *sleg Loga* (the spear of Lug), and *coire in Dagda* (the cauldron of the Dagda). Other versions are incorporated into the tale of the Second Battle of Mag Tuired and into the *Lebor Gabála*.

110. MS: BL Harley 5280.

    EDITIONS: Stokes, W. 1891 The second battle of Moytura. *Revue Celtique* **12**, 52–130 (with translation).
    Thurneysen, R. 1918 Zu irischen Texten: III. Cath Maige Turedh. *Zeitschrift für celtische Philologie* **12**, 401–6.
    Lehmacher, G. 1931 Die zweite Schlacht von Mag Tured und die keltische Götterlehre. *Anthropos* **26**, 435–59 (partial German translation).
    Gray, E.A. 1982 *Cath Maige Tuired: The Second Battle of Mag Tuired* (with translation). Irish Texts Society, 52. Naas.

    DATE: Ninth century (with later reworking).

    An account of the epic battle between the Túatha Dé Danann and the Fomoiri. The most recent edition includes an extensive introduction covering many aspects of the mythology of *Cath Maige Tuired*.

    TARA: (Gray) 24 §3; 40 §72. The text tells how the *Lia Fáil* was brought by the Túatha Dé Danann to Tara from the city of Falias (see no. 109). Its association with Tara is regarded as being in the past: *A Falias tucad an Lía Fáil buí a Temraig. Nogésed fo cech ríg nogébad Érinn* ('From Falias was brought the Lia Fáil which was in Tara. It used to cry under every king who would take Ireland'). A second episode in the tale recounts a contest between Lug and the champion Ogma, who flung a flagstone (*márlíacc*) out of the royal hall at Tara towards Lug. Lug reciprocated by hurling the stone back into the hall.

111. MS: RIA 24 P 9 (no. 739).

    EDITION: Ó Cuív, B. 1945 *Cath Muighe Tuireadh. The second battle of Magh Tuireadh*. Dublin.

    DATE: Early Modern Irish.

    A later version of *Cath Maige Tuired* than that in no. 110.

    TARA: 51.1219–20. This reference gives Tara its alternative name *Cathair Cróuinn*.

112. Gray, E.A. 1981–3 *Cath Maige Tuired*: myth and structure. *Éigse* **18**, 183–209; **19**, 1–35, 230–62.

    An extensive analysis of the text known as *Cath Maige Tuired*, in particular the three major aspects of sovereignty, legitimacy, and material power/royal hospitality. These are regarded as symbolising the reciprocal relationship between king and tribe.

    TARA: 17–28. The author explains the context of the episode involving the god Lug entering Tara and discusses the descriptions of *Feis Temro* and of the *Tech Midchúarta*. By inviting his people to feast with him, Núadu, the king, not only offered them entertainment but also confirmed the hierarchical nature of their relationships with him and with each other. By establishing the correct seating order at a royal feast, the king symbolically confirmed all the traditional prerogatives of those assembled there.

113. Ó Cathasaigh, T. 1983 *Cath Maige Tuired* as exemplary myth. In P. de Brún, S. Ó Coileáin and P. Ó Riain (eds), *Folia Gadelica. Essays presented by former students to R.A. Breatnach,* 1–19. Cork.

An analysis of *Cath Maige Tuired*, the myth of the War of the Gods between the Túatha Dé Danann and the Fomoiri, in which the latter were vanquished.

TARA: 6–12. The author discusses the role of Lug, with particular reference to his association with the kingship of Tara, comparing him to Cormac mac Airt and Conaire Mór in their roles as kings of Tara.

114. Ó Cathasaigh, T. 1989 Three notes on *Cath Maige Tuired*. *Ériu* **40**, 61–8.

Three notes on phrases of syntactical or grammatical significance in the text *Cath Maige Tuired*.

TARA: 64–6 n. 2. This note deals with the phrase *ní tocus-sa i Temraig* (*CMT* §67) and the possibility that it is a form of the verb *do-cing* 'steps, strides forward, approaches'. The author notes that in two prophetic texts *do-cing* is used in connection with accession to the kingship of Tara. In *Baile Chuinn* it is used of approaching the liquor which symbolises the sovereignty of Tara (*dos-cich Furbaide*), and in *Baile in Scáil* there is a repeated use of the phrase *do-da-cich, no-da-íba* 'he shall approach it, he shall drink it'. While the construction and context in *Baile Chuinn* and *Baile in Scáil* are somewhat different to those in *Cath Maige Tuired,* the author suggests that it is not unlikely that the use of this verb (*do-cing*) by Lug in *Cath Maige Tuired* is portentous. Lug is entering Tara to seek the kingship of Tara, which he succeeds ultimately in wresting from Núadu.

115. Carey, J. 1989–90 Myth and mythography in *Cath Maige Tuired*. *Studia Celtica* **24–5**, 53–69.

This important analysis of *Cath Maige Tuired* attempts to provide a historical basis for the text which dates it to *c*. 900, associating its theme with the conflict between the Vikings and the Uí Néill at that time.

Q. Ulster Cycle

The Ulster Cycle, the centre-piece of which is *Táin Bó Cuailnge*, consists of heroic sagas and poems relating to the Ulaid. Emain Macha is the main centre of activity in this cycle, as a result of which Tara is mentioned only on rare occasions. Despite this, some of these references are interesting in that they retain traditions relating to Tara not always to the fore in other literary cycles. Two kings are associated with Tara in different tales. They are Lugaid Reóderg and Cairpre Nia Fer, both of whom belong to Leinster tradition. (For comprehensive guides to studies on the *Táin* see J.P. Mallory (ed.), *Aspects of the Táin* (Belfast, 1992), and J.P. Mallory and G. Stockman (eds), *Ulidia. Proceedings of the first international conference on the Ulster cycle of tales* (Belfast, 1994).)

116. *Fled Bricrenn*

MSS: Lebor na hUidre; BL Egerton 93; TCD H 3 17 (no. 1336); Leyden University MS (Codex Vossianus); National Library of Scotland 72.1.40.

EDITION: Henderson, G. 1899 *Fled Bricrend. The Feast of Bricriu* (with translation). Irish Texts Society, 2. London.

DATE: Possibly the eighth or ninth century.

The Ulster Cycle tale *Fled Bricrenn*, the Feast of Bricriu.

TARA: 2 §2; 146–7 (n.). The *tech midchúarta* built by Bricriu for Conchobar mac Nessa and the Ulaid is described in detail and is compared to the *Tech Midchúarta* at Tara. While it is very fanciful, this account may be influenced by contemporary descriptions of medieval royal edifices (see nos 26–34).

117. *Mesca Ulad*

MSS: Lebor na hUidre; Book of Leinster; NLI G4 (fragment of Yellow Book of Lecan); National Library of Scotland 72.1.40.

EDITION: Watson, J.C. 1941 *Mesca Ulad*. Mediaeval and Modern Irish Series, 13. Dublin.

DATE: Two redactions survive, the earliest (Lebor na hUidre) possibly dating from the ninth century, the later (Book of Leinster) from the first quarter of the twelfth century.

The Ulster Cycle saga which tells of the intoxication of the Ulstermen, part of which is located in Temair Lúachra.

TARA: xxxvi–ix. In an additional note to the introduction, T.F. O'Rahilly speculates on the transference of the tale to Temair Lúachra in the south from Temair Breg (Tara, Co. Meath). He suggests that there were three stages to the development of the tale: (i) an oral tradition of an attack by the Ulaid on the Goidelic Tara, (ii) early written versions in which the raid was tactfully represented as having been made on the Tara of the Érainn, and (iii) a later recension in which Tara became the imaginary Temair Lúachra, supposed to be the capital of the Érainn and to be situated in the south-west of Ireland.

118. *Fochond loingse Fergusa meic Roig*

MS: Book of Leinster.

EDITION: Hull, V. 1930 The cause of the exile of Fergus mac Róig. *Zeitschrift für celtische Philologie* **18**, 293–8 (with translation).

DATE: Possibly the ninth century.

A fragmentary Old Irish tale which explains the reason for the exile of Fergus mac Róich from Ulster to Connacht.

TARA: 295. The text mentions the three main assemblies of Ireland, namely *Feis Temro*, *Feis Emna* and *feis i n-iarthur Chonnacht*.

119. *Tochmarc Emire*

MSS: Lebor na hUidre; RIA D iv 2 (no. 1223); 23 N 10 (no. 967); BL Harley 5280; Book of Fermoy; BL Egerton 92; Bod Rawlinson B 512.

EDITIONS: Meyer, K. 1888 The wooing of Emer. *The Archaeological Review* **1**, 1–4 (with translation).
Meyer, K. 1890 The oldest version of the *Tochmarc Emire*. *Revue Celtique* **11**, 434–57.

Meyer, K. 1900 Mitteilungen aus irischen Handschriften: *Tochmarc Emire la Coinculaind*. *Zeitschrift für celtische Philologie* **3**, 229–63.

Van Hamel, A.G. 1933 *Compert Con Culainn and other stories*. Mediaeval and Modern Irish Series, 3. Dublin.

DATE: Tenth or eleventh century.

This tale from the Ulster Cycle tells of Cú Chulainn's wooing of Emer, daughter of Forgall Monach.

TARA: 20 §§1–2. There is a description from the tale *Tochmarc Emire* of a *tech midchúarta*, apparently located at Emain Macha but understood to be comparable to the better-known *Tech Midchúarta* at Tara (*fo intamail Tighe Midchúarta*). The architectural features of the structure are of interest, possibly being influenced by descriptions of some medieval royal edifice. The description is almost identical with the description of the structure built by Bricriu in the tale *Fled Bricrenn*.

120. *Serglige Con Culainn*

MSS: Lebor na hUidre; TCD H 4 22 (no. 1363).

EDITIONS: Dillon, M. 1953 *Serglige Con Culainn*. Mediaeval and Modern Irish Series, 14. Dublin.

Dillon, M. 1953 The wasting sickness of Cú Chulainn. *Scottish Gaelic Studies* **7**, 47–88.

DATE: Two recensions survive, one dating possibly from the ninth century, the second from the eleventh century.

A Middle Irish prose text which describes Cú Chulainn's visit to the Otherworld and his wasting sickness (*serglige*).

TARA: 8–11 §§21–7. This passage describes Cú Chulainn's instructions to Lugaid Reóderg. A bull-feast (*tarbfes*) is held by Ailill and Medb, Cú Roí mac Dáiri, Tigernach Tétbannach mac Luchtai and Finn mac Rossa to determine who will be king of Tara. Lugaid Reóderg is chosen. According to the editor (introduction, x), Lugaid's instructions belong to the group of *tecosca* (instructions), of which *Tecosca Cormaic* is the best-known example. The description of a means of divination called *tarbfheis* 'bull-feast' (§23) is perhaps borrowed from the tale *Togail Bruidne Da Derga* (no. 127).

121. Dillon, M. 1941–2 On the text of *Serglige Con Culainn*. *Éigse* **3**, 120–9.

An analysis of the text of *Serglige Con Culainn*, with specific reference to the Lebor na hUidre version.

TARA: 124. A note on the *tarbfheis* and the elevation of Lugaid Reóderg to the kingship of Tara. (For the most recent discussion of the *tarbfheis* see J. Carey, 'The uses of tradition in *Serglige Con Culainn*', in J.P. Mallory and G. Stockman (eds), *Ulidia: Proceedings of the first international conference on the Ulster cycle of tales* (Belfast, 1994), 77–84.)

122. *Táin Bó Cuailnge*

MSS: Recension 1: Lebor na hUidre; Yellow Book of Lecan; BL Egerton 1782; RIA O'Curry MS I(C). Recension II: Book of Leinster; RIA C vi 3 (Stowe) (no. 740).

Recension III: BL Egerton 93; TCD H 2 17 (no. 1319) (fragments).

EDITIONS: O'Rahilly, C. 1967 *Táin Bó Cúalnge from the Book of Leinster* (with translation). Dublin.
O'Rahilly, C. 1976 *Táin Bó Cúailnge Recension 1*. Dublin.
O'Rahilly, C. 1978 *The Stowe version of Táin Bó Cuailnge*. Dublin.

DATE: Possibly the ninth century (Recension I).

The three recensions of *Táin Bó Cúailnge*. Tara hardly features in the *Táin*, but what references there are are important for their possible early dating and their independence from the *dindshenchas*.

TARA: Note O'Rahilly's indexes. Two kings are associated with Tara in the *Táin*, Cairpre Nia Fer and his son Erc, who appear to be of Leinster origin. Tara features in another incident, where Cú Chulainn asks his charioteer to instruct him on the main strongholds in Mag mBreg (Book of Leinster and Stowe), between Tara and Kells (Lebor na hUidre). Whereas the Lebor na hUidre version does not list the strongholds, the Book of Leinster version lists Tara and Tailtiu, *Cleittech, Cnogba, Brug meic inn Óóc* and *Dún mac Nechtain Scéne* (29.1059–60).

123. *Cath Bóinde/Ferchuitred Medba*

MSS: Book of Lecan; Bod Rawlinson B 512.

EDITIONS: O'Neill, J. 1905 Cath Boinde. *Ériu* **2**, 173–85 (with translation).
Meyer, K. 1913 Ferchuitred Medba. *Anecdota from Irish Manuscripts* **5**, 17–22. Dublin.

DATE: Middle Irish.

A Middle Irish text on Medb's acquisition of a series of spouses. The text cites Medb's associations with the kingship of Tara and Crúachain.

124. *Cogadh Ferghusa agus Chonchobair*

MSS: RIA 23 K 37 (no. 152); E iv 3 (no. 11); BL Egerton 106.

EDITION: Dobs, M. C. [alias Dobbs, M.E.] 1923 La guerre entre Fergus et Conchobar. *Revue Celtique* **40**, 404–23 (with French translation).

DATE: Middle Irish.

A Middle Irish tale which tells of the enmity between Fergus mac Róich and Conchobar mac Nessa. The text includes many topographical details relating to Meath.

TARA: 406 §2. Reference is made to a road to Tara known as *Slighe na Sochaidhe*. In 410 §4 Tailtiu is otherwise known as *Cnoc Lughach*.

R. Cycle of Kings

The Cycle of Kings provides the most extensive source of material relating to Tara in early medieval Irish literature. Its tales cover the reigns and activities of legendary and heroic kings (e.g. Conaire Mór and Cormac mac Airt), of proto-historic kings (e.g. Lóegaire mac Néill) and of historic kings (e.g. Diarmait mac Cerbaill). They are complex tales insofar as they consist of traditional themes, such as the theme of kingship and sovereignty (as personified by a goddess) and the idea of the just ruler, combined with contemporary political connotations. It is possible that echoes of earlier prehistoric or proto-historic times are embedded in these tales, though the unclear nature of the archaeological record of the period renders it most difficult to assess their value as genuine records. The three cycles which hold the greatest import for Tara are those of Conaire Mór, Cormac mac Airt and Eochaid Mugmedóin and his sons, most notably Níall Noígíallach.

Conaire Mór

125. *De Shíl Chonairi Móir*

    MSS: Book of Lecan; Book of Ballymote; TCD H 2 17 (no. 1319).

    EDITION: Gwynn, L. 1912 De Shíl Chonairi Móir. *Ériu* **6**, 130–43 (with translation).

    DATE: Possibly the eighth century.

    The Old Irish text *De Shíl Chonairi Móir* ('Of the Race of Conaire Mór') is a very important text in relation to Tara in that it recounts the birth of Conaire Mór and the manner of his assumption of the kingship of Tara. The description of his induction as king of Tara is of particular importance in that it purports to detail the regalia of the kingship of Tara — the chariot of kingship (*carpat na flatha*), the cloak of kingship (*casal ríg*), the two stones Blocc and Bluigne which opened before the rightful king, and Fál crying out against his chariot-axle (*gloedad in Fal fri fonnad in charpait*).

126. *De Maccaib Conaire*

    MS: Book of Leinster.

    EDITION: Gwynn, L. 1912 De Maccaib Conaire. *Ériu* **6**, 144–53 (with translation).

    DATE: Possibly the eighth century.

    The Old Irish text relating the vengeance of the sons of Conaire Mór on Nemed mac Srobcinn, who slew their father. The opening passage relates how the sons of Conaire were at Tara *i norbbu Féine* ('in the patrimony of the Féni') — the Féni, according to the text, being the Múscraige, Dál Matti, Corcu Duibne and the Laigin.

127. *Togail Bruidne Da Derga*

    MSS: Yellow Book of Lecan; RIA D iv 2 (no. 1223); BL Egerton 1782. (For a list of complete and fragmentary manuscript versions see Knott, xiv–xv.)

    EDITION: Knott, E. 1936 *Togail Bruidne Da Derga*. Mediaeval and Modern Irish Series, 8. Dublin.

    DATE: Ninth century.

    This Old Irish text recounts the tale of Conaire Mór, his assumption of the kingship of Tara and his ultimate downfall, having broken the many taboos placed upon him when he became king. The text incorporates a description of the initiation rites of the king of Tara (5 §§14–15) and also the list of the taboos placed upon Conaire as king of Tara (6 §16). Its importance lies in the possibility that it retains, relatively uninfluenced by monastic learning, elements of the sacred attributes of the kingship of Tara.

128. Gwynn, L. 1915 The recensions of the saga *Togail Bruidne Da Derga*. *Zeitschrift für celtische Philologie* **10**, 209–22.

An analysis of the manuscripts in which the Old Irish text *Togail Bruidne Da Derga* is preserved.

TARA: 209. The author remarks that though the text is probably later than the *Táin*, the origin of the tale may be more archaic, the status and importance of Tara being reflected to a greater degree than in the *Táin*.

See also nos 91 and 190.

129. *Tochmarc Étaíne*

MS: NLI G4 (fragment of the Yellow Book of Lecan); Lebor na hUidre.

EDITION: Bergin, O. and Best, R.I. 1938 Tochmarc Étaíne. *Ériu* **12**, 137–96 (with translation).

DATE: Ninth century.

The Old Irish tale known as the Wooing of Étaín, which forms part of the Conaire Mór cycle. The story centres on Eochaid Airem, whose residence is at Tara and who marries Étaín, daughter of Étar.

TARA: 162 §§1–2; 174 §1; 182 §§13–15; 190 §22. The text describes how Eochaid could not hold *Feis Temro* when he became king as he had no queen, for a king could not celebrate the *Feis* without a queen (*ní theclomdais feis Temra do ríg cen rigan lais*). It also includes mainly fanciful references to structures at Tara, the terraces of Tara (*for tsosta na Teamrach*), and the royal house (*for lar an rigthaighe; for forles an tighi*) ('in the middle of the royal house; through the roof-window of the house').

Conn Cétchathach

130. *Airne Fíngein*

MSS: Book of Fermoy; Liber Flavus Fergusiorum; RIA D iv 2 (no. 1223); Book of Lismore.

EDITION: Vendryes, J. 1953 *Airne Fíngein*. Mediaeval and Modern Irish Series, 15. Dublin.

DATE: Possibly the ninth or tenth century.

A Middle Irish text which describes the birth of Conn Cétchathach. Conn's birth is marked by wonderful events.

TARA: 9–11 §vi. Among the many wonders to manifest themselves on the birth of Conn are the five roads leading to Tara (*Slige Midlúachra, Slige Cúaland, Slige Asail, Slige Tola* (variant of *Slige Dála*) and *Slige Mór*), which are discovered by a series of mythical persons on their way to Tara.

131. *Aided Chuinn*

MS: Book of Lecan.

EDITION: Bergin, O. 1912 The death of Conn of the Hundred Battles. *Zeitschrift für celtische Philologie* **8**, 274–7 (with translation).

DATE: Middle Irish.

A prose version of the tale which tells of the death of Conn Cétchathach at the hands of Tipraite mac Máil, a king of Ulster, while preparing for *Feis Temro* (276–7).

132. MS: Book of Fermoy.

EDITION: Ní C. Dobs, M. [alias Dobbs, M.E.] 1936 From the Book of Fermoy. *Zeitschrift für celtische Philologie* **20**, 161–84.

DATE: Possibly the thirteenth century or earlier.

A miscellany of material relating to Conn Cétchathach and to Cormac mac Airt, including a version of the death and burial of Conn Cétchathach.

TARA: There are many references to Tara. Those included in the tale of Conn Cétchathach are not specific and relate in many instances to the convening of *Feis Temro*. Of Cormac mac Airt, the text states that he constructed *Raith Aichlí* (?Achall, Skreen) close to Tara, where he spent his last years (see no. 150).

133. FIRST LINE: *Ardrí dár gabh Érinn uill*.

MS: National Library of Scotland 72.1.19.

EDITION: Ó Macháin, P. 1986 Ar bhás Chuinn Chéadchathaigh. *Éigse* **21**, 53–65 (with translation).

DATE: Possibly the thirteenth century.

An Early Modern Irish poem on the death of Conn Cétchathach.

TARA: 59 §20. Tara is referred to as *Tulach in Trír*. On the death of Conn, Tara will scream (20c *bíaidh gáir ag Tulaigh i[n] Trír*).

Art mac Cuinn

134. *Echtra Airt meic Cuinn 7 Tochmarc Delbchaíme*

MS: Book of Fermoy.

EDITION: Best, R.I. 1907 The adventures of Art son of Conn, and the courtship of Delbchaem. *Ériu* **3**, 149–73 (with translation).

DATE: Early Modern Irish version.

A text relating the adventures of Art mac Cuinn in the Otherworld and his encounters with Otherworldly women, good and evil. The text includes many references to the associations between fertility, peace and prosperity in Ireland, the kingship of Tara and the character of the king of Tara's spouse. There is also a reference to human sacrifice (154–6 §8) made at the behest of the druids, who regard it as the only way in which the land might be cleansed of the evil influence of Art's association with an unworthy woman.

135. Meyer, K. 1905 Miscellanea: III — Human sacrifice among the ancient Irish. *Ériu* **2**, 86.

A note on the reference in the tale *Echtra Airt* to the sacrifice of the son of a sinless married couple at Tara, whose blood would be mixed with the soil of Tara so as to ensure the return of fertility and prosperity to Ireland.

Cormac mac Airt

136. *Genemuin Chormaic*

    MSS: Yellow Book of Lecan; Book of Ballymote.

    EDITION: Hull, V. 1952 Geneamuin Chormaic. *Ériu* **16**, 79–85.

    DATE: Middle Irish, possibly incorporating pre-eighth-century material (see no. 148).

    A Middle Irish text concerning the birth and fosterage of Cormac mac Airt and his assumption of the kingship of Tara. Cormac is associated in his childhood with the Luigne, Greccraige and Fir Chúl, all of whom are north Connacht people, and two of whom, the Luigne and Fir Chúl, have associations with Tara. The episode of Cormac's assumption of the kingship of Tara is linked to the origin of the *Clóenfherta* (Sloping Trenches) at Tara. The tale attributes the 'reconstruction' of Tara to Cormac mac Airt (84.105–7 *Con·rotacht didiu in Temair do athnuidhed lais amal na·roibi ro[ime] eter taigi 7 claidi 7 cumdaigi ol-cheana, eter loech-thigib 7 griananaib 7 tigib talman*).

137. FIRST LINE: *Faīd guil ar faichthi Temra*.

    MSS: RIA 24 P 25 (no. 475); UCD Mac Fir Bhisigh Book of Genealogies.

    EDITION: Carney, J. 1939 A miscellany of Irish verse: 1. A lament for Lugna Fer Trí. *Éigse* **1**, 239–43 (with translation).

    DATE: Pre-eighth century, with possible tenth-century additions (see no. 148).

    A lament by Cormac mac Airt on the death of his half-brother and co-fosterling Nia Mór, son of Lugna Fer Trí, who is described as sub-king of Connacht. This title was bestowed upon him by Cormac, king of Tara, thus signifying the subservient status of Nia Mór to Cormac.

138. MS: TCD H 2 7 (no. 1298).

    EDITION: Carney, J. 1940 Nia son of Lugna Fer Trí. *Éigse* **2**, 187–97 (with translation).

    DATE: Pre-eighth century, with possible tenth-century additions (see no. 148).

    A further version of the death of Nia Mór, son of Lugna Fer Trí, the co-fosterling of Cormac mac Airt. An important text in attempting to explain the relationship between Cormac mac Airt and Nia Mór. The text also includes a subtext (entitled 'Cormac's Dream' by the editor) where Cormac dreams that the captives' pillar (*coirthi na ngiall*) at Tara is lifted out of the ground by Eochu Gunnat, king of Ulster, and brought to Crúachain. Eochu carries away Cormac's wife, Eithne Thóebfhota (goddess of sovereignty). His druids explain that this dream signifies that Cormac will be banished from the kingship of Tara.

139. FIRST LINES: *Cáin do Dena Den doma addonrúacht.*
Beir mo scíath, sceo fri úath.
A maccáin na cí cia-so dogra ar-ataí.

MSS: Lebor na hUidre; Book of Leinster.

EDITION: MacNeill, J. [alias E.] 1893–6 Three poems in Middle Irish, relating to the Battle of Mucrama. *Proceedings of the Royal Irish Academy* **19**, 529–63.

DATE: Middle Irish.

Three Middle Irish poems relating to *Cath Maige Mucrama*, which relates how Art mac Cuinn goes to battle against Lugaid mac Con to contest the kingship of Tara. Art begets Cormac before the battle, fights Mac Con and dies. Mac Con becomes king of Tara. The first poem recounts Art mac Cuinn's prophecy before the battle and ultimate conversion to Christianity.

TARA: 534 §13 refers to Tara as *Temair Fáil,* while 536 §21 describes Tara as *Temair in trír.*

140. FIRST LINE: *Abbair fri síl nEógain móir.*

MSS: Bod Laud Miscellany 610; Book of Leinster.

EDITION: Meyer, K. 1918 Mitteilungen aus irischen Handschriften: Senchán Torpeist cecinit so sís. *Zeitschrift für celtische Philologie* **12**, 378–9.

DATE: Middle Irish.

A poem on the tale of Lugaid mac Con, reputed king of Tara.

TARA: 378–9 §§10–11. The poet alludes briefly to Lugaid residing at Tara and leaving it with the arrival of Cormac mac Airt. No specific reference is made to the story of the origin of the *Clóenfherta.*

141. MS: Yellow Book of Lecan.

EDITION: Dillon, M. 1945 The death of Mac Con. *Publications of the Modern Language Association of America* **60**, 340–5 (with translation).

DATE: Possibly the eleventh century.

Part of the Middle Irish text *Cath Maige Mucrama* which deals with the death of the king of Tara, Lugaid mac Con, following his expulsion from Tara at the hands of Cormac mac Airt.

TARA: 341 §1. The text opens with the tale of the false judgement which led to the collapse of the royal house at Tara.

142. MSS: *Cath Maige Mucrama* — Book of Leinster; NLI G 7.
Scéla Eógain 7 Cormaic — Bod Laud Miscellany 610; TCD H 3 17 (no. 1336).
Scéla Moshauluim 7 Maic Con 7 Luigdech — Bod Laud Miscellany 610.
Cath Cinn Abrad — RIA C i 2 (no. 1234); Book of Lecan.

EDITION: O Daly, M. 1975 *Cath Maige Mucrama* — The Battle of Mag Mucrama (with translation). Irish Texts Society, 50. Dublin.

DATE: Ninth century.

Four texts from the Cormac mac Airt cycle, *Cath Maige Mucrama, Scéla Eógain 7 Cormaic, Scéla Moshauluim* and *Cath Cinn Abrad*.

The editor's introduction is important in its analysis of the Lugaid mac Con and Cormac mac Airt cycle. A common theme in the four tales is the conflict between Mac Con, heir to the kingship of the Corco Loígde (a branch of the Érainn of Munster), and Ailill Ólomm, king of Dergthene (described by the editor as 'southern Goidels', i.e. ancestors of the Eóganachta), and his son Eógan. Of *Cath Maige Mucrama* the editor believes that the story in its original form had nothing to do with Cormac mac Airt or Tara, that it was purely a Munster tale which originated among the Corco Loígde and which was later altered and added to by the partisans of the Connachta in order to lend support to the claim of the race of Conn to the kingship of Tara (see no. 146).

143. *Esnada Tige Buchet*

MSS: Bod Rawlinson B 502; Rawlinson B 512; Book of Leinster; Yellow Book of Lecan; TCD H 2 17 (no. 1319).

EDITIONS: Stokes, W. 1904 The songs of Buchet's house. *Revue Celtique* **25**, 18–39, 225–7.
Hayden, M. 1912 The songs of Buchet's house. *Zeitscrift für celtische Philologie* **8**, 261–73 (metrical version from Rawlinson B 502 only; with translation).
Greene, D. 1955 *Fingal Rónáin and other stories*, 27–44. Mediaeval and Modern Irish Series, 16. Dublin.

DATE: Old Irish (prose); early eleventh century (metrical version).

An Old Irish tale, *Esnada Tige Buchet*, relates how Cormac mac Airt came upon Eithne Thóebfhota, daughter of Catháir Mór, who had been taken from her father by Buchet the herdsman. Eithne, who is ultimately a goddess of sovereignty, gives birth to Cormac's son, Cairpre Liphechair, and becomes his queen.

TARA: Apart from incorporating elements of the theme of the king (Cormac) being legitimised by the goddess of sovereignty (Eithne), the tale seems to incorporate the idea that it was the Leinstermen who bestowed the right to the kingship of Tara on Cormac. Cenannus (Kells, Co. Meath) is regarded as the royal residence for kings awaiting their turn to become king of Tara: *Buī Cormac matan moch fecht and i Cenannas iar ngabáil ríge* (29.511–12). This idea is made even clearer in the *dindshenchas* text explaining the name Odor (Odder, close to Tara), which is included into *Esnada Tige Buchet: Is ann didiu ro boí Cormac hua Cuind i Cenannas riasiu no gabad ríge nErenn, ar nīro léic Medb Lethderg hi Temraig iar n-écaib a athar .i. i fail Airt ro boí in Medb Lethderg do Laignib, ocus ar·robert-side in ríge iar n-ēcaib Airt. Ba hé domsad na rríg didiu Cenannus. Conid iar ngabáil ríge do Chormac ro clas lais in Temair* . . . (31.555–60) ('Then Cormac was in Kells before he could assume the kingship of Ireland, because Medb Lethderg did not allow him into Tara after his father's death. Medb Lethderg of the Laigin was Art's consort [in his company] and she took the kingship when Art died. Hence Kells was the residence of the kings. It was after Cormac assumed the kingship that Tara was built [lit. dug] by him').

144. *Comram na Clóenfherta*

MS: Bod Rawlinson B 502.

EDITION: Ó Cuív, B. 1976 Comram na Cloenfherta. *Celtica* **11**, 168–79 (with translation).

DATE: Old to Middle Irish.

An account of the slaying of maidens at Tara by Dúnlang, king of Leinster, in the time of Cormac mac Airt. The tale forms part of the introduction to the saga *Bórama Laigen*, which centres on the tribute levied by the kings of Tara on the Leinstermen. It alludes also to the blinding of Cormac mac Airt, to Cairpre Liphechair's accession to the kingship of Tara, and to the cause of the expulsion of the Déssi from Tara. While no reference is made to the *Clóenfherta Temrach*, except in the title, the *Clóenfherta* at Tara are associated with the incident of the slaying of the thirty maidens in Leinster sources. (See editor's note on the title, 173.)

145. Dobbs, M.E. 1930 Who was Lugaid mac Con? *Journal of the Royal Society of Antiquaries of Ireland* **60**, 165–87.

A detailed discussion of the legendary king of Tara, Lugaid mac Con, based on extensive documentary references.

TARA: 186–7. The author links Lugaid mainly with Munster, adding that any connection with Tara seems to be due to the linking of Mac Con's story to that of Cormac mac Airt in tales such as *Cath Maige Mucrama*.

146. Ó Cathasaigh, T. 1977 *The heroic biography of Cormac mac Airt*. Dublin.

An important analysis of the texts which recount the career and attributes of Cormac mac Airt. The cycle of tales relating to Cormac is analysed as a 'heroic biography' (e.g. birth-tale, the hero in the Underworld, his reign as king of Tara). Many references to Cormac's associations with Tara occur throughout this study. Of particular note is the section on 'The historicity of Cormac mac Airt' (101–4), which the author regards as 'purely speculative' owing to the nature of existing documentation. An edition of the tale *Scéla Eógain 7 Cormaic* is also included in this study (see no. 142).

147. Ó Cathasaigh, T. 1980–1 The theme of *lommrad* in *Cath Maige Mucrama*. *Éigse* **18**, 211–24.

A discussion of the theme of *lommrad* 'act of laying bare' (extended to mean also 'shearing sheep, melting away') and the appearance of the theme in the Old Irish text *Cath Maige Mucrama*, which is linked to the concepts of kingship, fertility, and man versus the Otherworld.

TARA: 213–16. The author analyses the episode in which Lugaid mac Con and Cormac mac Airt give conflicting judgements on the matter of the sheep which had consumed the queen's *glassen* (woad), and which ultimately led to the royal house at Tara collapsing as a result of the false judgement proclaimed by Lugaid. Hence the *Clóenfherta* (Sloping Trenches). The notion that the fertility of the land was contingent upon the truth and justice of the king is central to the Irish ideology of kingship. It is a dominant notion relating to the reign of Cormac mac Airt as king of Tara and in particular to this episode.

148. Ó Corráin, D. 1986 Historical need and literary narrative. In D. Ellis Evans, J.G. Griffith and E.M. Jope (eds), *Proceedings of the 7th International Congress of Celtic Studies, Oxford, 1983*, 141–58. Oxford.

A historical perspective and analysis of early Irish texts, which attempts to explain their context and purpose.

TARA: 144–56. The author provides a historical context for a number of texts closely associated with Tara, namely the tale concerning the sons of Eochaid Mugmedón and tales from the Cormac mac Airt cycle (*Genemuin Cormaic, Scéla Eógain 7 Cormaic,* and the tale of Nia Mór, son of Lugna Fer Trí).

149. *Echtra Cormaic*

MSS: I. *Echtra Cormaic i Tir Tairngiri, ocus Ceart Claidib Cormaic* — Yellow Book of Lecan; Book of Ballymote.
II. *Echtra Cormaic maic Airt* — Book of Fermoy (for an explanation of the versions of the account of Cormac's *echtra,* see Hull, 871–5).

EDITIONS: I. Stokes, W. 1891 The Irish ordeals, Cormac's adventures in the land of promise, and the decision as to Cormac's sword. *Irische Texte* (3rd ser.) **1**, 183–229. Leipzig.
II. Hull, V. 1949 Echtra Cormaic maic Airt, 'The adventure of Cormac mac Airt'. *Publications of the Modern Language Association of America* **64**, 871–83.
See also: O'Grady, S.H. 1857 *Faghail Craoibhe Chormaic mhic Airt*: How Cormac mac Airt got his branch. *Transactions of the Ossianic Society* **3**, 212–29 (with translation). (This is a Modern Irish version preserved in late MSS. O'Grady does not specify which MS he used for his edition.)

DATE: Early Modern Irish, possibly based on a Middle Irish exemplar.

Versions of the tale (and associated tales) which tell of Cormac mac Airt's adventures in the Otherworld, the fruits of which enabled him to gain the kingship of Tara.

TARA: (Stokes) 187–8 §§8–11. The text describes the Cauldron of Plenty placed by Cormac mac Airt in the *Tech Midchúarta*.

150. 'The Expulsion of the Déssi' and associated tales

MSS: Bod Rawlinson B 502; Laud Miscellany 610; TCD H 2 15 (no. 1316).

EDITIONS: Meyer, K. 1901 The expulsion of the Déssi. *Y Cymmrodor* **14**, 101–35.
Meyer, K. 1907 The expulsion of the Déssi. *Ériu* **3**, 135–42.
Meyer, K. 1907 *Tucait indarba na nDéssi. Anecdota from Irish Manuscripts* **1**, 15–24.

DATE: Possibly the eighth century.

An Old Irish text concerning the expulsion of the Déssi from Tara and their subsequent wandering and settlement in the south of Ireland.

TARA: *Ériu* **3**, 135–6. The text deals with the tale of the blinding of Cormac mac Airt at the hands of Óengus Gaíbúaibthech of the Déssi and Cormac's banishment, as a result of his blinding, to Achall (the Hill of Skreen). The Rawlinson B 502 version (*Y Cymmrodor* **14**, 106 §3) incorporates a topographical note on Achall: *Is desin rognid Ocheill* (= Achall) *for Temraig sechtair .i. clasa rath la Cormac, conid inte nofoihed som dogres, ar ni ba hada ri co n-anim do fheis i Temraig* ('Hence Achaill was built by the side of Tara, that is to say, a *rath* was dug by Cormac in which he would always sleep; for it was not lawful [lucky] for a king with a blemish to sleep in Tara').

151. FIRST LINE: *Cid frisndechaid assa thír.*

MSS: Bod Rawlinson B 502; Book of Leinster.

EDITION: Meyer, K. 1912 An Old-Irish parallel to the motive of the bleeding lance. *Ériu* **6**, 157–8 (with translation).

DATE: Tenth century.

A Middle Irish poem based on the theme of the bleeding or bloody lance.

TARA: Eochaid Finn Fúath nAirt, chief of the Fothairt, is driven from Tara by Art mac Cuinn for violating Tara by secretly and mischievously bringing a bloody head on a pole made from the rowan-tree while Art is holding a feast at Tara.

152. Ó Cathasaigh, T. 1984 The Déisi and Dyfed. *Éigse* **20**, 1–33.

A discussion of the context of the text 'The Expulsion of the Déssi'.

TARA: 10–14. This involves a textual discussion of the blinding of Cormac mac Airt and his banishment to Achall.

Eochaid Mugmedóin and his sons

153. *Echtra mac nEchdach Mugmedóin*

FIRST LINE: *Temair Breg, baile na fian*.

MSS: Bod Rawlinson B 502; Book of Leinster.

EDITION: Joynt, M. 1910 Echtra mac Echdach Mugmedoin. *Ériu* **4**, 91–111 (with translation).

DATE: Eleventh century.

A Middle Irish poem *Temair Breg, baile na fian*, ascribed to the poet Cúán úa Lothcháin (d. 1024). The tale tells of how Níall Noígíallach, progenitor of the Uí Néill and son of Eochaid Mugmedón, gained the kingship of Tara for himself and his descendants by mating with a hag, who in reality was the goddess of sovereignty. This text is important as a further example of the association between the kingship of Tara and goddesses of sovereignty. It is also a key text in determining the mythological, prehistoric and contemporary propaganda facets of the kingship of Tara. That it is attributed to Cúán úa Lothcháin, promoter of the cause of Máel Sechnaill II, king of Tara (d. 1022), hints at its contemporary purpose to bolster the claims of the Uí Néill against the rising star of Brían Bóruma.

154. MSS: Yellow Book of Lecan; Book of Ballymote.

EDITION: Stokes, W. 1903 The death of Crimthann son of Fidach, and the adventures of the sons of Eochaid Muigmedóin. *Revue Celtique* **24**, 172–207 (with translation).

DATE: Twelfth century.

The late Middle Irish prose version of *Echtra mac nEchdach Mugmedóin*, which relates how the Uí Néill concede sovereignty to the descendants of Níall Noígíallach's brother, Brión (regarded as the ancestor of the Uí Chonchobair of Connacht).

155. FIRST LINE: *Tairnic in sel-sa ac Síl Néill*.

MSS: Book of Uí Maine; RIA A v 2 (no. 744).

EDITION: Ó Cuív, B. 1983 A poem composed for Cathal Croibhdhearg Ó Conchubhair. *Ériu* **34**, 157–74 (with translation).

DATE: Late twelfth or early thirteenth century.

A bardic poem which retells the story of the sons of Eochaid Mugmedón and their encounter with the sovereignty of Ireland in the form of a hag. The poem concludes with a prophecy about the fortunes of the Uí Chonchobair dynasty from Toirdelbach (d. 1156) to Cathal Croibhdhearg (d. 1224). The importance of the poem lies in its retelling of the tale *Echtra mac nEchdach Mugmedóin*, in line with *Aided Crimthainn*, to bolster the claims to the kingship of Tara of a dynasty other than that about which the tale was composed originally. The Uí Chonchobair of Connacht replace the Uí Néill in the text.

156. Ó Corráin, D. 1987 Legend as critic. In T. Dunne (ed.), *The writer as witness: literature as historical evidence*, 23–38. Historical Studies 16. Cork.

    An analysis of legend and tradition in early Ireland.

    TARA: 31–5. An explanation of the context of the tales *Echtra mac nEchdach Mugmedóin* and *Aided Crimthainn*. The author argues that, on internal evidence, the first tale is to be regarded as Uí Néill propaganda, though some elements of the tale may be as old as the eighth century. The second tale explains the order of precedence among the royal lines of Connacht in the twelfth century.

See also nos 13 and 148.

Lóegaire mac Néill (d. ?461)

157. *Comthoth Lóegaire co creitim 7 a aided*

    MS: Lebor na hUidre.

    EDITION: Plummer, C. 1883–5 Irish miscellanies: the conversion of Loegaire and his death. *Revue Celtique* **6**, 162–72 (with translation).

    DATE: Middle Irish.

    A Middle Irish text which serves as an explanation for the conversion to Christianity of Lóegaire mac Néill, king of Tara. This tale is a version of 'The pseudo-historical prologue to the *Senchas Már*' (see no. 51).

    TARA: 165; 168. The text describes how Lóegaire was buried in his armour in the outermost ditch or bank (*isin chlud imechtrach*) to the south-east of *Ráith Lóegaire* (*ríg ratha Loegairi hi Temraig*), facing his enemies, the Leinstermen. The text concludes with the comment that *Ráith Lóegaire* was at that time the *Tech Midchúarta* of Tara and that was why Lóegaire asked to be buried there.

158. Mac Eoin, G.S. 1968 The mysterious death of Loegaire mac Néill. *Studia Hibernica* **8**, 21–48.

    A detailed discussion of various versions of the death of Lóegaire mac Néill (and of his son Lugaid), one of the kings most frequently associated with Tara.

Muirchertach mac Erca (d. 536)

159. *Aided Muirchertaig meic Erca*

    MSS: Yellow Book of Lecan; TCD H 2 7 (no. 1298).

    EDITION: Nic Dhonnchadha, L. 1964 *Aided Muirchertaig meic Erca*. Mediaeval and Modern Irish Series, 19. Dublin.

    DATE: Possibly the eleventh century.

    A late Middle Irish tale relating how Muirchertach mac Erca, king of Tara (d. 536), met his threefold death following his dalliance with Sín, a woman of the *síd*.

    TARA: 31 §49. Sín identifies herself as daughter of Sige mac Déin, who was killed by Muirchertach and whose people, *Sentuatha Temrach*, were dispossessed by him. Sín has returned to seek revenge on the king.

See also no. 203.

Diarmait mac Cerbaill (d. ?565)

160. *Aided Bresail*

    MSS: Book of Leinster; RIA B iv 2 (no. 1080); RIA 23 P 3 (no. 1242); Book of Lismore.

    EDITION: Meyer, K. 1910 Mitteilungen aus irischen Handschriften: Aided Bresail. *Zeitschrift für celtische Philologie* **7**, 305–7.

    DATE: Middle Irish.

    A Middle Irish text on the death of Bressal, son of Diarmait mac Cerbaill, king of Tara. The text notes that Kells was Diarmait's main stronghold at the time (. . . *Cenandus, ar ba hé ba [a] prímdún an tan sin*, 306).

See also nos 58–61.

Diarmait mac Áedo Sláine (d. 665)

161. *Tochmarc Becfhola*

    MSS: Yellow Book of Lecan; TCD H 3 18 (no. 1337); BL Egerton 1781; RIA B iv 1 (no. 236).

    EDITION: Bhreathnach, M. 1984 A new edition of *Tochmarc Becfhola*. *Ériu* **35**, 59–91 (with translation).

    DATE: Late ninth or early tenth century.

    Two versions of a Middle Irish tale of the meeting of Diarmait mac Áedo Sláine (d. 665), king of Tara, with a mythical woman (Becfhola) and of her betrayal of the king.

TARA: 61 n. 10. The editor cites the prose *Banshenchas* to the effect that one of Diarmait mac Áedo Sláine's wives was named Temair, daughter of Áed Builc, king of the Déssi, an interesting use of the name, perhaps with associations of sovereignty. (Another wife was Mugain, a name which also has connotations of sovereignty.) (For a list of women named Temair see M. Dobbs, 'The *Ban-shenchas*', *Revue Celtique* **49** (1932), 452.)

162. Ó Coileáin, S. 1974 The structure of a literary cycle. *Ériu* **25**, 88–125.

A detailed analysis of the literary cycle concerning Guaire Aidne, with particular reference to the cycle's development in Munster.

TARA: 105–7. The author discusses the historical and genealogical background to the tale and especially the relationships between Guaire and the ecclesiastics Cummíne Fota and Mac dá Cherda (Comgán). The latter is shown to have belonged to the Uí Rossa of the Déssi and to have been a close relative of Temair, wife of Diarmait mac Áedo Sláine (see genealogical table, 106).

Domnall mac Áedo (d. 642)

163. *Fled Dúin na nGéd* and *Cath Maige Raith*

MSS: Yellow Book of Lecan; RIA 23 K 44 (no. 58); B iv 1 (no. 236); Bibliothèque Royale Brussels 3410.

EDITIONS: O'Donovan, J. 1842 *The banquet of Dun na nGedh and the battle of Magh Rath, an ancient historical tale. Now first published from a manuscript [Yellow Book of Lecan col. 321] in the Library of Trinity College, Dublin, with a translation and notes*. Dublin. Irish Archaeological Society.
Lehmann, R. 1964 *Fled Dúin na nGéd*. Mediaeval and Modern Irish Series, 21. Dublin.

DATE: Late eleventh or early twelfth century.

A late Middle Irish tale of a banquet held in a dwelling called *Dún na nGéd* 'Fort of the Geese', the dwelling-place of Domnall mac Áedo, king of the northern Uí Néill and reputed king of Ireland.

TARA: 1–2.8–37. The opening passage of the tale explains that Domnall resides at Dún na nGéd and not at Tara as a result of the curse placed upon Tara by Rúadán. Describing Dún na nGéd (sited on the Boyne) as being built along lines similar to Tara, the text includes a list of monuments at Tara, most of which do not appear in the *dindshenchas* texts — *in midchúairt móradbal, in long Muman, in long Laigen, in chóisir Connacht, in eachrais Ulad, carcair na ngíall, rétla na filed, gríanán in énúaitne.*

164. MS: Yellow Book of Lecan.

EDITIONS: O'Donovan, J. 1842 *The banquet of Dun na nGedh and the battle of Magh Rath, an ancient historical tale. Now first published from a manuscript [Yellow Book of Lecan col. 321] in the Library of Trinity College, Dublin, with a translation and notes*. Dublin. Irish Archaeological Society.
Marstrander, C. 1911 A new version of the Battle of Mag Rath. *Ériu* **5**, 226–47 (with translation).

DATE: Tenth century.

A version of the Middle Irish tale *Cath Maige Rath*, which is a romanticised description of the great battle fought in 637 between Domnall mac Áedo, king of the northern Uí Néill (d. 642), and Congal Cáech, king of the Ulaid, and Domnall Brecc of Dál Riata.

TARA: 232–5. The tale opens with a description of *Feis Temro* (one of the three feasts of Ireland) held by the king of Ireland, Domnall mac Áedo maic Ainmirech. The passage includes a schematised description of the seating arrangement for the kings of the provinces, Domnall being seated in the centre of the royal house at Tara (*for lar in righthaigi a Temair*, 232.4).

165. Herbert, M. 1989 *Fled Dúin na nGéd*: a reappraisal. *Cambridge Medieval Celtic Studies* **18**, 75–87.

A study of the style and context of the tale *Fled Dúin na nGéd*, incorporating comments also on *Cath Maige Rath*. The author dates the latter to the tenth century and suggests that these tales cannot be regarded generically as companion tales, though their subject-matter is similar. *Fled Dúin na nGéd* is described as a *tour de force* of intertextual composition, whose author borrowed phrases, lists and descriptive passages from other tales. The text may be dated to the early twelfth century, to a time when the northern Uí Néill king, Domnall úa Lochlainn (d. 1121), had fraught relations with the Ulaid, a theme that is most prominent in *Fled Dúin na nGéd*.

Cano mac Gartnáin (d. 688)

166. *Scéla Cano meic Gartnáin*

MS: Yellow Book of Lecan.

EDITION: Binchy, D.A. 1963 *Scéla Cano meic Gartnáin*. Mediaeval and Modern Irish Series, 18. Dublin.

DATE: Possibly the ninth century.

A historical romance concerning Cano mac Gartnáin, king of Alba, in which fragments of a romantic legend are associated with a historical character.

TARA: 22 n. 39; 35 n. 456f. While Tara does not play any significant role in this tale, two incidental comments by the editor are worth noting. The first concerns the claim in the text that two sixth-century Uí Néill kings of Tara made a circuit of the lands of the Ulaid, an act which would have been 'utterly impossible' in the sixth century and which even in the ninth century (to which the editor dates the text) would have been 'extremely dangerous'. A reference in the text, 17 §20.457 *berta do chorm[u]im Cearnai*, is noted by the editor as being perhaps 'an oblique reference to the Tara monarchy . . . for the king of Tara is at least once called king of Cernae, where many of the royal line were buried'. Cernae is described elsewhere in the text as being a hillock in Mag mBreg, where enchanted swans used to rest. They were disturbed by Cano (§10.149–71), probably transgressing the taboo of the kings of Tara not to pursue *cláenmíla Cernai* 'the crooked beasts of Cernae' (see nos 127 and 369).

S. Fenian Cycle *(Fíanaigecht)*

The cycle of tales describing the career of Finn mac Cumaill, the *Fíanaigecht*, associated Finn with activities around Tara on occasion. The corpus of genealogies provides him with a Leinster pedigree, while in certain tales he is linked with the Luigne Temrach. *Acallam na Senórach*, a tract incorporating much topographical detail, includes references to monuments at Tara.

167. MS: Bod Laud Miscellany 610.

    EDITIONS: Meyer, K. 1881–3 Macgnimartha Find. *Revue Celtique* **5**, 195–204. Meyer, K. 1904 The boyish exploits of Finn. *Ériu* **1**, 180–90 (translation only).

    DATE: Possibly the twelfth century.

    A Middle Irish text concerning the boyhood adventures of Finn mac Cumaill.

    TARA: *Revue Celtique* **5**, 198 §3.14; 200 §14; *Ériu* **1**, 181; 184 §14. There are two references to the Luigne Temrach; it is implied in one case that they are opposed to Finn and his family, and in the other that he uses their name as an alias.

168. *Acallam na Senórach*

    MSS: Bod Laud Miscellany 610; Bod Rawlinson B 487; Book of Lismore. (For the most recent discussion of *Acallam na Senórach*, including the manuscript tradition, see N. Ó Muraíle, 'Agalamh na Senórach', *Léachtaí Cholm Cille* **25** (1995), 96–127.)

    EDITION: Stokes, W. 1900 Acallamh na Senórach. *Irische Texte* (4th ser.) **1**, 223–4 (with partial translation). Leipzig.

    DATE: Possibly the twelfth century.

    A famous colloquy between Patrick and Caílte, where many natural features and man-made monuments are described and explained.

    TARA: 223–4. This passage is an explanation of the origin of two monuments at Tara, *lighi ind Abaic* (see also nos 84–6) and the *Lia Fáil*. The existence of the *Lia Fáil* at Tara is regarded as in the past, e.g. line 8004 states (*Ocus cia ro thócaib*) *in leac sin nó ruc a hErinn í?* ('And who raised that flagstone or took it from Ireland?').

169. *Cath Cnucha*

    MS: Lebor na hUidre.

    EDITION: Hennessy, W.M. 1873–5 The Battle of Cnucha. *Revue Celtique* **2**, 86–93 (with translation).

    DATE: Middle Irish.

    A Middle Irish prose text which includes the tale of the birth of Finn mac Cumaill.

    TARA: 86–8. The opening lines of the text refer to the period when Cathaír Mór, progenitor of the Leinstermen, held the kingship of Tara, and when Conn Cétchathach was residing at Kells (*hi ferand rígdomna*), waiting to become king of Tara.

170. FIRST LINE: *Cnucha cnoc os cionn Life*.

MSS: Book of Lismore; RIA 23 O 39 (no. 83); Book of Lecan; RIA Stowe MS D ii 2 (no. 1222).

EDITIONS: Power, M. 1917 Cnucha cnoc os cionn Life. *Zeitschrift für celtische Philologie* **11**, 39–55 (with translation).
Ní Shéaghdha, N. 1945 *Agallamh na Seanórach*, vol. 3, 169–80. Dublin.

DATE: Possibly the twelfth century.

A late Middle Irish poem from *Acallam na Senórach*, incorporating the *dindshenchas* of Cnucha and a regnal list of the kings of Ireland from Conn Cétchathach and Eógan Taídlech to the three Collas. A prose introduction describes how the poem was recited by Caílte during the reign of Diarmait mac Cerbaill.

TARA: (Power) 42–4 §§25–30; 34–5; 41; 62–3. The most interesting stanza concerning Tara is that which claims that *Ráith Medba* was built by the Leinstermen for Medb Lethderg: §28 *Claidhset Laighin ar in leirg/ Raith Medhbha do Meidbh Lethdeirg/ is Raith Mheadhbha osin amach/ a hainm do lethaibh Themhrach* ('The Leinstermen built Ráith Meadhbha on the slope for Meadhbh Lethderg and thenceforth Raith Meadhbha was the name of one side of Temhair'). The poem also recounts that not until Cormac mac Airt was united with Medb did he become king of Ireland (§30 *nocor fhaidh Medbh lesin mac/ nir bo righ Eirenn Cormac*).

T. Verse

Tara appears frequently in poems as part of stock phrases which convey ideas of strength, nobility and legitimacy of power. There are, however, many poems that go beyond the use of stock phrases, providing information which either corroborates or deviates from details known from other sources. Poems which use Tara as a central theme or motif are listed in this section. Bardic poetry continues to use Tara and expands on its use in stock phrases. The idea of Tara as a place granting legitimacy to the authority of a lord or king becomes a literary device upon which complete poems are based.

Middle Irish poetry

171. FIRST LINE: *Atá sunn senchus nách súaill*.

    MS: RIA B iv 2 (no. 1080).

    EDITION: Meyer, K. 1912 Mitteilungen aus irischen Handschriften: Der Tribut des Königs von Ess Rúaid. *Zeitschrift für celtische Philologie* **8**, 115–16.

    DATE: Middle Irish.

    A Middle Irish poem on the rights and tributes of the kings of Ess Rúaid (Cenél Conaill).

    TARA: 116 §§9–12. The poem sets out briefly the relationship between the king of Cenél Conaill and the king of Tara, who is regarded as the high-king of Ireland, at times when the former does not hold that elevated office himself.

172. FIRST LINE: *Doluidh Ailill isin caillid*.

MS: Book of Fermoy.

EDITION: Meyer, K. 1918 Mitteilungen aus irischen Handschriften: Cináed húa Artagáin .cc. *Zeitschrift für celtische Philologie* **12**, 358–9.

DATE: Late Middle Irish.

Part of a poem ascribed to Cináed úa hArtacáin (d. 974) on the fate of various kings and their descendants.

TARA: §§1–4. The poet details the dynasties (branches of Síl nÁedo Sláine) in the hinterland of Tara, including Congal, from whom Clann Chellaig and Clann Chongalaig are descended, Diarmait, from whom Clann Chernaig meic Diarmata are descended (*conid úaid síardes im Temraig*), and Conall, from whom Uí Írgalaig (*isin Cerna*) are descended.

173. FIRST LINE: *Innid scēl scaīlter n-airich*.

    MS: Yellow Book of Lecan.

    EDITION: Mulchrone, K. 1949–50 Flannacán mac Cellaich Rí Breg hoc carmen. *Journal of Celtic Studies* **1**, 80–93 (with translation).

    DATE: Late ninth century.

    An Old Irish poem on the deaths of Irish heroes ascribed to Flannacán mac Cellaig, king of Brega (d. 896).

    TARA: 85 §18 refers to the deaths of Núadu and Loingsech, *Dardaīn Nūadad hi Temair;/ diardaín Loingsich a Foraich* ('The Thursday of Núadu in Tara; the Thursday of Loingsech from Forach'). The editor notes (n. 91 §18b) that a place-name Forach (now Farrow) is found near Skreen, Co. Meath. The incident may refer to Loingsech mac Óengusso, king of Tara (696–703).

174. FIRST LINE: *Fíanna bátar i n-Emain*.

    MSS: Book of Leinster; Bod Laud Miscellany 610; BL Egerton 1782.

    EDITION: Stokes, W. 1902 On the deaths of some Irish heroes. *Revue Celtique* **23**, 303–48 (with translation).

    DATE: Tenth century with twelfth-century additions.

    Composite poem on the deaths and graves of Irish heroes ascribed to the poet Cináed úa hArtacáin (d. 974), possibly added to by Bishop Finn of Kildare in the twelfth century.

    TARA: §§1, 7, 12, 17. A possible reference to the *Lia Fáil* (§7), described as being located *i n-uachtar Bruidne* ('in the upper part of the Bruiden'). See, however, editor's note §7 (333).

175. FIRST LINE: *Apraid a éolchu Elga*.

    MS: BL Egerton 1782.

    EDITION: Thurneysen, R. 1921 Das Gedicht der vierzig Fragen von Eochaid ua Cērīn. *Zeitschrift für celtische Philologie* **13**, 130–6.

    DATE: Eleventh century.

Versification of forty questions of general knowledge ascribed to Eochaid úa Céirín, an eleventh-century poet.

TARA: 131 §6. The question is posed as to who reigned in Tara when an unusual shower of snow fell. The answer: Énna Airctheach reigned when a shower of silver fell on Tara and a shower of wine fell on the whole of Ireland.

Bardic poetry

176. FIRST LINE: *Dúnta in tech i-táit na ríg.*

    MS: NLI G 3.

    EDITION: Carney, J. 1969 The Ó Cianáin miscellany. *Ériu* **21**, 122–47 (with translation).

    DATE: Early eleventh century.

    TARA: 142–7. This is a poem lamenting the death of Máel Sechnaill II, king of Tara (d. 1022), which is ascribed to Flann Ó Rónáin (Flann na Marb) and which the editor maintains is contemporary. It includes an allusion to the Battle of Tara, fought in 980, in which Máel Sechnaill defeated the Vikings (of Dublin) somewhere in the vicinity of Tara. Tara is among the places associated with Máel Sechnaill: §8 *forad torc Temra, teg nAirt* ('A seat of the heroes of Tara, the house of Art'). Other places include *Loch Ainninn* (Lough Ennel), *Cnogba* and *Cerna*.

177. FIRST LINE: *Maoil Sechloinn sinnser Gaoidhel.*

    MS: Brussels 5057–9.

    EDITION: O'Keefe, J.G. 1934 On Mael Shechlainn, king of Ireland, †1022, and his contemporaries. In J. Fraser, P. Grosjean and J.G. O'Keefe (eds), *Irish Texts Fasc.* **4**, 30–3. London.

    DATE: Eleventh century or later.

    A poem in praise of Máel Sechnaill II, king of Tara, which incorporates a list of his contemporaries.

    TARA: 31 §6. The poet refers to the Battle of Tara (980) and the killing by Máel Sechnaill of the king of the Vikings: *Rí Lochlonn na long sotla/ a ccath Temhrach taobhchorcra,/ do thuit díni in róid reabaigh/ coig míle do mhíledhuibh.*

178. FIRST LINE: *[B]aile suthach síth Emhna.*

    MSS: Book of Fermoy; RIA 23 H 8 (no. 703).

    EDITION: Ó Cuív, B. 1956–7 A poem in praise of Raghnall, king of Man. *Éigse* **8**, 283–301 (with translation).

    DATE: Late twelfth or early thirteenth century.

    A poem praising Raghnall, king of Man (d. 1229), great-grandson of Gofraid Meránach, king of Dublin (d. 1095).

    TARA: 289 §10. The poet alludes to Raghnall's claim to the kingship of Tara: 'Dá Thí's great ridge awaits thee' (*Radruim [sic] Dá Thí ar thí h'errla*), *Radhruim Dá Thí* being a poetic name for Tara. He continues: 'thou wilt obtain, O noble son of Sadhbh, speech from the flagstone on the side of Tara' (*do-ghébha, a m[e]ic shaeir Shadbha, labra ón leic a taeib Themra*). The editor notes (n. 299.10b) that the reference to the flagstone implies that the *Lia Fáil* was believed to have been at Tara about the end of the twelfth century.

179. FIRST LINE: *Uathad mé a Temraig anocht.*

    MS: Bod Rawlinson B 514.

    EDITION: O'Keefe, J.G. 1934 A prophecy on the high-kingship of Ireland. In J. Fraser, P. Grosjean and J.G. O'Keefe (eds), *Irish Texts Fasc.* **4**, 39–41. London.

    DATE: Possibly the twelfth century.

    A poem foretelling the kings of Tara, the coming of Christianity and the downfall of Tara as a result. The poet predicts the coming of the prophetic king Aedh Anglonnach (see no. 14), who will banish foreigners (*Goill*) from Ireland (41 §14 *ticfa Aedh Anglonnach ann/ dibeorus Goill da bfherand*).

180. FIRST LINE: *An tú arís, a ráith Teamhrach?*

    MSS: RIA 23 L 17 (104); A iii 2 (no. 735); A v 2 (no. 744); Book of O'Gara; Book of the O'Conor Don.

    EDITION: Quiggin, E.C. 1913 O'Conor's house at Cloonfree. In E.C. Quiggin (ed.), *Essays and studies presented to William Ridgeway,* 333–52 (with translation). Cambridge.

    DATE: Early fourteenth century.

    A poem (whose author is not readily identifiable) concerning the house built at Cloonfree, Co. Roscommon, by Aodh Ó Conchobhair, grandson of Ruaidrí úa Conchobair (d. 1309). The theme of the poem is of interest in that the author sees the erection of the house as the reconstruction of Tara at Cloonfree. §3 *Do-thógbhais ceann a gClúain Fráoich/ ar leirg úaine an fheóir fhionnmháoith,/ a ráith cheathardhruimneach Chuinn/ leathan-bhruighneach bhláith bheandchruinn* ('Thou [Rath of Tara] hast appeared in Cloonfree above the verdant slope of the fair-smooth sward, rath of Conn of the fourfold ridge, spaciously palatial, smooth, with round pinnacles').

181. FIRST LINE: *Mór ar bfearg riot a rí Saxan.*

    MS: RIA A iv 3 (no. 743).

    EDITIONS: Bergin, O. 1913 A poem by Gofraidh Fionn Ó Dálaigh. In E.C. Quiggin (ed.), *Essays and studies presented to William Ridgeway,* 323–32 (with translation). Cambridge.
    Bergin, O. 1970 *Irish bardic poetry*, 73–81, 244–8. Dublin.

    DATE: Fourteenth century.

    A poem composed in honour of Maurice Fitzmaurice (Muiris Óg), second earl of Desmond (d. 1358), by the poet Gofraidh Fionn Ó Dálaigh (d. 1387). The poem is of interest in that, in the context of praising Muiris Óg, the poet retells the tale of Lug entering Tara: §49 *Cosmhail cúairt Logha ó lios Eamhna/ d'fhoghluim ghairggníomh,/ as cúairt Muiris go lios Lonndún,/ d'fios an airdríogh* ('Alike are the journey of Lugh from the court of Eamhain [to Tara], to learn fierce deeds, and the journey of Maurice to the court of London, to visit the high-king').

182. FIRST LINE: *A toigh bheag tiaghar a tteagh mór.*

MS: Book of the O'Conor Don.

EDITION: Mac Kenna, L. 1952 A poem by Gofraidh Fionn Ó Dálaigh. *Ériu* **16**, 132–9 (with translation).

DATE: Fourteenth century.

A eulogy to Diarmuid 'na gCaisleán' Ó Briain, king of Thomond (d. 1364), by Gofraidh Fionn Ó Dálaigh.

TARA: 133 §§11, 13. Diarmuid's residence is transferred from *Teach Táil* in Munster to Tara. By enabling Diarmuid to reside at Tara, the poet grants his patron a national status contrary to his actual position. He was deposed in 1343 and again in 1360. This literary device of transferring a king's residence to Tara appears to have been prevalent in thirteenth- and fourteenth-century bardic poems.

183. O Riordan, M. 1990 *The Gaelic mind and the collapse of the Gaelic world.* Cork.

An analysis of the political aspects of the bardic poetry of late medieval Ireland and its use as a historical source for the sixteenth and seventeenth centuries.

TARA: 33–4; 37–50; 59–61. The author touches on the use of Tara as a symbol of authority and legitimacy by the bardic poets.

See also no. 14.

LITERARY INTERPRETATION OF THE SOURCES

AA.	General studies	184–9
BB.	Kingship and sovereignty	190–208
CC.	Inauguration rites	209–14
DD.	Lug	215–19

AA. General studies

184. O'Rahilly, T.F. 1946 *Early Irish history and mythology*. Dublin.

    A very elaborated and sustained attempt at combining literature and history in an effort to present a context for the earliest period of Irish history. The author also deals in detail with the context of Irish mythology.

    TARA: 171–83 ('The Five Provinces'). The author expounds his theory of the Midland Goidels, who, he claimed, established themselves at Tara, which remained their capital until the seventh century. Originally known as the Connachta, they became the Uí Néill and established a kingship of Tara superior to that of other provinces. There are many other references in the book which touch on the prehistory and history of Tara, such as his discussion of the Luigne (390–4).

185. O'Rahilly, T.F. 1950 Notes on *Early Irish history and mythology*. *Celtica* 1, 387–402.

    Additional comments and corrections by O'Rahilly to his book *Early Irish history and mythology*.

    TARA: 387–91; 394–5. The author revises his theory that Túathal Techtmar was the progenitor of the 'fifth' (*cóiced*) of Mide. It existed long before the time of Túathal Techtmar. He also revises his view of the origins of Cormac mac Airt, claiming that Cormac was taken over from the pre-Goidelic inhabitants of the Tara district, as evidenced by the tradition of his being fostered by Lugna Fer Trí.

186. Rees, A. and Rees, B. 1961 *Celtic heritage: ancient tradition in Ireland and Wales*. London.

    An analysis of Celtic tradition based on the evidence of religion, myth and anthropology. It incorporates many references to Tara, a constant preoccupation of the authors being Tara's role as part of the centre, geographically and in society. See especially chapter 7, 'The Centre', 146–72.

187. Dillon, M. (ed.) 1959 *Irish sagas*. Thomas Davis Lecture Series. Cork and Dublin.

    A series of papers on Irish sagas.

    TARA: 15–23 (*Tochmarc Étaíne*, M. Dillon); 24–37 (*Cath Maige Tuired*, B. Ó Cuív); 107–21 (*Togail Bruidne Da Derga*, M. O Daly); 152–66 (*Cath Maige Muccrime*, J. Carney).

188. McCone, K. 1990 *Pagan past and Christian present in early Irish literature*. Maynooth.

    A study of medieval Ireland's literature in which the author argues that this literature is rooted in *senchas* (lore) adapted, synthesised and modified by monastic men of letters from the Bible and other Latin writings, in conjunction with vernacular tradition both oral and written.

    TARA: (Main observations) 75–6 (the context of the Middle Irish tales *Airne Fíngein* and *Do Shuidigud Tellaich Themra*); 119–20 (*Aided Meidbe, Cath Bóinde, De Shíl Chonairi Móir* and *Esnada Tige Buchet*); 130–7 (sovereignty and the kingship of Tara); 159–60 (aspects of the tale *Esnada Tige Buchet*).

189. Ó hÓgáin, D. 1990 *Myth, legend and romance: an encyclopaedia of the Irish folk tradition.* New York.

A comprehensive key to the popular literature of Ireland; it includes entries on individuals, on peoples and families, on places and on general topics.

TARA: 400–2. A useful general description of the most important persons, traditions and events associated with Tara.

BB. Kingship and sovereignty

The sacred and unusual nature of the kingship of Tara has been the theme of many scholarly works. Ritual inaugurations and assemblies, taboos, associations with certain goddesses who represent the sovereignty of Tara, the Otherworldly nature of the kingship, and concepts of truth and justice leading to prosperity and fertility are aspects of early kingship which occur frequently in the published material. Particular reference is made to the heroic and mythological kings of Tara, Conaire Mór and Cormac mac Airt, the proto-historical kings, Níall Noígíallach and Lóegaire mac Néill, and the historical king Diarmait mac Cerbaill. The attributes of the goddesses Medb and Eithne, the god Lug and the ritual assembly, *Feis Temro,* are given consistent notice by scholars.

190. Baudiš, J. 1916 On the antiquity of the kingship of Tara. *Ériu* **8**, 101–7.

A discussion of the antiquity of the kingship of Tara and of its attributes, mainly based on evidence from the Conaire Mór cycle. Baudiš concludes that the tradition of the kingship of Tara preserves to a remarkable degree the characteristics of a priest-kingship. He surmises that 'before the coming of the Milesian race, Tara was anciently a place of importance, and that the importance of the king of Tara was due to his priestly nature'.

191. Ó Máille, T. 1928 Medb Chruachna. *Zeitschrift für celtische Philologie* **17**, 129–46.

A detailed consideration of the traditions and attributes of Medb, her consorts, her other manifestation as Medb Lethderg, the sovereignty of Ireland and the origin of the name Medb. The author refers throughout to Medb's associations with Tara.

192. Thurneysen, R. 1930 Allerlei Keltisches: 7. Göttin Medb? *Zeitschrift für celtische Philologie* **18**, 108–10.
Thurneysen, R. 1933 Zur Göttin Medb. *Zeitschrift für celtische Philologie* **19**, 352–3.

Notes on Medb, the goddess associated with the inauguration of kings, and her attributes in direct response to the extensive article by Ó Máille in *Zeitschrift für celtische Philologie* **17**.

193. O'Rahilly, T.F. 1946 On the origins of the names *Érainn* and *Ériu*. *Ériu* **14**, 7–28.

A discussion of the origin — etymologically, historically and mythologically — of *Érainn* and *Ériu*. The article includes a discussion of concepts such as earth mother-goddesses, kingship and the *banfheis* (the ritual marriage of goddess and king), and connections between place-names and goddesses.

TARA: 14–21. The author discusses the associations between the goddess Ériu (and other goddesses such as Medb), sovereignty and the kingship of Tara. See also O. Bergin's refutation of the author's etymology of *Ériu* in same volume, 147–53.

194. Mac Cana, P. 1955–9 Aspects of the theme of king and goddess in Irish literature. *Études Celtiques* **7** (1955–6), 76–114, 356–413; **8** (1958–9), 59–65.

A detailed study of the theme of sovereignty as manifested in the relationship between goddess and king. Specific reference is made to the traits and role of Mór or Mugain in Munster. Mór is sometimes identified as the historical Mór, daughter of Áed Bennán of the Eóganachta Irluachra (d. 632), though this identification is doubtful. The author argues that Mór played the part of the territorial goddess associated with the kingship of Munster, who took over from the earlier Mugain, goddess of the Érainn (similar to Medb at Tara).

195. Wagner, H. 1970 Studies in the origins of early Celtic civilisation. *Zeitschrift für celtische Philologie* **31**, 1–58.

A detailed study, based on comparative linguistics and mythology, of aspects of Irish and Welsh literature and language.

TARA: There are many references to Tara. Note in particular 15–19 (symbols of kingship); 21–30 (sites of open-air assemblies, Lug, *Óenach Tailten*); 37 (*Feis Temro*); 42–5 (kingship and goddesses); 58 n. 2 (the king of Tara as sun-god); 58 n. 3 (*Lia Fáil*). In his note on the *Lia Fáil*, the author argues that the element *Fál* is etymologically identical with Gwawl, the name for the Otherworld king in the Welsh *Mabinogi*. The *Lia Fáil* represents the voice of the ancestor-deity of Tara, Lug.

196. Borgeaud, W.A. 1971 Hibernica: Echu–Echoch, Echoid–Echdach, Temair. *Beiträge zur Namenforschung* **6**, 40–4.

A note on the etymology of the name *E(o)chaid*, *E(o)chu*, a name associated with a horse-god and with death.

TARA: 42–3. The author suggests that the name *Temair* originates from a word meaning 'twilight' or 'darkness'. He points to the existence of a number of *Temair* place-names in Ireland, and draws a parallel with the use of the word *Pylos* 'Gate of the Dead' in place-names in the Peloponnese. He also alludes to the connection between Eochaid's daughter Medb, whose name is associated with drunkenness, and the existence of the *Tech Midchúarta*, 'the house of regular imbibing'.

197. Wagner, H. 1975 Studies in the origins of early Celtic traditions. *Ériu* **26**, 1–26.

A wide-ranging discussion, based on linguistic and literary evidence, of parallels between Celtic and other cultures.

TARA: 20–1. The author quotes as significant the reply given by Emer, Cú Chulainn's wife, to her future spouse when he asks her her name (*Tochmarc Emire* §18). She answers: '*Temair ban, báine ingen . . .*', which is explained in what seems to be a gloss *amal atá Temair ós cach thulaig, sic atúsa ós cach mnaí* ('as Tara is above every hilltop, so am I above every woman'). The author surmises that just as Cú Chulainn is the son of Lug, the progenitor god of Tara, so Emer represents the hilltop-goddess Temair, and is therefore ultimately identical with Medb, whose name is another epithet of the ancestor-goddess of Tara. In his linguistic analysis of the name *Temair* (21 n. 39) he suggests that it could be related to Old Irish *temel* (darkness) and cognate with, among other words, Latin *tenebrae*, the darkness associated with the ancestor-goddess of Tara.

198. Wagner, H. 1977 The archaic *Dind Ríg* poem and related problems. *Ériu* **28**, 1–16.

A study of the Old Irish poem *Dind Ríg rúad-túaim tenbath* on the destruction of Dind Ríg. Particular emphasis is placed on Leinster–British connections found in personal and place-names in the Leinster tradition.

TARA: 13. The author points to similarities between the Celts and other ancient civilisations, including the fact that the former considered their political and religious centres, such as Temair, Crúachain and Emain, to be replicas of the palaces of the gods of the Otherworld.

199. Ó Cathasaigh, T. 1977–9 The semantics of *síd*. *Éigse* **17**, 137–55.

An important analysis of the Old Irish word *síd/síth,* which can mean both 'Otherworld hill or mound' and 'peace'. The author's primary objective is to establish whether the two are etymologically related. In the course of his discussion he touches on subjects of great relevance to Tara such as the earliest forms of kingship, with specific reference to Conaire Mór and Cormac mac Airt. Two attributes of legitimate kingship are identified (which also show the relationship between the two meanings of *síd*), namely that legitimate kingship has its source in the Otherworld and that the reign of a righteous king is marked by peace and plenty. He reinforces the oft-quoted argument that an essential part of the inauguration ceremonies of kings was their location on or close to tumuli. In this connection, 150 n. 52, concerning the etymologically associated words *forad* ('a mound or platform', see the *Forad* at Tara) and *gorsedd* (Welsh), is important. According to Ó Cathasaigh, the Irish *forad* seems to have had an early connection with druidical functions. He quotes a reference from the early stratum of the 'Expulsion of the Déssi', where a *forad* is opened before the druid Díl delivers a prophecy.

200. Wagner, H. 1979 Origins of pagan Irish religion and the study of names. *Bulletin of the Ulster Place-names Society* (2nd ser.) **2**, 24–40.

A detailed discussion on the theme of the *síd*, on sacred places, gods and goddesses based on comparative philology and literary analysis.

TARA: 26. The author suggests a contrast between Temair and Tailtiu, Temair meaning 'the Dark One' and Tailtiu 'the Beautiful One', reflecting 'the same dual function of the goddess of life and death' which is also found in connection with river names.

201. McCone, K.R. 1980 Fírinne agus torthúlacht. *Léachtaí Cholm Cille* **11**, 136–73. Maigh Nuad.

A study of the associations between truth and fertility in the context of kingship. Relevant to the kingship of Tara and its associations with the goddesses Medb and Eithne, as well as its connections with fertility and sovereignty.

202. Wagner, H. 1981 Origins of pagan Irish religion. *Zeitschrift für celtische Philologie* **38**, 1–28.

A slightly expanded version of no. 200.

TARA: 6–7 §9. The author considers the significance of the association between the earth-goddess and sacred hills (e.g. Tailtiu, Temair). He takes Temair to mean 'the Dark One', which may reflect the goddess's dual function of life and death. He maintains that it is almost certain that Temair derives from the root *tem- (Old Irish *temel* 'darkness').

203. Bhreathnach, M. 1982 The sovereignty goddess as goddess of death? *Zeitschrift für celtische Philologie* **39**, 243–60.

A discussion of the theme whereby the goddess of sovereignty reappears as the goddess of death to unjust kings and withdraws sovereignty from them. The author makes extensive reference to the kingship of Tara in discussing the tales of Conaire Mór and Muirchertach mac Erca.

204. McCone, K.R. 1983 Scéla Muicce Meic Da Thó. *Léachtaí Choim Cille* **14**, 5–38. Maigh Nuad.

The author addresses motifs and contexts of the epic tale *Scéla Muicce Meic Da Thó*. The conclusion on the kingship of Tara (36–7), which is also based on another tale, *Esnada Tige Buchet*, is of interest. It is argued that *Esnada Tige Buchet* tells of the shift in power in the kingship of Tara from the Leinstermen to the Dál Cuinn (Uí Néill). Eithne is the goddess of sovereignty symbolising the kingship of Tara, and Catháir Mór (Leinster) and Cormac mac Airt (Uí Néill) are the protagonists (see no. 146).

205. Mac Cana, P. 1985 Early Irish ideology and the concept of unity. In R. Kearney (ed.), *The Irish mind. Exploring intellectual traditions*, 56–78. Dublin.

A discussion of the traditional concept of unity as portrayed in Irish literature, a concept which lay in the cultural unity of the island. The learned, literary language was fashioned and cared for by endless generations of druids and *filid* until the collapse of Gaelic society in the seventeenth century.

TARA: 70. The author regards Tara as the ritual centre of sovereignty in Ireland, though its king was not in any real and practical sense king of all Ireland. Assuming that Tara was established as the seat of sacred kingship *par excellence* by the Gaelic colonisers who seized dominion over large areas of the northern half (who according to the author come to be known as the Uí Chuinn, 'descendants of Conn Cétchathach'), its spiritual precedence failed to become a political reality because the Uí Chuinn failed to gain effective control over the whole of Ireland. Elsewhere (71) he speaks of 'the cult of the central kingship of Tara' and of Tara as part of the *topos* of unity in bardic poetry (75).

206. Mac Cana, P. 1988 Placenames and mythology in Irish tradition: places, pilgrimages and things. In G.W. MacLennan (ed.), *Proceedings of the First North American Congress of Celtic Studies held at Ottawa from 26th–30th March, 1986*, 319–41. Ottawa.

A study linking place-names with sacred history (e.g. scenes of mythic events) which determined the origin and subsequent evolution of a tribe or nation. Such places were often the sites of ritual ceremonies and celebrations, guarded by a bank or other form of enclosure.

TARA: 323; 333. The author notes that Tara and other royal or ritual sites are located on the tops of hills or mountains, some modest but all commanding a wide view over the surrounding countryside. They are the spot at which the earth comes nearest the sky, the replica of the sacred mountain which touches the sky and which therefore stands, as the Axis Mundi, at the centre of the world.

207. Ní Chatháin, P. 1991 Traces of the cult of the horse in early Irish sources. *Journal of Indo-European Studies* **19**, 123–31.

A discussion of indications of the cult of the horse in early Ireland with specific reference to kingship rites and the role of the goddess. Note the possible association between Lagore, Co. Meath (*Loch Dá Gabar* 'the lake of the two horses'), and resonances of an equine cult (124–5). (For similar associations with Tara, see no. 196.)

208. Kelly, P. 1992 The *Táin* as literature. In J.P. Mallory (ed.), *Aspects of the Táin*, 69–102. Belfast.

A study of *Táin Bó Cúailnge* as a work of literature.

In the excerpt entitled 'Medb: Sovereignty Goddess or All-too-human', the author deals with the differences between Medb's better-known role as goddess of sovereignty and the more negative (and less godly) role assigned to her in the *Táin*.

CC. Inauguration rites

Historical evidence for the physical manifestation of the kingship of Tara in its ritual and sacral aspects is not immediately available. The two descriptions of the inauguration of a king of Tara, in the Conaire Mór cycle and in the Life of Colmán mac Lúacháin, are unlikely to reflect the historical formula of inauguration at Tara. There are, however, attributes common to historical and fanciful descriptions of inauguration rites which are available from Irish and Scottish sources (e.g. the use of prehistoric tumuli as sites for the rite, and the involvement of a priestly caste (Christian and non-Christian)). These may provide some supporting evidence for the ceremonies which supposedly took place at Tara.

209. Dillon, M. 1973 The consecration of Irish kings. *Celtica* **10**, 1–8.

A discussion of the attributes of the consecration of kings (the use of the straight white rod, the chariot-race, the ritual steps towards each of the five regions) based on various Irish texts, and including Indian and classical parallels.

TARA: 2; 3; 4. The author illustrates his argument with references to the inauguration of kings of Tara. He cites the description from the Conaire Mór cycle and the passage in the Life of Colmán mac Lúacháin, which he describes as a fanciful account.

210. Bieler, L. 1975 Hagiography and romance in medieval Ireland. *Medievalia et Humanistica. Studies in Medieval and Renaissance Culture* (new ser.) **6**, 13–24.

A discussion of aspects of Irish hagiography.

TARA: 17. The author draws a parallel between the motif of prophecy of the birth of a saint and the test concerning the claim to the throne of Tara — the axle screeching against the *Lia Fáil*.

211. Watson, A. 1981 The king, the poet and the sacred tree. *Études Celtiques* **18**, 165–80.

   A discussion of the nature and function of the sacred tree in the pagan Irish religious system and its relations to the social role of king and poet.

   TARA: 175–6. The author mentions trees sometimes associated with Tara, namely *Bile Tortan* (at Ardbraccan, Co. Meath) and *Bile Dathí* (barony of Farbill, Co. Westmeath). (See also A.T. Lucas, 'The sacred trees of Ireland', *Journal of the Cork Historical and Archaeological Society* **68** (1963), 16–54. This is a comprehensive study of the subject, though no reference is made to Tara.)

212. Doherty, C. 1985 The monastic town in early medieval Ireland. In H.B. Clarke and A. Simms (eds), *The comparative history of urban origins in non-Roman Europe: Ireland, Wales, Denmark, Germany, Poland and Russia from the ninth to the thirteenth century*, 45–75. BAR International Series 255(i). Oxford.

   A detailed examination of the development of 'Christian cult centres' in Ireland between the introduction of Christianity and the coming of the Anglo-Normans.

   TARA: 47–53. The author makes a series of pertinent comments concerning Tara in discussing the concept of the celestial city in Ireland. The text *Do Shuidigud Tellaich Themra* is regarded as a fusion of biblical, Christian and native ideas which see Tara and Uisnech as focal points in Ireland. The reference to the marking out of a *forrach* at Uisnech is seen as the raising of a pagan shrine or sanctuary there, and is taken to be related to the existence of a *forad* on a site. Of the *forad*, the author states: 'Originally the *forad* was probably associated in particular with kingship. Some of them may have been prehistoric tumuli. They were regarded as the home of the gods, and kings were inaugurated upon them. The king, therefore, seated upon his *forad*, was the intermediary between his people and the otherworld' (52).

213. de Pontfarcy, Y. 1987 Two late inaugurations of Irish kings. *Études Celtiques* **24**, 203–8.

   A discussion of the description in Giraldus Cambrensis's *Topographia Hibernica* of the inauguration of the king of Tír Chonaill, and the description in the twelfth-century Life of Colmán mac Lúacháin of the inauguration of the king of Tara. The author suggests that these descriptions 'recall very archaic rituals which belong without any doubt to the Indo-European and Celtic tradition. They show, in different ways, a similar well-structured relationship of symbols which expresses the cosmic dimension of the creation of a king as the child and genitor of the people–land–sovereignty' (208).

214. Bannerman, J. 1989 The king's poet and the inauguration of Alexander III. *Scottish History Review* **68**, 120–49.

   A description of the inauguration of Alexander III of Scotland at Scone in 1249. Parallels are drawn with what is known of Irish inaugurations.

DD. Lug

Lug, the omnicompetent god (*samildánach*), seems to be the divine manifestation of the kingship of Tara. The connection between him and Tara appears consistently in the sources. He is recognised as the *samildánach* in the episode describing his entry into Tara in *Cath Maige Tuired*. His role in legitimising a king's authority over Tara is emphasised in the regnal list *Baile in Scáil*. *Óenach Tailten*, which is associated closely with the kings of Tara, was reputedly held at Lugnasad, Lug's festival.

215. MacNeill, M. 1962 *The festival of Lughnasa. A study of the survival of the Celtic festival of the beginning of harvest*. Dublin and Oxford.

    The primary study of the festival of Lughnasa, the rite of the beginning of harvest, often associated with Lug.

    TAILTIU: 311–38. A detailed description of the *Óenach Tailten* held at Lughnasa. Included at the end of the book are maps and plans of Tailtiu based on those provided by John O'Donovan for the Ordnance Survey in the nineteenth century.

216. MacNeill, M. 1965 Trespass and building in the Lughnasa legends. *Journal of the Royal Society of Antiquaries of Ireland* **95**, 115–19.

    The account of Lug's arrival at Tara in *Cath Maige Tuired* describes how he built a structure called the *Cró Logo*. The author attempts to explain this incident with reference to the motifs of trespass, house-building and the celebration of the harvest festival found in popular literature.

217. Ó Riain, P. 1978 Traces of Lug in early Irish hagiographical tradition. *Zeitschrift für celtische Philologie* **36**, 138–56.

    A discussion of pagan deities and Christian saints with particular reference to Molua, Molacca and Lachténe and their derivation from the god Lug.

    TARA: 151–3. This part discusses the attributes of the legendary king of Tara, Lugaid mac Con, and of his possible Christian reflex, Lugaid Maccan, referred to in the Life of Molua. The author argues that they belong to a Munster tradition and that the Tara tradition is intrusive, while preserving intact the ancestral names, Lug (Lugaid mac Con) and Corp (Cormac mac Airt, Cormac Cas, Cairpre Liphechair).

218. Tovar, A. 1982 The god *Lugus* in Spain. *Bulletin of the Board of Celtic Studies* **29**, 591–9.

    A listing of references to the god Lug from the Continent, Britain and Ireland.

    TAILTIU: 598. A passing reference to *Óenach Tailten*.

219. Gray, E.A. 1989–90 Lug and Cú Chulainn: king and warrior, god and man. *Studia Celtica* **24–5**, 38–52.

    An extensive discussion of the relative attributes of Cú Chulainn and his divine father, Lug.

    TARA: 41. The author argues that as master of all the arts Lug is equivalent to all the *áes dáno* in Tara, who themselves represent the entire society. In equality, however, there is distinction. Núadu rises to honour Lug, showing deference to the authority of kingship.

HISTORICAL INTERPRETATION OF THE SOURCES

EE.	General studies	220–3
FF.	The high-kingship of Tara	224–46
GG.	*Feis Temro*	247–9
HH.	Tara and Iona	250–3
II.	Tara and Cashel	254–7
JJ.	The Gailenga and the Luigne	258–66

EE. General studies

220. Dillon, M. (ed.) 1954 *Early Irish society*. Thomas Davis Lecture Series. Dublin.

    A series of lectures on aspects of early Irish society.

    TARA: 36–51 ('Irish origin-legends', M.A. O'Brien); 52–65 ('Secular institutions', D.A. Binchy); 66–78 ('The impact of Christianity', J. Carney).

221. Mac Niocaill, G. 1972 *Ireland before the Vikings*. The Gill History of Ireland 1. Dublin.

    A general discussion of the history of Ireland from *c*. AD 450 to 800, chapters being divided according to the main tribes, dynasties and kingdoms of Ireland.

    TARA: The greatest part of the discussion of Tara relates to the kingship of Tara and is found in the chapters dealing with the rise of the Uí Néill. In the discussion a chronology is suggested, though it has been superseded by more recent work.

222. Ó Corráin, D. 1972 *Ireland before the Normans*. The Gill History of Ireland 2. Dublin.

    A synthesis of the history of Ireland from the ninth century to the twelfth century.

    TARA: Many valuable comments are made. Of particular note are the sections on 'The concept of kingship' (32–5), 'The ceremony of inauguration' (35–7), and 'The struggles of the overkings' (96–101).

223. Byrne, F.J. 1973 *Irish kings and high-kings*. London.

    An extensive study which attempts to elucidate early medieval Ireland from a wide range of sources. The author concentrates on the theme of kingship and, in that context, chapters 1–6 are of vital importance to any consideration of the historical interpretation of Tara. Chapter 4, 'The kingship of Tara', is of particular significance.

FF. The high-kingship of Ireland

The existence of a high-kingship of Ireland, centred at Tara, has been for centuries (and remains) a national doctrine. Its authenticity has been questioned by scholars since Eoin MacNeill suggested that the concept of a national monarchy was created by the Irish 'synthetic historians', who compiled and wrote the annals, genealogies and pseudo-historical works of early medieval Ireland, in the eleventh and twelfth centuries. It is clear that the idea of a high-kingship was fostered from an early period by propagandists who promoted the cause of the Uí Néill dynasts. The rise of Armagh as the primatial see in Ireland contributed also to the Uí Néill claims to a primacy in political power. That they had authority in all parts of the country from the seventh century onwards is not borne out by the annalistic records. Their position was threatened on occasion by kings of Munster and their propagandists. Whatever about the reality of a high-kingship of Ireland, it is notable that Tara was a potent symbol whose sacred past was regenerated at various times by MacNeill's synthetic historians to boost the claims of ambitious and weak kings alike.

224. Rhys, J. 1890–1 The early Irish conquests of Wales and Dumnonia. *Journal of the*

Royal Society of Antiquaries of Ireland **21**, 642–57.

Early theories about the conquest of Ireland by the Celts and about Irish settlements in Wales. The author speculates that the Celts started in Mide and conquered Ireland from there, Tara being their focus-point. He states that Mide was the first Celtic, and in fact the first Aryan, settlement in Ireland.

225. MacNeill, E. 1919 *Phases of Irish history*. Dublin.

A pioneering work in the analysis of early Irish history, many conclusions of which remain relevant today.

TARA: 233–6. The author argues that the tale of Rúadán's curse of Tara and its subsequent desertion is a Middle Irish tale which does not reflect the real reason why Tara was abandoned. Tara does not stand alone; Crúachain and Dún Ailinne were abandoned at the same period. 'It was military kings who ruled from these strongholds, surrounded by strong permanent military forces. My first visit to Tara convinced me that what we see there is the remains of a great military encampment.' This militarisation died with the absence of booty from Britain and Gaul, and this ultimately caused the abandonment of Tara. The importance of Tara was also reduced when Clann Cholmáin won the hegemony of the southern Uí Néill from Síl nÁedo Sláine, who still kept Tara in their possession until the close of the tenth century.

226. MacNeill, E. 1921 *Celtic Ireland*. Dublin.

An attempt to establish a critical basis for the study of the early history of Ireland. References to Tara are scattered throughout the work. Note especially chapter 3 (25–42) on the influence of what the author termed 'the Irish synthetic historians' on the creation of an early monarchy. He adduces evidence from the status accorded to holders of the title *rígdomna Temrach* for his arguments regarding dynastic succession in general (130–3).(For notes updating MacNeill's work see the 1981 edition, which includes an introduction and additional notes by D. Ó Corráin.)

227. MacNeill, E. 1927 Miscellanea: Pre-Christian kings of Tara. *Journal of the Royal Society of Antiquaries of Ireland* **57**, 153–4.

A note emphasising that the alleged unbroken father-to-son line of the kings of Tara from Lugaid, first king of Tara recorded in the *Annals of Tigernach*, to Níall Noígíallach was virtually impossible. 'We have to infer therefore that the ancient chronicler, having no continuous record of the kings of Tara before Niall, filled the blanks with the most suitable and similar material known to him, Niall's pedigree containing doubtless names, notably that of Cormac, associated in tradition with the kingship of Tara.'

228. Binchy, D.A. 1958 The date and provenance of *Uraicecht Becc*. *Ériu* **18**, 44–54.

A discussion of the date and context of the law-tract *Uraicecht Becc*. The author concludes that the tract is of Munster origin (note the phrase *ollam uas rígaib rí Muman*) and of an early date (?seventh century).

TARA: 51. The author indicates that he intends to explain in a future article that 'the over-lordship of the king of Tara was not admitted in Munster before the middle of the ninth century'. He refers to the relationship between Cathal mac Finguine, king of Munster (d. 742), and kings of Tara.

229. Binchy, D.A. 1962 The passing of the old order. In B. Ó Cuív (ed.), *The impact of the Scandinavian invasions on the Celtic-speaking peoples c. 800–1100 A.D.*, 119–32. Dublin. (Proceedings of the International Congress of Celtic Studies held in Dublin, 6–10 July, 1959.)

An important paper in which the author explains, among other topics, his views on the kingship of Tara, the high-kingship of Ireland and the impact of the Vikings.

TARA: 124–32. The Ireland of *c.* 800 found by the Vikings was 'a *congerie* of tribal states tenuously linked together in five larger groups. Two of these groups, the Uí Néill and the Eoghanacht dynasties, were of outstanding importance, the head of the former being usually the most powerful monarch in the whole country' (126). The impact of the newcomers was to jolt the country out of its old tribal framework and to create 'if not a modern sense of nationalism, at least a feeling of "otherness" among peoples whose only loyalty had hitherto been to their local kings' (131).

230. Byrne, F.J. 1962–3 Review of B. Ó Cuív (ed.), *The impact of the Scandinavian invasions on the Celtic-speaking peoples* (Dublin 1962). *Irish Historical Studies* **13**, 269–71.

A review of the papers given at the Celtic Congress of 1959, the main theme of which was the impact on Ireland of the Scandinavian incursions.

TARA: 270. The author reviews Binchy's paper, 'The passing of the old order', in which the latter maintained that the king of Tara held a status no higher than that of a *rí ruirech* (provincial king). The reviewer contests this view, arguing among other points that the king of Tara had a higher status on the basis that the title *rí ruirech* could be claimed by the king of either the northern or southern Uí Néill, as well as the king of the Airgíalla, all of whom were subject to the king of Tara. The tribute, be it token or real, exacted from the Laigin by the king of Tara is cited as further evidence of the latter's higher status.

231. Byrne, F.J. 1962–3 Review of K. Hughes, 'The church and the world in early Christian Ireland', in *Irish Historical Studies* **13**, 99–116. *Irish Historical Studies* **13**, 263–6.

In his review the author comments (264) on the connection between the claims of Armagh and the establishment of a high-kingship over all Ireland (apparently not stressed by Hughes). He notes that the first king of Tara to assert himself as king of Ireland was Máel Sechnaill in the mid-ninth century, and that the establishment of a high-kingship was no doubt supported by responsible ecclesiastics who needed strong kings to enforce their *cána* (laws/tributes).

232. Kelleher, J.V. 1963 Early Irish history and pseudo-history. *Studia Hibernica* **3**, 113–27.

A study on Tara, the Uí Néill and concepts of high-kingship, all of which, according to the author, are inextricably linked. Whereas the annals and *Baile in Scáil*, the 'official Uí Néill documents', attempt to present an agreed account of pre-tenth-century history, the author concludes that evidence is not lacking for the existence of older and quite different traditions about the kingship of Tara and the Christianisation of Ireland. It is possible to see how the story kept changing, and how the claims kept expanding, from century to century (126).

233. Byrne, F.J. 1965 The Ireland of Saint Columba. *Historical Studies* **5**, 37–58.

An analysis of events in Ireland *c.* 550–650, with particular reference to the northern half of Ireland and to events which might have had an effect on Columba and his kinsmen, the Uí Néill.

TARA: 42 (the existence of the high-kingship of Tara); 44 (Diarmait mac Cerbaill and the celebration of *Feis Temro*); 47–8, 52 (the Ulaid's claim to the kingship of Tara); 58 n. 91 ('Recent opinion is returning to Macalister's view that the importance of Tara lay in the religious realm rather than the political realm . . .').

234. Byrne, F.J. 1967 Seventh-century documents. *Irish Ecclesiastical Record* **108**, 164–82.

A survey of documents which can be dated with certainty to the seventh century.

TARA: 168. The author deals with the regnal list *Baile Chuinn*, apparently written during the reign of Fínnachta Fledach (675–95) or just before his accession to the kingship of Tara. The text displays some interesting variants from the accepted Uí Néill doctrine in that it includes kings who may have been outsiders, e.g. *Feachno*, who is to be identified possibly with Fiachnae mac Baetáin (d. 626) of the Dál nAraidi of the Ulaid. Moreover, it seems to confirm that the kingship of Tara was not an ordinary tribal kingship succeeded to immediately on the death of the previous holder, but was a prize to be achieved only by the most outstanding. The list shows many periods of interregnum.

235. Byrne, F.J. 1969 *The rise of the Uí Néill and the high-kingship of Ireland*. O'Donnell Lecture Series, 13. Dublin.

An in-depth analysis of the concept of high-kingship and its particular association with the Uí Néill. The author argues that the high-king over all the Uí Néill and their dependencies bore the title *rí Temro*, king of Tara. Tara was a sacral kingship; its holder was not a high-king, but was in a position of prestige. *Feis Temro* was a pagan fertility rite which accompanied the inauguration of the king of Tara. Of the Uí Néill he states: 'They ruled over peoples largely of alien stock, from whose gods they were not descended. Tribal kingship survived but was everywhere subjected to a new kind of over-kingship, dynastic in principle' (22).

236. Binchy, D.A. 1970 *Celtic and Anglo-Saxon kingship*. O'Donnell Lecture Series. Oxford.

A study of the attributes and development of kingship in Celtic, early Irish and Anglo-Saxon society.

TARA: 31–46. The author deals with the developments and relations between the provinces, the rise of the Uí Néill and the kingship of Tara. According to the author (43), from the end of the fifth century to the middle of the ninth century there were two major kingdoms in Ireland, Tara and Cashel. While the king of Tara was normally the most powerful king in Ireland, he was not the king of Ireland (37). Of *Feis Temro* he states that it was in origin a ritual marriage between the new king of Tara and the goddess Medb (11).

237. Byrne, F.J. 1974 *Senchas*: the nature of Gaelic historical tradition. *Historical Studies* **9**, 137–59.

A discussion of *senchas*, which is defined as 'the traditional lore of Irish culture' and which is very important as a basis for understanding source material and interpretations.

TARA: 145–6. The author touches on relations between the Uí Néill and vassal tribes such as the Cíannachta, Luigne and Airgíalla. He comments also that by the twelfth century 'all claimants to the high-kingship saw Dublin rather than Tara as the symbol of monarchy' (140).

238. Byrne, F.J. 1971 Tribes and tribalism in early Ireland. *Ériu* **22**, 128–66.

A survey of the political, economic and social structures of early Ireland, which attempts to elucidate the concept of the tribe as presented in early Irish society.

TARA: 149. The author describes the Uí Néill as having 'organised their conquest in the North and the midlands on a territorial and dynastic basis. They seem to have taken over the hieratic kingship of Tara as a symbol of suzerainty which cut across the ancient provincial divisions.' He argues further that 'the original functions of that pagan kingship [Tara] were soon rendered obsolete by the advent of Christianity, but under ecclesiastical influence it was to germinate into a high-kingship of all Ireland, particularly after Armagh [situated in the Uí Néill vassal kingdoms of Airgíalla] had won recognition as the primatial church in Ireland, thus establishing an ecclesiastical unity to which a national monarchy seemed the natural corollary'.

239. Dillon, M. and Chadwick, N. 1967 *The Celtic realms*. London.

A summary of the history and culture of the Celtic peoples from prehistory to the Norman arrival in Britain.

TARA: 155–8; 181–2. The authors summarise the mythological traditions of Tara and theories concerning the rise of the Uí Néill and their associations with Tara.

240. Binchy, D.A. 1976 Irish history and Irish law: II. *Studia Hibernica* **16**, 7–45.

A detailed critique of modern studies in early Irish history, with particular reference to the study of the law-tracts and to F. J. Byrne's *Irish kings and high-kings*.

TARA: 18–20. The author comments on Byrne's views of high-kingship and suggests that the high-kingship can be regarded 'as a claim asserted quite early by Uí Néill propagandists, like Adomnán, but never realized in practice by any monarch of that race, nor even (as Professor Byrne rightly insists) by the "usurper" Brían Bóruma or any of those provincial kings who during the eleventh and twelfth centuries fought for what was by then at least a national monarchy *in Werden*.' He expands also on Byrne's view that the term *ard-rí* is not 'very old' by explaining that had it been known to the classical jurists as a technical term, the name for a more exalted grade of monarch than *ruiri* (< *ro-rí*), it would have been a similar 'close' compound *airdri, gen. *airdrech (like *ruirech*).

241. Ó Corráin, D. 1978 Nationality and kingship in pre-Norman Ireland. In T.W. Moody (ed.), *Nationality and the pursuit of national independence*, 1–35. Historical Studies 11. Belfast.

A discussion of the concept of *natio* (sense of identity; nationality) in pre-Norman Ireland, the existence of which the author proposes.

TARA: 7–8. The author quotes, as evidence that the Irish had a sense of nationality from an early stage, Muirchú's view of Tara as *Temoria que est caput Scottorum* ('Tara which is the *caput* of the Irish') and Adomnán's description of Diarmait mac Cerbaill as *totius Scotiae regnatorem a deo ordinatum* ('the ruler of all Ireland, ordained by God').

TAILTIU: 20. The author cites the revival of *Óenach Tailten* as a political institution in the eleventh and twelfth centuries as an example of the influence of the synthetic historians and poets of the period.

242. Ó Corráin, D. 1977–9 High-kings, Vikings and other kings. *Irish Historical Studies* **21**, 283–323.

    A detailed review of A.P. Smyth's *Scandinavian kings in the British Isles* (Oxford, 1978), concerning mainly ninth-century Viking activity in Britain and Ireland.

    TARA: 301–13. The reviewer comments on the status of the king of Tara in the mid-ninth century, particularly in the person of Máel Sechnaill mac Maíle Ruanaid, and his relations with other provinces, the Vikings and with the rest of the Uí Néill. Of Máel Sechnaill he remarks that he was an over-king of the southern Uí Néill, who succeeded to the paramountcy of the whole of the Uí Néill (traditionally called the kingship of Tara) in 846 and ruled until his death in 862. He expanded his power greatly and his success lent considerable substance to the long-standing claim of the kings of Tara to be kings of Ireland (302).

243. Smyth, A.P. 1982 *Celtic Leinster: towards an historical geography of early Irish civilization A.D. 500–1600*. Dublin.

    A history of Leinster combining historiography, historical geography and topography.

    TARA: 9; 17–18. The author postulates that, since the hillforts at Tara and Knockaulin are of similar construction and associated with the Fir Domnann (related to the Dumnonii of Cornwall and northern Britain), it is possible that Ireland's eastern royal forts were constructed by an invading aristocracy which came from western Britain. He also alludes to hints that Cormac mac Airt once belonged to the Leinster tradition before he was taken over by the usurping Uí Néill dynasty.

244. Breatnach, L. 1986 Varia VI: 3. *Ardri* as an old compound. *Ériu* **37**, 192–3.

    A note on an old compound word *ardri*, gen. *ardrech*, later re-formed as *ardrí*, gen. *ardríg*.

    TARA: 193. In response to Byrne's and Binchy's comments that the term *ard-rí* is a late formation, the author quotes a passage from the Old Irish text on status, *Míadshlechta*, where the first of the types of king there distinguished is the *tríath*, of whom it is said: *Tríath .i. ríg, amail is-beir: Tríath trom trem[i]-ætha* (MS *termætha*) *Érind túath[a] óthuind co tuind . . . Cóic cóicid Érenn term[i]-aetha a mánu uile, amail ro chét do Concobur: Ardmac rígh/ romac Nesa/ nenaisc íathu/ Fer Féne* (CIH 583.7–12) ('A *tríath* i.e. a king, as [the following] states: The mighty *tríath*, he goes through the kingdoms of Ireland from wave to wave [i.e. from sea to sea] . . . The five provinces of Ireland, he goes through all their submissions, as has been sung concerning Conchobar: The exalted son of a king, the great son of Nes, he secured the lands of the Irish'). The author concludes that 'clearly someone of higher standing than a king with dominion in his own province alone is indicated by this passage from the Old Irish laws'.

245. Simms, K. 1987 *From kings to warlords: the changing political structure of Gaelic Ireland in the later Middle Ages*. Suffolk.

An investigation of the changing perceptions of Irish kingship in the late Middle Ages (thirteenth to seventeenth centuries), with discussion of aspects such as succession, inauguration, the king's public life, deposition and death.

TARA: 15; 21; 35–6; 41–2 (inauguration of the king of Tara). The author notes that the *Lia Fáil* is the only inauguration stone referred to before the fifteenth century.

246. Wormald, P. 1986 Celtic and Anglo-Saxon kingship: some further thoughts. In P.E. Szarmach (ed.), *Sources of Anglo-Saxon culture*, 151–83. Studies in Medieval Culture 20. Kalamazoo.

   A reassessment of the view that Celtic kingship was archaic in comparison with Germanic and Scandinavian kingship of the early medieval period. The author argues that this archaism was due more to those who preserved and composed the documents on which scholars rely for their source material than to any immense differences in the real exercise of kingship in Ireland during that period.

See also no. 68.

GG. *Feis Temro*

Feis Temro, the Feast of Tara, was one of the few physical manifestations of the kingship of Tara. The genuine *feis*, not to be confused with the parliamentary assembly described by Geoffrey Keating in his history of Ireland *Foras Feasa ar Éirinn*, seems to have been a fertility rite which celebrated the divine nature of the king of Tara. The last *feis* seems to have been celebrated *c*. 560 during the reign of Diarmait mac Cerbaill, a period which appears to mark the beginning of a transition of the kingship of Tara from paganism to Christianity.

247. Ó Ceithearnaigh, S. [alias Carney, J.] 1949 An dara Pádraig — an taon Phádraig amháin. *Comhar* **8** (11) (Samhain), 3–4.

   A summarised version of a paper concerning the Patrician controversy.

   TARA: 4. A brief paragraph on *Feis Temro*, which the author viewed as an inauguration (*teacht i gcoróinn*).

248. Binchy, D.A. 1958 The Fair of Tailtiu and the Feast of Tara. *Ériu* **18**, 113–38.

   An important discussion and evaluation of previous discussions on:
   (i) the Assembly (*mórdáil*) at Uisnech, which the author describes as an invention of *dindshenchas* pseudo-historians, though there may have been some sort of fire-cult centred on Uisnech in an earlier period;
   (ii) the Fair of Tailtiu (*Óenach Tailten*), not the national assembly held by the 'high-king' of Ireland, but an old burial place and the site of an old *óenach*; *Óenach Tailten* was the most important assembly in Ireland because it was held under the aegis of the king of Tara who, as titular head of all the Uí Néill kingdoms and their dependent tribes, was normally the most powerful monarch in Ireland;
   (iii) the Feast of Tara (*Feis Temro*) was 'a primitive fertility rite culminating in the apotheosis of the sacred king. It was last held by Diarmait mac Cerbaill in 560, after which it was discarded as a relic of paganism.' The concept of the sacred

feast was revived more than three centuries later by pseudo-historians in the form of a constitutional organ of high-kingship (137–8).

249. Cunningham, B. 1986–7 Seventeenth-century interpretations of the past: the case of Geoffrey Keating. *Irish Historical Studies* **25**, 116–28.

   An analysis of the contemporary context of Geoffrey Keating's history of Ireland, *Foras Feasa ar Éirinn,* and of Keating's objectives in compiling and writing the text.

   TARA: 124. It would seem that the seventeenth-century Old English preoccupation with a parliament may have prompted Keating's reinterpretation of *Feis Temro* as a parliamentary gathering when (to quote Keating) 'the entire assembly sat for the purpose of determining and completing the laws and customs of the country'.

See also nos 36 and 92.

HH. Tara and Iona

The monastery of Iona had a vested interest in the fortunes of the Uí Néill since their founder and successive abbots belonged to the Cenél Conaill, the northern branch of that dynasty. Their interest in the kingship of Tara, as portrayed through the works of the monastery's most renowned chronicler, Adomnán, abbot of Iona (d. 704) (who does not refer to Tara in his *Vita Columbae*), is less obvious than that of Armagh's propagandists such as Muirchú, biographer of Patrick. This may reflect Armagh's proximity to (and Iona's distance from) Tara and to the southern branches of the Uí Néill, consistent rivals of the northern branches.

250. Picard, J.-M. 1982 The purpose of Adomnán's *Vita Columbae*. *Peritia* **1**, 160–77.

   A discussion of the background to the compilation of Adomnán's *Vita Columbae* in the context of Tírechán, Muirchú, Armagh and Uí Néill expansion versus the Columban confederation and its relations with the Uí Néill.

   TARA: 171. The author queries why the Uí Néill chose to favour Armagh and not Iona, despite Adomnán's clear statement of the over-kingship of Tara (for example, describing Diarmait mac Cerbaill (d. ?565) as 'king of the whole of Ireland'). The answer is that, besides Armagh's strategic importance for the Uí Néill, it was a rising community rather than one in decline, as was Iona after the Easter controversy.

251. Enright, M.J. 1985 *Iona, Tara and Soissons: the origin of the royal anointing ritual.* Arbeiten zur Frühmittelalterforschung, Bd. 17. Berlin and New York.

   This is a discussion of concepts of kingship, royal authority and the consecration of kings based on 'Celtic and Germanic' evidence. Despite the title, little is said of Tara apart from describing it as 'the chief cult center of the old religion' (14).

252. Enright, M.J. 1985 Royal succession and abbatial prerogative in Adomnán's *Vita Columbae*. *Peritia* **4**, 83–103.

A discussion of Adomnán and royal succession in Ireland and Scotland.

TARA: 96–9. A discussion on the relationship between the Columban confederation and the Uí Néill kings of Tara. The author suggests that, despite Adomnán's kinship with the Uí Néill, the distance between Iona and Tara, 'the centre of political decision-making', in comparison to the distance between Tara and Armagh placed the latter in a more advantageous position.

253. Herbert, M. 1988 *Iona, Kells, and Derry: the history and hagiography of the monastic familia of Columba*. Oxford.

A study of the history and documentary records of the federation of the Columban monasteries of Iona, Kells and Derry. In her extensive study of the Columban hagiography, the author refers to the relations between the founder of the federation, Colum Cille, and his successors and the kings of Tara to the twelfth century, especially in the context of the over-kingship of the Uí Néill.

II. Tara and Cashel

The differences between Tara and Cashel, the capital of Munster, are assumed to be that Tara reflected an old ritual and non-Christian capital and that Cashel had Christian associations from an early date, though this assumption ignores the many non-Christian elements associated with the kingship of Munster. Cashel continued to be inhabited into the early medieval period, unlike Tara. The similarities between the two have not been noted, the most striking of which is the domination of both by two powerful and rival dynasties, the Uí Néill and the Eóganachta, both of whom obscured the authority other people held over Tara or Cashel prior to their ascent to power.

254. Ryan, J. 1941–2 Historical addendum (Uí Echach Muman). In S.P. Ó Ríordáin, 'Excavation of a large earthen ring-fort, Garranes, Co. Cork'. *Proceedings of the Royal Irish Academy* **47**C, 145–50.

A note attempting to identify Garranes with Ráith Raithlenn, stronghold of the Uí Echach Muman.

TARA: 148. In his discussion of the kingship of Tara alternating between the northern and southern Uí Néill dynasties, Ryan maintains that while Tara was a 'meeting-place of the nation' and a 'symbol of supreme authority', it was not the residence of kings. Similarly Cashel was not the residence of Eóganacht kings, though it differed from Tara in that it was 'something of a town with a permanent population'.

255. Dillon, M. 1958 On the date and authorship of the Book of Rights. *Celtica* **4**, 239–49.

A discussion on the date and provenance of the *Lebor na Cert* based on references to the status of the various kings and provinces. The author concludes that it is an eleventh-century compilation of antiquarian learning.

TARA: 246–7; 248. The author cites as evidence for an eleventh-century date the fact that the king of Tara is presented as king of Mide, not as king of Ireland, a status accorded to him from the early eleventh century onwards. Commenting on the poem

Temair teach a mbuí mac Cuind, which is separate from the main body of the text, the author regards the exaltation of Tara above Cashel as a sign of an even later date, perhaps the work of a northern *fili* wishing to refute the Book of Rights, gathered in with the rest by the compiler. (For further discussion and edition of this poem see M. Dillon, *Lebor na Cert. The Book of Rights* (Dublin, 1962), xi–xii, 122–47 (Irish Texts Society, 46).)

256. Dillon, M. 1977 The Irish settlements in Wales. *Celtica* **12**, 1–11.

    A discussion of early connections (secular and ecclesiastical) between Ireland and Wales, and of Irish migrations to Wales.

    TARA: 10. The author notes 'the remarkable contrast' between Tara and Cashel. Tara was an old pagan sanctuary, but Cashel (a name said to be borrowed from Latin *castellum*) from the first was Christian. Several of the early kings of Cashel were bishops, and, as Dillon surmises, there was no conflict with the church such as led to the collapse of Tara.

257. Sproule, D. 1984 Origins of the Eóganachta. *Ériu* **35**, 31–7.

    An analysis of the origin of the term *Eóganacht* and of its adoption by unrelated septs in Munster, who formed the loose hegemony known as the Eóganachta. This term is likely to have been an imitation of the word *Connacht*. Furthermore, it is postulated that there was a north–south parallelism, that these Munster septs made an effort to create a southern equivalent to the Uí Néill and Connachta.

See also nos 21 and 228.

JJ. The Gailenga and the Luigne

Among the substratum of population ruled over by the Uí Néill in the hinterland of Tara were the Cíannachta, the Gailenga and the Luigne. The Gailenga and the Luigne formed population groups in north Connacht and in Mide and Brega. Their close proximity to the Uí Néill led MacNeill to suggest that they represented the deliberate colonisation of the midlands and border areas by the Connacht ancestors of the Uí Néill with their vassals. There are hints that they all have the same origins and that the Gailenga and the Luigne were branches of the same group who were less successful than the group of dynasties who became known as the Uí Néill. The Luigne, in particular, were closely linked with Tara to the extent that they are sometimes called *Luigne Temrach* or *colomain na Temra(ch)*.

258. Cochrane, R. and Rhys, J. 1898 Notes on the newly-discovered ogam-stones in County Meath. *Journal of the Royal Society of Antiquaries of Ireland* **28**, 53–60.
    Rhys, J. 1899 Miscellanea: The Cairan Ogam Stone. (A correction.) *Journal of the Royal Society of Antiquaries of Ireland* **29**, 426–7.

    Descriptive notes on the discovery, dimensions and readings of (i) the Painestown Stone, Co. Meath (includes map of the site close to Seneschalstown House), and (ii) St Cairan's (*sic*) Stone from St Cairan's (*sic*) churchyard (Castle Kieran, Co. Meath), approximately three miles from Kells. This stone reads COVAGNI MAQUI MUCOI LUGUNI, a reference to one of the Luigne.

259. Macalister, R.A.S. 1945 *Corpus inscriptionum insularum Celticarum,* vol. 1. Dublin.

Vol. 1, 46–7, no. 41. A reading and a description of the ogham stone from Castle Kieran (Macalister: Castlekeeran), Co. Meath (see no. 258). Note also the existence of two 'Luigne' ogham stones in the barony of East Muskerry (112–14, nos 112–13) and one in the barony of Middle Third (295, no. 307).

260. MacNeill, E. 1907 MOCU, MACCU. *Ériu* **3**, 42–9.

A discussion of the form MOCU, MACCU found on ogham inscriptions and in early texts such as Adomnán's *Vita Columbae*. MacNeill comments: 'I have found no instance of *mocu* referrable to any branch of the dynasties of Tara and Cashel' (43). Note also 46(d), the Luigne inscriptions.

261. MacNeill, E. 1934–5 Colonisation under early kings of Tara. *Journal of the Galway Archaeological and Historical Society* **16**, 101–24.

The author argues that occupation of Tara by kings of Connacht is shown to have been accompanied or followed by plantations of colonies of subject peoples from Connacht (e.g. Cíannachta, Gailenga, Luigne) to hold border territories which had previously belonged to the kings of Emain. He assigns this occupation to the second half of the third century AD.

262. Knott, E. 1946 Varia II: 1. Colomain na Temra. *Ériu* **14**, 144–6.

A note on the 'quasi-tribal name' *Colomain na Temra(ch)*, which in its most frequent use is specifically applied to Luigne Temra. The word *colomain*, according to Knott, is borrowed from Latin *columna*.

263. O'Connell, P. 1958–61 Early colonisation of Breifne. *Breifne* **1**, 3–16.

A summary of the early history of the kingdom of Bréifne, incorporating ideas expounded by MacNeill and O'Rahilly.

TARA: 5–7. The author repeats MacNeill's idea that east Bréifne (Gailenga and Luigne) was used as a buffer state by the Uí Néill dynasty of Tara.

264. Byrne, F.J. 1967–8 Historical note on Cnogba (Knowth). In G. Eogan, 'Excavations at Knowth, Co. Meath, 1962–1965'. *Proceedings of the Royal Irish Academy* **66**C, 383–400.

A detailed note on the dynasties, kings and tribes of Mide and Brega, based on references incorporating a wide range of sources such as the annals, genealogies and *dindshenchas*, with specific reference to the dynasties occupying Knowth (northern Brega) and Lagore (southern Brega). It includes important references to the Gailenga and the Luigne.

265. Wagner, H. 1972 Beiträge in Erinnerung an Julius Pokorny: 16. Zum irischen Stammesnamen *Luaigni/Luigni*. *Zeitschrift für celtische Philologie* **32**, 87–9.

On the etymological origin and associations of the Luigne, in response to O'Rahilly's theories as expounded in his *Early Irish history and mythology* (391–4). The author argues that the name Luigne stems from the element *leug-/leuk-* (Old Irish *lugae* 'an oath'), possibly connected with the name of the god Lug. He postulates that the original homeland of the Luigne may have been in Silesia, where a tribe known as the *Lugii* were settled in the La Tène period.

266. Ahlqvist, A. 1976 Two ethnic names in Ptolemy. *Bulletin of the Board of Celtic Studies* **26**, 143–6.

    A discussion of Ptolemy's *Logi* in Scotland. Of particular note are the author's comments on the origins of the tribal name Luigne (146). A certain number of Irish personal and other names would seem to be connected with the element *-lugu-* (see no. 265). The Luigne are of particular interest, not only because of the attestation of their name in ogham but also because a corresponding name may exist in Spain, among the inhabitants of the town of Paelontium in Asturia.

See also no. 148.

ARCHAEOLOGY AND TOPOGRAPHY

KK.	General studies	267–82
LL.	Surveys of Tara	283–93
MM.	Monuments at Tara	294–312
NN.	Roadways	313–15
OO.	Excavations	316–41
PP.	Objects	342–60
QQ.	The hinterland of Tara	361–83
RR.	Popular descriptions and local notes	384–91
SS.	Tara in Ireland and Scotland	392–400
TT.	The characteristics of royal sites	401–5

KK. General studies

267. Wakeman, W.F. 1848 *A handbook of Irish antiquities*. Dublin.

    An illustrated guide to the monuments of Ireland. Revised by J. Cooke, *Wakeman's handbook of Irish antiquities* (Dublin, 1903).

    TARA: 40–5 (revised edition 9, 165–9). Brief descriptions of the *Lia Fáil*, placed in its present position, according to the author, in 1824, and of Tara as a royal residence.

268. Wilde, W.R. 1849 *The beauties of the Boyne and its tributary the Blackwater*. Dublin.

    A travelogue of the countryside through which the rivers Boyne and Blackwater flow. The work includes very fine engravings by Wakeman. For an abridged third edition see C. Ó Lochlainn, *Wilde's Boyne and Blackwater* (Dublin, 1949).

    TARA: 122–6 (Ó Lochlainn, 102–6). In general, Wilde follows Petrie's description of the hill. He agrees with Petrie that the *Lia Fáil* is not that now in Westminster Abbey but 'we are not by any means convinced that this *round pillar stone*, now placed over the croppies' grave is *the* stone. Perhaps the *flat sculptured stone*, latterly called the Cross of St Adamnan, may have been it.'

269. O'Curry, E. 1873 *On the manners and customs of the ancient Irish* (3 vols). Dublin.

    A monumental work containing information from all possible sources, documentary and material, on 'ancient' Irish society. It must be used with caution, however, as many conclusions are reached in an uncritical manner, as might be expected for a work of the period.

    TARA: There are numerous references. Vol. 1, cccxxxiii (*Múr Tea*); cccli–ii (*Tech Midchúarta*). Vol. 2, 8–23 (a lengthy discourse on, among other topics, *Feis Temro*); 106–7 (the importance of the poem *Fíanna bátar i nEmain*, ascribed to the Meath poet Cináed úa hArtacáin); 137–49 (the importance of the Meath poet Cúan úa Lothcháin). Vol. 3, 5–6 (*Rath na Righ* at Tara); 6–8 (the 'Great House of the Thousand Soldiers'); 12 (the *Foradh* at Tara); 172 (a description of the two torques found at Tara).

    TAILTIU: Vol. 1, cccxxvi (the Fair of Tailté).

270. Wood-Martin, W.G. 1895 *Pagan Ireland: an archaeological sketch, a handbook of Irish pre-Christian antiquities*. London.

    A general account of the antiquities of Ireland (see no. 267).

    TARA: 316–17. A description of the *Lia Fáil*, regarded by the author as the 'supposed magic-stone, which roared like a lion when a legitimate king stood on it'. He is not convinced by Petrie's argument that the stone at Tara known as the *Lia Fáil* is genuine. He comments that the 'Irish kings would have had a very uncomfortable seat if perched on top of this pillar'.

271. Westropp, T.J. 1902 The ancient forts of Ireland: being a contribution towards our knowledge of their types, affinities, and structural features. *Transactions of the Royal Irish Academy* **31**, 579–730.

A comprehensive study of so-called ancient forts, a term which, for Westropp, covers a wide range of monuments in Ireland, primarily stone forts, ringforts and hillforts.

TARA: 686–7 (fig. 19). Tara is classified as a royal residence. A brief description of the principal monuments and their measurements is provided along with a simplified plan.

272. Evans, E.E. 1966 *Prehistoric and Early Christian Ireland. A guide*. London.

A field-guide to the monuments of Ireland.

TARA: 174–7. This description provides the most detailed summary account of the archaeology of the hill. It summarises the results of the excavations at the Mound of the Hostages, at Ráith na Ríg and at the Rath of the Synods.

273. Killanin, Lord and Duignan, M.V. 1967 *The Shell guide to Ireland* (2nd edn, revised with index). London.

A general guide to the archaeological and historical monuments of Ireland as well as to things of artistic and literary interest.

TARA: 435–6. An excellent summary of the history and archaeology of Tara based on Duignan's astute and knowledgeable comments. For a revised and updated edition see P. Harbison, *The Shell guide to Ireland* (Dublin, 1989), 288–9.

274. Norman, E.R. and St Joseph, J.K. 1969 *The early development of Irish society: the evidence of aerial photography*. Cambridge.

A summary of the results of the extensive survey carried out in Ireland by the Cambridge Committee for Aerial Photography, with particular reference to evidence for human settlement and natural conditions in early Ireland.

TARA: 11–12 (fig. 5), 76–8 (fig. 44). The authors provide a summary of the results of the excavations undertaken in the 1950s. They also comment on the possibility of settlement patterns in the hinterland of Tara. In pointing to the existence of a farmstead 'comprising a rath re-planned more than once' to the south-east of Tara (fig. 5), they speculate on 'whether the surroundings of such royal residences may not have been dotted with the substantial farmsteads necessary to support the population concentrated there' (12).

275. Harbison, P. 1970 *Guide to the National Monuments in the Republic of Ireland (including a selection of other monuments not in state care)*. Dublin.

A guidebook of monuments arranged by county.

TARA: 192–4. A brief history and description of the monuments, including a plan of the hill (after Ó Ríordáin, see no. 290).

276. Harbison, P. 1976 *The archaeology of Ireland*. London.

A general guide to the archaeology of Ireland from the earliest period to the Spanish Armada.

TARA: 62–4. A brief account of how a certain Mr Groome, said to have been associated with the British Israelites, was led to believe that the Ark of the Covenant was to be found at Tara. (Uncertainty about the involvement of the British Israelites in the project was fuelled by Hubert Butler in his essay 'The British Israelites at Tara', now reprinted in R.F. Foster (ed.), *The sub-prefect should have held his tongue and other essays* (London, 1990), 68–70.) See no. 341.

277. Herity, M. and Eogan, G. 1977 *Ireland in prehistory*. London.

    A study of the economy, technology, burial customs, art and society of prehistoric Ireland from the Neolithic to the first centuries of the first millennium AD.

    TARA: There are many references to Tara scattered throughout the study. It is useful as a general guide to the context of the monuments and finds from the hill.

278. Caulfield, S. 1981 Celtic problems in the Irish Iron Age. In D. Ó Corráin (ed.), *Irish antiquity: essays and studies presented to Professor M.J. O'Kelly,* 205–15. Cork.

    An attempt to reconcile the archaeological and linguistic evidence for the Celticisation of Ireland.

    TARA: 212. The late implantation of the two earthen ringforts at Tara, identified as *Tech Cormaic* and the *Forad*, on much earlier sites demonstrates that what exists today is 'a palimpsest of monuments which were clearly not in contemporaneous use'. A parallel example is to be found at Clogher, Co. Tyrone.

279. Harbison, P. 1988 *Pre-Christian Ireland. From the first settlers to the early Celts*. London.

    A general guide to the prehistory of Ireland.

    TARA: 187–91. A description of Tara, its monuments and the history of excavations carried out there.

280. O'Kelly, M.J. 1989 *Early Ireland. An introduction to Irish prehistory*. Cambridge.

    A synthesis of Irish prehistory which provides an account of the development of Irish society from the Ice Age to the Iron Age.

    TARA: 325–7. A note on the history of excavations at Tara.

281. Raftery, B. 1991 Tara, County Meath. In C. Tanzi (ed.), *The Celts,* 612. Milan.

    A catalogue and commentary on aspects of the Celts in Europe, archaeological, historical, literary and mythological.

    TARA: 612. A useful summary of information relating to Tara, its function, its monuments and literary descriptions associated with it.

282. Raftery, B. 1994 *Pagan Celtic Ireland. The enigma of the Irish Iron Age*. London.

    A detailed account of the archaeological evidence for developments in Ireland in the millennium before the advent of Christianity. It includes (fig. 36) a plan of the features uncovered in Ó Ríordáin's excavations at the Rath of the Synods (see also nos 337 and 340).

TARA: 65–70. A useful résumé of the evidence for activity at Tara and of possible functions for the site.

LL. Surveys of Tara

The monumental descriptions of Tara produced by John O'Donovan (1836), George Petrie (1839) and R.A.S. Macalister (1917) continue to be the most extensive studies of the site to date. Subsequent descriptions have tended to be based on these early works or to be extensions of them. The value of the monograph by S.P. Ó Ríordáin (1954) lies in the brief accounts of the excavations carried out by him and by R. de Valéra (outlined in a supplementary note), and added to by Evans and others in brief notes on the excavations.

283. O'Donovan, J. 1836 Letters containing information relative to the antiquities of the County of Meath collected during the progress of the Ordnance Survey in 1836.

    TARA: 219–38. One of the first antiquarian descriptions of Tara. Among the more important topographical details noted by O'Donovan is the possible location of *Sescend Temrach* (the Moor/Marsh of Tara), which he identifies with a 'spot extending from the ash tree under which there was a well called Tober-Fin southwards to the road'. In this area there was 'spewy land', which in the memory of a local farmer was drained by the proprietor of the land shortly before 1798 (234).

284. Petrie, G. 1839 On the history and antiquities of Tara Hill. *Transactions of the Royal Irish Academy* **18**, 25–232.

    The most comprehensive treatise on the Hill of Tara to date. In his landmark work, Petrie covered the descriptions of Tara in the *dindshenchas* material, covered (in great detail) the Patrician connection with Tara and also the associations between Tara and heroic kings such as Cormac mac Airt. He also provided a wealth of documentation on the monuments at Tara. The value of Petrie's work today lies in the amount of material relating to Tara which he included in his paper and which, though often unreferenced, wrongly translated or lacking critical analysis, is of much use as a guide to the documentary sources on Tara.

285. Murphy, D. and Westropp, T.J. 1894 Notes on the antiquities of Tara (*Teamhair na Righ*). *Journal of the Royal Society of Antiquaries of Ireland* **24**, 232–42.

    A description of the origin, history and monuments of Tara, including maps. It is based on an uncritical analysis of the documentary evidence and makes much use of Petrie's essay 'On the history and antiquities of Tara Hill'. Note the passing reference to the finding of the gold torques (239), found, according to the authors, near the modern church, on clearing away a bank in 1810. Also note (242) that the well *Adlaic* was covered in 1837.

286. O'Daly, B. 1913 Tara of the kings. *Irisleabhar Muighe Nuadhad* (1913), 91–105.

    A description of the monuments at Tara as found on a visit in 1913. It includes early engravings and photographs.

287. Macalister, R.A.S. 1917–19 Temair Breg: a study of the remains and traditions of Tara. *Proceedings of the Royal Irish Academy* **34**C, 231–399.

One of the more important papers concentrating solely on Tara, regarded by the author as an updating of Petrie's monograph. Divided into sections: (1) introduction, (2) the topography of Temair, (3) the origin of Temair, (4) the kingship of Temair, (5) the voice of Fál, (6) the gods and the cults of Temair, and (7) the place of Temair in European culture. The section relating to the topography of Tara (234–78) is the most useful, attempting to correct some of Petrie's interpretations of the *dindshenchas*, not always successfully (see for example Macalister's incorrect re-identification of *Tech Cormaic* and the *Forad*). Otherwise Macalister includes many useful references, though he relies much on classical and anthropological parallels and as a consequence comes to strange conclusions.

288. Macalister, R.A.S. 1931 *Tara. A pagan sanctuary of ancient Ireland*. London.

An extended version of Macalister's paper published in the *Proceedings of the Royal Irish Academy* (no. 287). Of particular interest is Macalister's description of the British Israelites' activities at Tara (39–43). For a brief review of Macalister's work see J. Vendryes's note in *Revue Celtique* **50** (1933), 181–3.

289. Macalister, R.A.S. ?1935 *Teamhair: Tara*. Official Guides to National Monuments. Dublin.

One of a number of official guides to the National Monuments of Ireland published by the Office of Public Works. The author provides a brief description of the main visible monuments at Tara.

290. Ó Ríordáin, S.P. 1954 *Tara: the monuments on the hill*. Dundalk.

A description of the monuments at Tara, combined with a brief survey of the documentary evidence, by the excavator of the Rath of the Synods. Its value is increased by the few hints published to date about the outcome of these excavations (21–2). See no. 322.

291. Swan, D.L. 1978 The Hill of Tara, County Meath: the evidence of aerial photography. *Journal of the Royal Society of Antiquaries of Ireland* **108**, 51–66.

A description of monuments at Tara identified through aerial photography and divided into three categories: (1) those hitherto unknown; (2) those confirming the observations of previous writers regarding more obscure sites and features; and (3) further evidence regarding doubtful sites. The author also attempts to identify monuments with references to sites detailed in early documents. Plans and photographs are included.

292. Moore, M.J. 1987 *Archaeological Inventory of County Meath*. Dublin.

Part of the Archaeological Inventory series produced by the Archaeological Survey of the Office of Public Works. It consists of all known archaeological sites in the county, arranged by monument type.

TARA: 197 (index). The hill is described as containing 'prehistoric earthworks', listed as a passage tomb, barrows, a tumulus, mounds, pit burials, a henge, standing stones, hillforts, ringforts, enclosure sites, earthworks and roadways.

293. Newman, C. 1993 The Tara survey. Interim report. *Discovery Programme Reports* **1**, 70–93. Dublin.

    A description of the objectives of the archaeological survey of Tara instituted under the auspices of the Discovery Programme. A preliminary report of the results of aerial, topographical and geophysical surveys of Ráith Ghráinne and the area immediately around the monument is also included in the study.

See also no. 272.

MM. Monuments at Tara

The individual monuments at Tara given most notice are the *Lia Fáil* and the *Tech Midchúarta* (Banqueting Hall). The authenticity of the *Lia Fáil*, its attributes and origins are topics which have been discussed most frequently. The function of the *Tech Midchúarta* has yet to be understood, though there has been much speculation on the matter.

Lia Fáil

294. Conwell, E.A. 1864–6 Has the Lia Fail on Tara Hill been inscribed? *Proceedings of the Royal Irish Academy* **9**, 539–40.

    A fanciful theory regarding inscribed lines and cup-marks on the pillar-stone at Tara known as the *Lia Fáil*.

295. O'Rourke, J. 1880 The *Lia Fail*, or Stone of Destiny. *Irish Ecclesiastical Record* (3rd ser.) **1**, 441–53.

    A traditional description of the *Lia Fáil* and discussion of the veracity of the claim that the Westminster coronation stone is the *Lia Fáil*.

296. O'Reilly, P.J. 1902 Notes on the Coronation Stone at Westminster and the *Lia Fáil* at Tara. *Journal of the Royal Society of Antiquaries of Ireland* **32**, 77–92.

    An explanation, based on an uncritical view of the sources though leading to the correct conclusion, of the fact that the stone at Westminster Abbey, the so-called Stone of Scone, is not the *Lia Fáil*.

297. Vendryes, J. 1930 Variétés: V. La Pierre de Kohima et la Pierre de Fál. *Revue Celtique* **47**, 206–8.

    Comparison of the properties of the *Lia Fáil* and the Manipur Stone at Kohima in Bengal.

298. Gogan, L.S. 1951 Dála Lia Fáil. *Feasta* **3** (2) (Feabhra), 10–12.

A note which attempts to explain why the Coronation Stone at Westminster Abbey is not the *Lia Fáil* and some comments on the nature of the *Lia Fáil,* including an argument that the *Lia Fáil* had particular associations with the tribe known as the *Menapii*, who originated from a region around the River Waal in Germany. The author surmises that the name Waal originates from Vacalos (Vahalos), which could also be the basis for the element *Fál*.

299. Nitze, W.A. 1956 The *Siège Perilleux* and the *Lia Fáil* or 'Stone of Destiny'. *Speculum* **31**, 258–62.

The author equates the attributes of the *Lia Fáil* with the stone under the vacant seat at the Round Table in the Arthurian tale *Didot-Perceval*. This stone splits and utters a cry (*brait*) which is followed by a great mist when Perceval first occupies the seat. Finally, after the Grail question is asked, it is joined together, again uttering a noise. The chair under which this stone is placed is known as the *siège perilleux*.

300. Pinault, J. 1961 *KRĀWO- et *WĀLO, *WALI- dans les langues celtiques. *Ogam* **13**, 599–614.

A detailed discussion of the term *cró* (as found in *cró Logo*, the building erected by Lug close to Tara). The author surmises that the word conveys the idea of a circle and possibly the space within a circle. He also discusses the origin of the word *Fál* and comes to the conclusion that the *Lia Fáil* meant the 'Stone of the Enclosure'.

301. Guyonvarc'h, C.J. 1964 Notes d'étymologie gauloises et celtiques xx; — (80) Irlandais *Lia Fáil* 'Pierre de Souveraineté'. *Ogam* **16**, 436–40.

A comprehensive note on the attributes of the *Lia Fáil* and on the possible etymological origin of the word *Fál*. The author incorporates many textual references to the *Lia Fáil* in his work, concluding that the stone signifies the 'Stone of Sovereignty' (as opposed to the 'Stone of the Enclosure', as postulated by Pinault).

302. Evans, E.E. 1976 The bull-roarer. *Ulster Journal of Archaeology* **39**, 71.

A note on the cry uttered by the *Lia Fáil*. The author suggests that the cry could have been produced by a bull-roarer, an example of which was found at Glenviggan, Co. Tyrone (*Ulster Journal of Archaeology* **38**, 16–18).

303. Ó Broin, T. 1990 *Lia Fáil*: fact and fiction in the tradition. *Celtica* **21**, 393–401.

A detailed discussion of the *Lia Fáil* and its attributes, including the possibility that it was a flagstone rather than a 'conical or cylindrical stone', its character as a goddess, and its part in inauguration rites and in the sacred marriage of kingship. As to the present-day identification of the *Lia Fáil*, the author doubts that the present stone is the genuine inauguration stone of Tara, and feels that of all the monuments at Tara the *Lia Fáil* had the least chance of surviving struggles and depredations and that it was removed or destroyed early on.

TARA: A SELECT BIBLIOGRAPHY

Cros Adomnáin

304. Rynne, E. 1987 A pagan Celtic background for sheela-na-gigs? In E. Rynne (ed.), *Figures from the past. Studies on figurative art in Christian Ireland*, 189–202. Dublin.

   A study of the possible non-Christian 'Celtic' origin of sheela-na-gigs, based primarily on the evidence of Iron Age sculpture and of associated fertility cults.

   TARA: 192–4 (pls 11:4 and 11:5). It is suggested, following the description of mythological inaugurations at Tara, that *Cros Adomnáin* and the smaller stone beside it are Blocc and Bluicne, which represent the female part, while the *Lia Fáil* represents the male.

Tech Midchúarta

305. Piggott, S. 1968 *The druids*. London.

   A general discussion of the evidence for 'Celtic religion', with particular reference to archaeological evidence.

   TARA: 72–4. A discussion of sacral enclosures (elongated subrectangular plan, illustrated in figs 20–2) in Aulnay-aux-Planches, Marne, and Libernice in Bohemia, which may be analogous to the *Tech Midchúarta* at Tara.

306. Ó Broin, T. 1973–4 '*Craebruad*': the spurious tradition. *Éigse* **15**, 103–13.

   A discussion of the term *cráebrúad* (the Red Branch) associated with the Ulster Cycle and of its use to describe a structure at Emain Macha.

   TARA: 109. The author notes that descriptions of houses at Emain are borrowed, insofar as, for example, the detailed account of the *Cráebrúad* tallies with that of the *Tech Midchúarta* at Tara. 'So lacking in identity is the famous "house of Conchobar" that it is sometimes called "the Midchúairt of the Ulstermen".'

See also nos 26–34.

Rath Lugh (*sic*)

307. Hickey, E. 1952 Miscellanea: Rath Lugh. *Journal of the Royal Society of Antiquaries of Ireland* **82**, 183–4.

   A description of a monument known as Rath Lugh (*sic*) in the townland of Lismullin, north-west of Tara. The author alludes to two historical references to Rath Lugh, both referring to *fert na ndruadh* ('burial place of the druids'), which she accepts as being the same as Rath Lugh. There are no references to Rath Lugh as such.

Rath Maeve (*sic*)

308. Stout, G. 1991 Embanked enclosures of the Boyne region. *Proceedings of the Royal Irish Academy* **91**C, 245–84.

The results of a survey of a major group of embanked enclosures in the lowland valleys of County Meath. The morphology, material culture and distribution of these monuments are discussed.

TARA: 257 (fig. 7 and pl. II). A detailed description of the monuments known as Rath Maeve in the townlands of Odder and Belpere, 1km south of Tara.

Ráith na Ríg

309. Collis, J. 1977 Iron Age henges? *Archaeologia Atlantica* **2**, 55–63.

    A paper which lists and discusses thirteen henge-type monuments in Britain, Ireland and Germany, including Ráith na Ríg at Tara (59), which may be of later Bronze Age or Early Iron Age date.

310. Newman, C. 1995 The Tara survey. Interim report. *Discovery Programme Reports* **2**, 62–7. Dublin.

    A summary of the surveying undertaken on Ráith na Ríg in 1993. This work revealed that earlier monuments were incorporated into the rampart of the hillfort and the possible existence of a barrow (*c.* 40m in diameter, due west of the *Forad*). The location and structure of the eastern and southern entrances, as identified by the geomagnetic survey, are also discussed.

Souterrains

311. Hickey, E. and Rynne, E. 1953 Two souterrains on the lower slopes of Tara. *Journal of the County Kildare Archaeological and Historical Society* **13** (4), 220–2.

    A report on two souterrains. The first, at Cabragh townland, located on the southern slopes of the Glen of Tara, extends for a distance of 60m from a low mound 30m in diameter and is partly rock-cut. It is illustrated with a plan and sections. The second, referred to by Orpen in the *Journal of the Royal Society of Antiquaries* **21** (1891), 153, was located some 300m west of the monument known as Rath Miles in Castletown townland.

Linear earthworks

312. Condit, T. 1993 Travelling earthwork arrives at Tara. *Archaeology Ireland* **7** (4), 10–12.

    A report on the discovery from aerial photographs of a linear earthwork, running north–south and traceable for a distance of 700m, located in Riverstown townland, some 1.2km west of the Hill of Tara.

NN. Roadways

The idea that five great roadways radiated from Tara to various parts of Ireland is based on interpretation of part of the early medieval Irish text *Airne Fíngein*, in which the five roads appear as a portent of Conn Cétchathach's birth. Evidence for the real existence of these roadways is present in a range of texts, though the assumption that they led through Tara is not proven.

313. Hamilton, G.E. 1913 The northern road from Tara. *Journal of the Royal Society of Antiquaries of Ireland* **43**, 310–13.

    Theories regarding the route of the *Slige Midlúachra*, the northern road from Tara, based on references from documentary sources (sagas, annals, etc.). The author claims that the route followed by the roadway was Tara–Boyne–Dundalk–Upper Fews–Newtown Hamilton–Emain Macha.

314. Dobbs, M.E. 1926 Some ancient place-names. *Journal of the Royal Society of Antiquaries of Ireland* **56**, 106–18.

    An attempt to identify place-names and possible roadways referred to in three late Middle Irish or Early Modern Irish texts: (i) the Battle of Leitir Ruibhe, (ii) the Wars of Fergus and Conchobar, and (iii) the Campaigns of Conall Gulban.

    TARA: 108; 110–11. Many of the roadways either begin at Tara, pass through Tara or are in the vicinity of Tara.

315. Ó Lochlainn, C. 1940 Roadways in ancient Ireland. In J. Ryan (ed.), *Féil-sgríbhinn Eoin mhic Néill*, 465–74. Dublin.

    A study of the possible major roadways which crossed Ireland in the early period (from *c.* AD 450 to 1000). Ó Lochlainn supposes that it would be natural for 'royal seats, such as Ailech, Crúachu, Temhair, Dind Rígh, Caiseal' to have been well supplied with roads (466). He investigates the tradition of the five great roadways radiating from Tara, delineating details of their routes: *An tSlighe Mhór, Slighe Dhála Meic Umhóir, Slighe Assail, Slighe Mhidhlúachra, Slighe Chualann* (470–3).

OO. Excavations

Tara has received the attention of professional and speculative excavators. A group known as the British Israelites came to Tara in 1899 to search for the Ark of the Covenant. In the course of their search they damaged the hill, most notably in the area of the Rath of the Synods. Later professional excavations of the Mound of the Hostages, of Ráith na Ríg and of the Rath of the Synods were carried out by S.P. Ó Ríordáin and R. de Valéra between 1955 and 1959. Though complete reports of these excavations are not available, it is known that the Mound of the Hostages was particularly significant in that it proved to be a Neolithic passage tomb, still containing its primary deposits, into which were inserted Bronze Age burials of various types. Excavation of the Rath of the Synods showed that it was surrounded by rock-cut fosses and by timber palisades. Finds from the site appeared to date from the first three centuries AD. Investigations at Ráith na Ríg uncovered a deep fosse dug into the bedrock and evidence of a palisade built into the inner side of this ditch.

316. Healy, J. 1900 Miscellanea: Tara. *Journal of the Royal Society of Antiquaries of Ireland* **30**, 176.

A note on the 'excavations' at Tara by the British Israelites, in which the author observed the 'two circular trenches cut in the rock, the inner one about 8 feet wide, and the outer one 18 feet wide'. The only finds noted were a collection of fifteen Roman coins, all belonging to the reign of Constantine the Great (possibly a hoax; see nos 323 and 326).

317. Ó Ríordáin, S.P. 1955 A burial with faience beads at Tara. *Proceedings of the Prehistoric Society* **21**, 163–73.

A detailed report on the excavation of the inhumed skeleton of a youth, buried in a flexed position, which was accompanied by a necklace of bronze, amber, jet and faience beads. The burial was among other Bronze Age burials inserted into the Mound of the Hostages.

318. de Paor, M. 1957 Notes on excavations in Eire, England, Northern Ireland, Scotland and Wales, during 1956. Mound of the Hostages, Tara, Co. Meath. *Proceedings of the Prehistoric Society* **23**, 220–1.

A summary report of the excavations carried out in 1955–6. The excavations concentrated on the clay layer which covered the Mound of the Hostages and into which some forty Bronze Age burials were inserted. All except one (see Ó Ríordáin, no. 317) were cremated. The site produced a remarkable richness of finds, including urns, food vessels, a stone battle-axe and a bronze dagger. The excavations also revealed the passage tomb which lay underneath the cairn and its clay layer.

319. Barley, M.W. and Lucas, A.T. 1958 *Council for Old World Archaeology (COWA) surveys and bibliographies*. British Isles, Area 1, No. I. Cambridge, Mass.

TARA: 10. A summary report of the excavation of the Mound of the Hostages carried out in 1955–6. See no. 318.

320. Barley, M.W. and Lucas, A.T. 1960 *Council for Old World Archaeology (COWA) surveys and bibliographies*. British Isles, Area 1, No. II. Cambridge, Mass.

TARA: 11. A summary report of the excavation of the Mound of the Hostages carried out in 1959. See no. 321.

321. Longworth, I. 1960 Notes on excavations, 1959 (Eire): Mound of the Hostages, Tara, Co. Meath [based on information provided by M.J. O'Kelly]. *Proceedings of the Prehistoric Society* **26**, 341–2.

A summary report of the completion of Ó Ríordáin's excavations by R. de Valéra in 1959. This involved the removal of the cairn and excavation of the passage tomb and of the pre-cairn deposits. The investigation revealed that Bronze Age 'food-vessel people' had entered the earlier tomb and had disturbed the primary deposits. The finds from the Mound of the Hostages at the time were regarded as the largest and most comprehensive collection so far available from an Irish cemetery of this type.

322. de Valéra, R. 1961 Excavation of the Mound of the Hostages. Supplementary note to 1961 edition of S.P. Ó Ríordáin, *Tara: the monuments on the hill*.

A summary report of the excavation of the Mound of the Hostages which was completed by de Valéra in 1959.

323. Dolley, M. 1968 Two numismatic notes: II. The mythical Roman coin-hoard from Tara. *Journal of the Royal Society of Antiquaries of Ireland* **98**, 62–5.

A note based on evidence given by one Wing-Commander Fowler, brought up in the vicinity of Tara, that the Roman coins found by the British Israelites were a hoax, apparently planted there in 1899 by the landowner who had given permission for the investigations to be carried out. The hoard had been accepted as genuine by S.P. Ó Ríordáin, 'Roman material in Ireland', *Proceedings of the Royal Irish Academy* **51**C (1947), 80.

324. Harbison, P. 1968–9 Catalogue of Irish Early Bronze Age associated finds containing copper or bronze. *Proceedings of the Royal Irish Academy* **67**C, 35–91.

TARA: 56. Ó Ríordáin's excavation of the Mound of the Hostages brought to light finds from a secondary burial dating to the Early or Middle Bronze Age (see no. 317). Items included a small dagger, bronze tubular beads, a possible awl, faience beads, amber beads and a jet bead.

325. Harbison, P. 1969 *The daggers and the halberds of the Early Bronze Age in Ireland*. Prähistorische Bronzefunde 6 (1). Munich.

TARA: 17 (nos 101, 101a). Two daggers from two separate burials. One (101) is from a secondary unburnt burial in the passage grave associated with beads of bronze, faience and jet (see Ó Ríordáin, no. 317), the other (101a) from a cremation burial with a battle-axe and a cordoned urn and food vessel found during the excavation of the Mound of the Hostages (see also no. 324).

326. Bateson, J.D. 1973 Roman material from Ireland: a re-consideration. *Proceedings of the Royal Irish Academy* **73**C, 21–97.

An assessment of Roman material found in Ireland: locations, dates, hoaxes, etc.

TARA: 59–60 (no. 73), the hoard of Roman coins reputed to be a hoax; and 71–2 (no. 21) from the excavations at the Rath of the Synods, a series of objects including sherds of Samian pottery, a lead sealing from a sealing box, a barrel padlock and fragments of glass said to be Roman.

327. Kavanagh, R.M. 1973 The encrusted urn in Ireland. *Proceedings of the Royal Irish Academy* **73**C, 507–617.

A catalogue and discussion of the vessels known as encrusted urns associated with Bronze Age burials.

TARA: 555–8 (nos 57–62); 600–2 (illustrations). Detailed descriptions of encrusted urns found with the Bronze Age burials which were inserted into the Mound of the Hostages.

328. Herity, M. 1974 *Irish passage graves. Neolithic tomb-builders in Ireland and Britain 2500 B.C.* Dublin.

A study of the Neolithic passage tombs of Ireland, based on their structure, art, burials and grave-goods.

TARA: 252–3 and *passim* (and figs 33, 96, 143). A summary report of the excavations carried out by Ó Ríordáin and de Valéra at the Mound of the Hostages and of the finds from the excavation. The author comments (41) that, though in structure it was a degenerate tomb, it produced a quantity of burials and finds unequalled in Ireland.

329. Kavanagh, R.M. 1976 Collared and cordoned cinerary urns in Ireland. *Proceedings of the Royal Irish Academy* **76**C, 293–403.

A description and discussion of the vessels known as collared and cordoned urns associated with Bronze Age burials.

TARA: 350–1 (nos 36–8); 388–9 (fig. 14, nos 36–7). Detailed descriptions of collared and cordoned urns found with the Bronze Age burials which were inserted into the Mound of the Hostages.

330. Kavanagh, R.M. 1977 Pygmy cups in Ireland. *Journal of the Royal Society of Antiquaries of Ireland* **107**, 61–95.

A description and discussion of the vessels known as pygmy cups associated with Bronze Age burials.

TARA: 86 (nos 36–7); 70 (illustrations). Detailed descriptions of vessels found with the Bronze Age burials which were inserted into the Mound of the Hostages.

331. Raftery, B. 1983 *A catalogue of Irish Iron Age antiquities*. Marburg.

TARA: Nos 79, 207, 361, 604, 617. The latter was a stone gaming-piece from the excavations at the Rath of the Synods of a type also found at Knowth, Co. Meath, and Freestone Hill, Co. Kilkenny.

332. Eogan, G. 1984 *Excavations at Knowth 1. Smaller passage tombs, Neolithic occupation and Beaker activity*. Dublin.

A detailed report of the excavation of the seventeen smaller passage tombs, the area of Neolithic settlement and the areas of Beaker domestic activity at Knowth.

TARA: 195. As part of the discussion of the smaller passage tombs, a comparison is made with other tombs of similar proportions, including the Mound of the Hostages at Tara. Comparative dating evidence is provided for the Mound of the Hostages, based on I.R. McAulay and W.A. Watts, 'Dublin radiocarbon dates I', *Radiocarbon* **3** (1961), 26–38.

333. ApSimon, A. 1985–6 Chronological contexts for Irish megalithic tombs. *Journal of Irish Archaeology* **3**, 5–15.

A definition of the chronological contexts of megalithic tombs, a subject vital to the study of these monuments.

TARA: 10. A comment on the radiocarbon dates for the passage tomb in the Mound of the Hostages.

334. Dwyer, M. 1987 Tara excavations. *The Lough Gur and District Historical Society Journal* (March 1987), 39–49.

The transcript of a diary kept by one of S.P. Ó Ríordáin's assistants on the excavations from June to August 1952. While scarce on precise archaeological detail, it is noteworthy in its references to accounts of eminent visitors to the site during that season.

335. O'Brien, E. 1990 Iron Age burial practices in Leinster: continuity and change. *Emania: Bulletin of the Navan Research Group* **7**, 37–42.

A discussion of burial practices in Leinster from the Late Bronze Age into the Iron Age, with reference to such practices as inhumation and cremation and such monuments as stone-lined and slab-lined graves.

TARA: 38. An extensive note is provided on the burials found during excavations at the Rath of the Synods, where the rites of crouched inhumation and cremation were used simultaneously. The burials appear to date to the first or second century AD, and seem to reflect the combination of a Romano-British rite (inhumation) and a native rite (cremation).

336. Waddell, J. 1990 *The Bronze Age burials of Ireland.* Galway.

A catalogue of known Irish burials of the Bronze Age.

TARA: 128. A brief entry on secondary burials inserted into the Mound of the Hostages.

337. Cooney, G. and Grogan, E. 1991 An archaeological solution to the 'Irish' problem? *Emania: Bulletin of the Navan Research Group* **9**, 33–43.

An attempt to elucidate developments during the transitional period from the Late Bronze Age to the Iron Age in Ireland. The authors argue that there is little or no evidence for a population intrusion of any scale but rather for direct continuity, especially in the area of ceremonial and ritual behaviour.

TARA: 38, fig. 8. One of the two published schematic drawings of part of the Iron Age complex at the Rath of the Synods at Tara (see also no. 340).

338. O'Brien, E. 1992 Pagan and Christian burial in Ireland during the first millennium AD: continuity and change. In N. Edwards and A. Lane (eds), *The early church in Wales and the West,* 130–7. Oxford.

A discussion of early Christian burial rites and practices in Ireland, with reference to evidence to earlier rites dating to the Iron Age.

TARA: 131. Reference is made to the existence of two types of practice found in the excavations at the Rath of the Synods, crouched and extended inhumation burial alongside cremation (see no. 335 for conclusion).

339. Ó Ríordáin, B. and Waddell, J. 1993 *The funerary bowls and vases of the Irish Bronze Age*. Galway.

A corpus of burials containing food vessels of the earlier Bronze Age from Ireland.

TARA: 127, no. 570; 273 (illustration). A summary note on a bipartite vase found at the Mound of the Hostages.

340. Cooney G. and Grogan, E. 1994 *Irish prehistory: a social perspective*. Dublin.

A study of Irish prehistory which follows an integrated approach to the archaeological record and which views this record as the result of human action.

TARA: 185–93 (fig. 10:2). The authors suggest a similarity of features between Dún Ailinne, Emain Macha and 'the pre-Rath of the Synods sequence of activity' at Tara. There are some five stages at Tara, possibly beginning around the same time as Dún Ailinne, which 'replicate many of the features of the two other sites' (Emain and Dún Ailinne) (189). The complexes of prehistoric monuments and their varying morphology at Tara and at Crúachain 'suggest a long-term ritualisation of the landscape' (191).

341. Lohan, R. 1994 *Guide to the archives of the Office of Public Works*. Dublin.

A description of the historical development of the Office of Public Works from the nineteenth century based on the Office's own records.

TARA: 110–12; 117 (figs 17–18). A discussion of the issues raised concerning interference with the monuments at Tara at the end of the nineteenth century. The question of landowners' rights and of powers of guardianship vested in the Board of Works was the main matter to be addressed.

See also nos 272 and 288.

PP. Objects

The finds associated with the excavations at Tara and the stray finds from the hill range in date from the Neolithic to the early medieval period. The limited number of finds, combined with knowledge of Tara's monuments, reflects an occasional reuse of the site. Continuous use of the hill, whether for settlement, burial or other purposes, since early prehistoric times has yet to be demonstrated. With regard to the object most closely associated with Tara in the popular mind, the 'Tara Brooch', it has been proven that it was found on the seashore at Bettystown, Co. Meath.

342. Petrie, G. 1841 On two gold torcs found at Tara. *Proceedings of the Royal Irish Academy* **1**, 274–6.

A note on the gold torcs found close to the church at Tara.

343. Wilde, W.R. 1861 *A descriptive catalogue of the antiquities of animal materials and bronze in the museum of the Royal Irish Academy*. Dublin.

TARA: 605. A bronze horsebit of Iron Age type (fig. 505), found with a pendant (fig. 516) 'and another bridle-bit on an ancient battle-field in the valley between the hills of Tara and Skreen, Co. Meath'. (See also Wilde, *A descriptive catalogue of the antiquities of gold in the museum of the Royal Irish Academy* (Dublin, 1862). TARA: 71–2. Illustrations and descriptions of the Tara torcs.)

344. More, A.G. 1870–9 On an ancient bronze implement, found near the Hill of Tara. *Proceedings of the Royal Irish Academy* **15**, 25–6.

   A description of an artefact of uncertain function found *c*. 1871 'close to the well-known Hill of Tara'. This object is identified by Raftery (*A catalogue of Irish Iron Age antiquities*, 133, no. 361) as a bronze tanged spearbutt. (See no. 331.)

345. Ball, V. and Stokes, M. 1892 On a block of red enamel said to have been found at Tara Hill with observations on the use of red enamel. *Transactions of the Royal Irish Academy* **30**, 277–94.

   A note on the discovery of a block of red enamel, reputedly found at Ráith Chaelchon at Tara. (A disputed provenance; also said to have come from near Kilmessan. See Raftery, *A catalogue of Irish Iron Age antiquities*, 225, no. 604, and Youngs, *'The Work of Angels'*, 201, no. 196.)

346. Armstrong, E.C.R. 1911 Note on the block of red enamel from Tara. *Journal of the Royal Society of Antiquaries of Ireland* **41**, 61–2.

   A note on the use and fabric of the block of red enamel reputedly found at Tara (see no. 345), which it is concluded was not intended to be re-fused, but was prepared to be cut into plaques or studs and attached, not fused, to objects.

347. Eogan, G. 1965 *Catalogue of Irish bronze swords*. Dublin.

   TARA: Nos 230, 494, 623; figs 34, 65, 83. Bronze Age swords reputedly found at or near Tara. With regard to no. 623, it is noted that 'it is unlikely that it is a genuine prehistoric antiquity'.

348. Eogan, G. 1967 The associated finds of gold bar torcs. *Journal of the Royal Society of Antiquaries of Ireland* **97**, 129–75.

   TARA: 138 (illustrated, pl. 13). A summary of the detail of the objects commonly known as 'Tara torcs', which form the basis of this discussion.

349. Harbison, P. 1969 *The axes of the Early Bronze Age in Ireland*. Prähistorische Bronzefunde 9 (1). Munich.

TARA: 48, no. 1353. An axehead of Ballyvalley type, a single find, now in the British Museum.

350. Eogan, G. 1972 'Sleeve-fasteners' of the Late Bronze Age. In F. Lynch and C. Burgess (eds), *Prehistoric man in Wales and the west. Essays in honour of Lily F. Chitty*, 189–209. Bath.

TARA: Nos 23–4. Two gold ornaments, known as 'sleeve-fasteners', possibly found near Tara.

351. Pryor, F. 1980 *A catalogue of British and Irish prehistoric bronzes in the Royal Ontario Museum*. Toronto.

TARA: Nos 183–4. Two decorated long bronze pins reputed to have come from Tara, but which find no ready parallels in Ireland. The author notes that this provenance seems suspect as Tara 'was often used to lend spurious authenticity to objects held by dealers which may not even have originated in Ireland'.

352. Burgess, C.B. and Gerloff, S. 1981 *The dirks and rapiers of Great Britain and Ireland*. Prähistorische Bronzefunde 4 (7). Munich.

TARA: 37, no. 266. A fragment of a bronze rapier now in the National Museum of Ireland.

353. Eogan, G. 1983 *The hoards of the Irish Later Bronze Age*. Dublin.

TARA: Nos 21, 22, 115 (figs 13, 15:A, 61:C). The three hoards from Tara, which consisted of two (possibly three) gold torcs (see nos 342–3 and no. 354), two gold earrings and two gold sleeve-fasteners (see no. 350) respectively.

354. Ryan, M. (ed.) 1983 *Treasures of Ireland. Irish art 3000 B.C.–1500 A.D.* Dublin.

TARA: 81–2, no. 9, a description of the two gold torcs from Tara (illustrated).

355. Raftery, B. 1984 *La Tène in Ireland. Problems of origin and chronology*. Marburg.

A commentary to accompany Raftery's *A catalogue of Irish Iron Age antiquities* (see no. 331).

TARA: Fig. 24 (no. 22, decorated horsebit, Tara–Skreen); fig. 34 (no. 12, decorated Irish pendant prong-terminal; also illustrated in pl. 17, no. 1); fig. 35 (no. 4, decorated Irish pendant stem-terminal).

356. Moore, M. 1984 Irish cresset-stones. *Journal of the Royal Society of Antiquaries of Ireland* **114**, 98–116.

TARA: 111, no. 5. A cresset-stone (stone lamp), dating from the eleventh or twelfth century AD, which is kept in the museum of the Louth Archaeological Society. It is listed in the antiquities of a certain Mr Redmond McGrath, with the comment 'found in the side of a well on the western slope of the [Tara] hill' (*County Louth Archaeological Journal* **1** (4) (1907), 105).

357. Youngs, S. (ed.) 1989 *'The Work of Angels': masterpieces of Celtic metalwork, 6th–9th centuries AD*. London.

    TARA: 97–8, no. 77. A ninth-century annular brooch, said to have been found at Tara (and not to be confused with the 'Tara Brooch').

The 'Tara Brooch'

358. Wheeler, H.A. 1949 The Tara Brooch: where was it found? *Journal of the County Louth Archaeological Society* **12** (1), 155–8.

    A note on the versions of the account that the Tara Brooch was found at Bettystown, Co. Meath.

359. Whitfield, N. 1974 The finding of the Tara Brooch. *Journal of the Royal Society of Antiquaries of Ireland* **104**, 120–42.

    A detailed examination of the background to the finding of the Tara Brooch, which was found at Bettystown, Co. Meath, and given the title 'Tara Brooch' by a firm of jewellers in the nineteenth century.

360. Whitfield, N. 1976 The original appearance of the Tara Brooch. *Journal of the Royal Society of Antiquaries of Ireland* **106**, 5–30.

    An examination of the condition of the Tara Brooch on the basis of nineteenth-century models and photographs.

QQ. The hinterland of Tara

Tara is located in Mag mBreg, the plain of Brega, from which is derived the extent of the kingdom of Brega, dominated in the early historic period by the Síl nÁedo Sláine, a branch of the southern Uí Néill. The literature links a number of places in its hinterland with the activities of the kings of Tara. Most notable among them are Tailtiu (Teltown, Co. Meath), where the king of Tara held *Óenach Tailten*, Cermna (?Carnes, Co. Meath), where the kings of Tara are reputed to have been buried, and Achall (Skreen, Co. Meath), the hill which faces Tara directly to the east.

Brega and Mide

361. Thunder, J.M. 1887–8 The kingdom of Meath. *Journal of the Royal Society of Antiquaries of Ireland* **18**, 507–25.

A useful, though uncritical, note on the extent of the kingdom of Mide.

362. O'Brien, M.A. 1932 Varia IV: 12. *Banba*. *Ériu* **11**, 167–8.

An important note on the origin of the name *Banba*. The author suggests that Banba was originally coterminous with north Leinster (i.e. Mag mBreg) and was derived from an early Welsh name for this, **Bann-fa*, **Banno-magos*. He quotes a poem by Cúán úa Lothcháin (d. 1024) which refers to Tara *Deis fri Banba, bél fri Bóin* ('with her right hand to Banba and her face to the Boyne'), indicating that even as late as the eleventh century Banba must mean the territory to the east, between Tara and the sea. (For a continuation of the discussion see E.P. Hamp, 'Varia I: 4. Banba again', *Ériu* **24** (1973), 169–71.)

363. Morris, H. 1937 Ancient Cualu: where was it? *Journal of the Royal Society of Antiquaries of Ireland* **67**, 280–3.

An uncritical analysis of references to the territory of Cúalu (south County Dublin) which contains some useful information.

TARA: 281–3. The author refers to the Luigne, Tara and Cúalu. While it may be somewhat uncritical in its analysis, it does provide some information as to who may have occupied the territories around Tara.

364. Walsh, P. 1940 Meath in the Book of Rights. In J. Ryan (ed.), *Féilsgríbhinn Eoin mhic Néill*, 508–21. Dublin.

A detailed description of the sub-kingdoms of Mide and Brega based on the *Lebor na Cert*, the Book of Rights. The details of each kingdom provided by the author form a necessary reference point for any study of the area.

365. Brady, J. 1956 The kingdom and county of Meath. *Ríocht na Midhe* **1** (2), 6–13.

A comprehensive guide to the history of County Meath. The earlier period, though treated knowledgeably, reflects the views of early twentieth-century scholars. It nevertheless incorporates useful references to Tara.

366. Brady, J. 1958 Early Christian Meath. *Ríocht na Midhe* **1** (4), 5–13.

A useful, though uncritical, description of the early ecclesiastical associations of Meath (Mide). It places a heavy reliance on Patrician documents.

367. Moran, W. 1958 The hereditary lands and royal *túath* of the O'Melaghlins. *Ríocht na Midhe* **1** (4), 33–44.

A survey of the tribes and kingdoms of Mide and Brega. Useful for the detail of the extent of lands held by various tribes, though it relies heavily on Paul Walsh's work. Largely uncritical.

368. Cuffe, P. 1964 History of Duleek. *Ríocht na Midhe* **3** (2), 140–51.

An uncritical introduction to the history of Duleek, relating its early history chronologically, in traditional manner. Divided into four sections: (1) Tara, AD 227–600; (2) Bregia, AD 600–800; (3) Meath, AD 800–1000; (4) Chaos, AD 1000–1169.

369. Ó Concheanainn, T. 1971 Topographical notes — I. Cermna in Meath. *Ériu* **22**, 87–96.

A study of the location and symbolic significance of the place-name *Cermna*, an unidentified territory often mentioned in association with Tara and confused with *Cerna* (?Carnes, Co. Meath). The author discusses the confusion between the two names *Cermna* and *Cerna*, as well as the link with another unidentified place-name, *Cera*, located in or near *Cermna*. In relation to the association between *Cermna* and the kingship of Tara, he argues that by poetic extension *Cermna* was associated with Tara and its king with *Mag mBreg* and Mide, and by further extension with all of Ireland.

370. Ó Corráin, D. 1971 Topographical notes — II. Mag Femin, Femen, and some early annals. *Ériu* **22**, 97–9.

A study of the location of *Femen* in which the author argues that early annalistic entries regarding *Femen* locate it in Brega and not in Munster. He maintains that *Femen* must have been an important centre of Uí Néill activity at an early period, as indeed was the whole area of Brega, and that the annalistic entries in question refer, insofar as they are historical, not to any events in Munster history but to the penetration of the Uí Néill into Brega.

See also no. 264.

Tailtiu

371. Conwell, E.A. 1870–9 On the identification of the ancient cemetery at Loughcrew, Co. of Meath; and the discovery of the tomb of Ollamh Fodhla. *Proceedings of the Royal Irish Academy* **15**, 72–106.

A lengthy and largely uncritical description of Loughcrew and Tailtiu, incorporating the argument that the 'tomb of Ollamh Fodhla' was located at Tailtiu. It includes an interesting plan of Tailtiu (84). See also same volume, 114–28, for continuation of argument as to the equation of Tailtiu with Loughcrew in S. Ferguson, 'On ancient cemeteries at Rathcroghan and elsewhere in Ireland (as affecting the question of the site of the cemetery at Taltin)'.

372. Morris, H. 1930 Where was Aonach Tailtean? *Journal of the Royal Society of Antiquaries of Ireland* **60**, 113–29.

An attempt to identify the location of *Óenach Tailten* by matching documentary evidence with monuments. It is rather uncritical and the analysis is unreliable. The author seems to conclude that the original site of the *óenach* was at Sliabh na Caillighe (Loughcrew Hills), not at Teltown, Co. Meath, but that it may have been transferred to Teltown at a later period.

373. Thurneysen, R. 1936 Allerlei Keltisches: 2. Tailtiu. *Zeitschrift für celtische Philologie* **20**, 368–9.

A note on the etymology of the name *Tailtiu*, which, the author argues, is cognate with the Welsh *telediw* 'beautiful, remarkable'. He also points to the female connections with the place-name, as in *Tailtiu ingen Magmóir*, an attribute common to many important sites.

See also no. 215.

Skreen

374. Hickey, E. 1952 St Mary's Abbey and the church at Skryne. *Journal of the Royal Society of Antiquaries of Ireland* **82**, 145–50.

A discussion on the founding of the Anglo-Norman church and settlement at Skreen under the patronage of Adam de Feypo. The granting of the church to St Mary's Abbey, Dublin, and the long-running opposition by the occupants of the old church of St Columba at Skreen to the new settlers is also described.

375. Otway-Ruthven, A.J. 1964 Parochial development in the rural deanery of Skreen. *Journal of the Royal Society of Antiquaries of Ireland* **94**, 111–22.

Details of the development from *c.* 1200 of parishes in the deanery of Skreen and their secular and ecclesiastical associations.

TARA: 122. Tara was held by the Hospitallers by 1233, and it is likely that its parochial organisation was established before the end of the twelfth century. The lords of Tara were the de Repenteni family, who are most prominent in County Louth.

376. Hickey, E. 1994 *Skryne and the early Normans*. Dublin.

A survey of early Anglo-Norman settlement in the parish of Skreen and surrounding areas.

TARA: 68. The author refers to the Irish Pipe Roll of King John 1211–12 (see no. 74) and suggests that the de Feypo claim to Tara and Trevet was an extension of his lands, possibly reflecting earlier pre-Norman divisions of land. A translation of the Charter of Ralph de Repenteni granting revenue from Tara to St Mary's Abbey, Dublin (see no. 75), is also provided (162).

Ocha

377. Morris, H. 1926 The battle of Ocha and the burial place of Niall of the Nine Hostages. *Journal of the Royal Society of Antiquaries of Ireland* **56**, 29–42.

An attempt to identify Ocha, the reputed burial-place of Níall Noígíallach, as Faughan Hill, Co. Meath, based mainly on an uncritical analysis of documentary evidence.

378. Walsh, P. 1916 Irish *Ocha, Ochann*. *Ériu* **8**, 75–7.

> The author identifies the place-name *Ocha, Ochann* as Faughan Hill, Co. Meath. Faughan Hill is in the parish of Martry, south of the River Blackwater, close to Teltown (Tailtiu).

Odba

379. Morris, H. 1939 Some places in the metrical *Dindsenchus*. *Journal of the Royal Society of Antiquaries of Ireland* **69**, 179–89.

> A note on various place-names referred to in the metrical *dindshenchas*. Note especially 186–9 (IV) Odba, which Morris identifies with Mullahow, east of Garristown.

380. Ó Murchadha, D. 1992–3 Odhbha and Navan. *Ríocht na Midhe* **8** (4), 112–23.

> A detailed note on the origin of the name Navan, Co. Meath, which it is suggested was originally a prehistoric burial mound called Odhbha. In the medieval period it was used as a fortified residence by the Uí Néill kings of the region and by the Vikings. The Normans transformed it into a motte-and-bailey fortification in 1176. It finally became Navan as a result of the name used for a twelfth-century monastery built near the mound (*Novan* derived from ★(*'n*)*Odhbha*(*n*)).

Belach Dúin

381. O'Connell, P. 1957 Castle Kieran. *Ríocht na Midhe* **1** (3), 17–33.

> A note on the ecclesiastical site known as Castle Kieran, three miles west of Kells (the earlier name for Castle Kieran seems to have been *Belach Dúin*), a foundation associated with Ciarán of Clonmacnoise. It is the location of the ogham stone which the author reads as COVAGNI MAGI MUCOI LUGUNI. (See nos 258–9.)

Tethba

382. Walsh, P. 1940–2 Tethbae. *Ériu* **13**, 88–94.

> A discussion on the extent of the two territories known as Tethba(e) and of the Uí Néill families who held power in the area. It includes an edition of a text describing the dispersal of the sons of Níall Noígíallach, *Fodlais dano Niall Noigiallach a chrich mbunaid eter a chlaind* ('Níall Noígíallach divided his ancestral land among his sons') (see no. 22).
>
> TARA: 92. Reference is made to Níall giving the supremacy of Tara to his son Lóegaire (*Dobert imorro follomnas Temrach do Laegaire*).

Uisnech

383. Moran, W. 1959 Uisneagh, Tara and the rise of monarchy. *Ríocht na Midhe* **2** (1), 3–17.

    An uncritical 'history' of Uisnech and Tara based on old-fashioned conclusions extracted from *Táin Bó Cuailnge* and Keating's *Foras Feasa ar Éirinn*. The author concludes that Tara was founded by Túathal Techtmar (and Uisnech similarly, citing Macalister's excavation as corroborating his theories); having been dispossessed of Uisnech he chose Tara, 'the next most sacred hill in the kingdom'. He also discusses Cormac mac Airt's career.

RR. Popular descriptions and local notes

Tara, in the popular mind, continues to be regarded as the seat of the high-kings of Ireland, the mystical residence of gods and goddesses, and the place where Saint Patrick had his greatest triumph over paganism. These views are perpetuated in the many pamphlets on and descriptions of Tara available in popular literature, a selection of which are noted here.

384. Healy, J. 1898 Tara, pagan and Christian. *Irish Ecclesiastical Record* (4th ser.) **3**, 97–117.

    An extensive traditional description of Tara, physical and historical, given as part of a lecture to clerical students in Maynooth, educating them in their heritage.

385. Dawson, A. 1901 *The Hill of Tara. A personal visit*. Dublin.

    A description of Tara as found on a visit in the summer of 1887. Of note is the author's reference (9) to what seems to have been the destruction of Duma na mBó some years prior to his visit.

386. Patterson, A.W. 1908–9 Tara restored. *Journal of the Ivernian Society* **1**, 21–30.

    A revivalist paper advocating the rebuilding of Tara as a national centre for music and art.

387. Elderkin, G.W. 1945 *Tara and Scythia*. Massachusetts.

    An unusual comparative study of Greek monuments and rituals and similar patterns thought by the author to be in Ireland. He is somewhat unfamiliar with Irish material. Similar sentiments are expressed by the author in 1961 (*Related religious ideas: Delphi, Tara and Jerusalem*).

388. Callary, R.R. 1955 *The Hill of Tara*. Dublin.

    A popular pamphlet based on the popular understanding of the 'history' of Tara and its monuments.

389. Hickey, E. 1955 *The legend of Tara*. Dundalk.

A publication incorporating all popular and traditional material concerning Tara. The tone of publication is set by the author at the beginning when she states: 'This book is not written for the scholar. If you are a scholar, shut it up at once. It is written to tell the ordinary person something of Tara and the people who lived there.'

390. Callary, R.R. 1957 Tara: the European background. *Ríocht na Midhe* **1** (3), 4–16.

A largely uncritical attempt to provide an archaeological and historical context for Tara in a European archaeological framework. The author's most perceptive comments are his questions: 'When and by whom was it [Tara] occupied? What were its culture, religion and social organization?' (4).

391. McGurl, M.K. 1958 The proposed museum at Tara. *Ríocht na Midhe* **1** (4), 61–5.

Comments on a proposal to locate a museum at Tara. It includes references to a dispute between Bord Fáilte Éireann and the Meath Archaeological Society on the matter.

SS. Tara in Ireland and Scotland

The name *Temair*, the original meaning of which remains obscure, is found as a place-name element in other locations in Ireland and Scotland. Various suggestions for its original meaning include 'a high place', 'a dark place' (hence 'an entrance to the Otherworld'), and 'a sacred space'. Of the other place-names containing the element *Temair*, *Temair Érann* or *Temair Lúachra* gain most notice in the early literature.

392. Bhreathnach, E. 1993 List of topographical details extracted from E. Hogan's *Onomasticon Goedelicum*. *Discovery Programme Reports* **1**, 103(d). Dublin.

A list of the places in Ireland containing the element *Temair*.

Temair Érann / Temair Lúachra

393. Westropp, T.J. 1918 Temair Erann, an ancient cemetery of the Ernai on Slievereagh, County Limerick. *Journal of the Royal Society of Antiquaries of Ireland* **48**, 111–20.

An attempt to identify *Temair Érann* and *Cenn Febrat* with the Ballyhoura Hills.

394. Westropp, T.J. 1921–4 The 'Mound of the Fiana' at Cromwell Hill, Co. Limerick, and a note on Temair Luachra. *Proceedings of the Royal Irish Academy* **36**C, 68–85.

A note on the extent and location of the monuments of places identified as *Temair Lúachra* and *Temair Érann*.

395. Doyle, J.J. 1927 Teamhair Luachra (Tara-Luachra). *Journal of the Royal Society of*

Antiquaries of Ireland **57**, 59–63.

A note identifying *Temair Lúachra* with Taur near Kingwilliamstown, Co. Cork.

396. O'Shaughnessy, D.F. and Carroll, P. 1931 Tara Luachra. *Journal of the Cork Historical and Archaeological Society* **36**, 69–75.

The authors argue that *Temair Lúachra* is to be identified with Mortellestown, Kilfinane, Co. Limerick.

The name Tara elsewhere in Ireland

397. Ó Ceallaigh, S. 1950 Old lights on place-names: new lights on maps. *Journal of the Royal Society of Antiquaries of Ireland* **80**, 172–86.

A study of place-names and their origins and various forms.

TARA: 179–80. A long table-top mountain in the Glens of Antrim is called 'The Three Taghmores', which local people explained as the three Teamhairs.

398. Walsh, P. 1955 Ancient Westmeath. *Ríocht na Midhe* **1** (1), 20–31.

A detailed description of the territorial and tribal divisions of what is now County Westmeath. It contains useful references to many tribal names. The place-name *Temair Singite* is identified as Turin, Co. Westmeath (28).

Scotland

399. Watson, W.J. 1904–5 Notes: Tara. *The Celtic Review* **1**, 286.

This is a topographical note in which the author attempts to corroborate the theory that *teamhair* means 'a place of prospect', commanding a wide view, by drawing attention to a Scottish place-name incorporating the name Tara. In Glencasley in Sutherland there is Dail Teamhair, a level plain by a river, of which the characteristic feature is a number of truncated conical mounds or hillocks. The author regards these hillocks as corresponding to the description 'a place of prospect' and that the meaning 'the Dale of Taras' seems appropriate.

400. Watson, W.J. 1926 *The history of the Celtic place-names of Scotland*. Edinburgh.

A study of the origins of the place-names of Scotland.

TARA: 505. The author includes references to Dail Teamhair and Poll Teamhair in Glencasley in Sutherland and to Druim Teamhra, north of Loch Gorm in Islay.

TT. The characteristics of royal sites and assemblies

Tara, in its manifestation as what is known as a 'royal site' in archaeological terminology, is often compared with the other 'royal sites' of Ireland — Emain, Dún Ailinne and Crúachain. Attempts to find common attributes between these sites are hampered by lack of information about their genuine comparability, chronologically and structurally. For detailed discussions and bibliographies relating to other royal sites in Ireland see *Emania: Bulletin of the Navan Research Group* **1–** (1986–).

401. Ettlinger, E. 1953–4 The association of burials with popular assemblies, fairs and races in ancient Ireland. *Études Celtiques* **6**, 30–61.

    A summary of all places associated with assemblies and the characteristics of such sites.

    TARA: 40–2; Tailtiu: 42–3; Tlachtga: 43–4; Emain: 44–5; Crúachain: 45.

402. Ó Riain, P. 1972 Boundary association in early Irish society. *Studia Celtica* **7**, 12–29.

    A discussion of evidence for the location of ecclesiastical sites and secular settlements on boundaries in Ireland, including evidence from Gaulish sources.

    TARA: 22. The author notes that four of the principal royal dwellings of Ireland, namely Ailech, Tara, Dún Ailinne and Cashel, 'served as territorial demarcation points, as did a host of other royal dwellings'.

403. Wailes, B. 1982 The Irish 'royal sites' in history and archaeology. *Cambridge Medieval Celtic Studies* **3**, 1–29.

    An attempt to address the evidence available (mainly archaeological) for the function and dating of Emain, Tara, Crúachain, Dún Ailinne and Uisnech. An important work in that it is one of the few articles to take a fresh, critical view of the relationship between historical and archaeological evidence.

404. Warner, R.B. 1988 The archaeology of early historic Irish kingship. In S.T. Driscoll and M.R. Nieke (eds), *Power and politics in early medieval Britain and Ireland*, 47–68. Edinburgh.

    An attempt to identify characteristics of royal sites in Ireland and to find compatible historical documentation. The author makes particular reference to the site of Clogher, Co. Tyrone.

405. Aitchison, N.B. 1994 *Armagh and the royal centres in early medieval Ireland. Monuments, cosmology and the past.* Suffolk.

    A detailed study, based on a particular perspective of the archaeological evidence and the source material, in which the author attempts to explain the 'mytho-historical' associations of the royal centres, and most especially Navan Fort, Co. Armagh (Emain Macha). Its central theme is the manner in which earlier, often prehistoric, archaeological sites in the Irish landscape were perceived during the early medieval period and invested with ideological meaning and value within both secular and ecclesiastical contexts.

INDEXES TO THE BIBLIOGRAPHY

(References are to entry numbers)

INDEX OF AUTHORS

Ahlqvist, A., 266
Aitchison, N.B., 405
Anderson, A.O., 15
ApSimon, A., 333
Armstrong, E.C.R., 346
Ball, V., 345
Bannerman, J., 214
Barley, M.W., 319–20
Bateson, J.D., 326
Baudiš, J., 190
Bergin, O., 32, 66, 129, 131, 181
Best, R.I., 16, 32, 66, 103, 129, 134
Bhreathnach, E., 69, 392
Bhreathnach, M., 161, 203
Bieler, L., 38, 39, 210
Binchy, D.A., 26, 36–7, 47–9, 51, 61, 166, 220, 228–9, 236, 240, 248
Borgeaud, W.A., 196
Brady, J., 365, 366
Breatnach, L., 36, 40, 244
Brooks, E. St John, 78–9
Burgess, C.B., 352
Butler, H., 276
Byrne, F.J., 16, 18, 223, 230–1, 233–5, 237–8, 264
Callary, R.R., 388, 390
Carey, J., 51, 101–2, 115, 121
Carney, J. (alias Ó Ceithearnaigh, S.), 24, 46, 137–8, 176, 187, 220, 247
Carroll, P., 396
Caulfield, S., 278
Chadwick, N.K., 239
Charles-Edwards, T.M., 34–5, 103
Cochrane, R., 258
Collis, J., 309
Condit, T., 312
Conwell, E.A., 294, 371
Cooke, J., 267
Cooney, G., 337, 340
Cuffe, P., 368
Cunningham, B., 249
Curtis, E., 76
Davies, O., 74
Dawson, A., 385
de Paor, L., 50, 55
de Paor, M., 318
de Pontfarcy, Y., 213
de Valéra, R., 322
Dillon, M., 90, 99, 107, 120–1, 141, 187, 209, 220, 239, 255–6
Dobbs, M.E. (alias Ní Con Dobs, M.), 19, 22, 105, 124, 132, 145, 161, 314
Doherty, C., 54, 212
Dolley, M., 323
Doyle, J.J., 395
Duignan, M.V., 273

Turim Tigi Temrach, 32–3
Uraicecht Becc, 228
Vita Columbae, *see* Adomnán
Vita Tripartita, 42–4

INDEX OF PROPER NAMES

Adomnán, author of the *Vita Columbae*, abbot of Iona (d. 704), 57, 240–1, 250, 252
Áed Eangach, fictitious king referred to in *Baile in Scáil*, 14, 179
Áed Sláine mac Diarmata, king of Brega (d. 604), 106
Ailill Molt, reputed king of Tara (d. 483), 43, 120
Ailill Ólomm, king of Dergthene, 142
Alexander III, king of Scotland (d. 1286), 214
Aodh Ó Conchobhair, grandson of Ruaidrí úa Conchobair (d. 1309), 180
Art mac Cuind, father of Cormac mac Airt, 134–5, 139, 143, 151
Bec mac Dé, prophet, 83
Berchán, a sixth-century prophet/saint, 15
Bodbchath, king of the Luigne, 57
Bressal mac Diarmata, 160
Brían Bóruma, king of Cashel and *imperator Scottorum* (d. 1014), 13, 240
Bríon, Níall Noígíallach's brother and ancestor of the Uí Chonchobair, 154–6
Búan mac Lóegaire Birn, ancestor of the Osraige, 20
Caílte mac Liatháin Cherddae, ancestor of the Caíltrige, 19
Caílte (mac Rónáin), hero of the Fíanna, 168, 170
Cairpre Liphechair, son of Cormac mac Airt, 28, 143–4, 217
Cairpre Nia Fer, mythical king of Tara, 122
Cano mac Gartnáin, king of Alba, 166
Cathaír Mór, eponymous ancestor of the Leinstermen, 18, 25, 143, 169, 204
Cathal Croibhdhearg Ó Conchobhair, king of Connacht (d. 1224), 155
Cathal mac Finguine, king of Munster (d. 742), 228
Ciarán mac int saír, founder of the monastery of Clonmacnoise (d. 548), 63
Cináed úa hArtacáin, poet (d. 974), 98, 172, 174, 269
Colmán mac Luacháin, founder of the monastery of Lynn, Co. Westmeath, 62, 209, 213
Columba, founder of the monastery of Iona (d. 597), 73, 82, 253
Colum Cille, *see* Columba
Conaire Mór mac Étarscéla, heroic king of Tara, 113, 125–7, 129, 190, 199, 203, 209
Conall Corc, ancestor of the Eóganachta, 21
Conall Grant, king of southern Brega, 57
Conchobar mac Nessa, heroic king of Ulster, 116, 124
Congal Cáech, king of the Ulaid (Cruithne) and reputed king of Tara (d. 637), 35, 164
Congalach Cnogba mac Maíle Mithig, king of Tara (d. 956), 15
Conn Cétchathach, grandfather of Cormac mac Airt and ancestor of the Uí Néill, 10–11, 18, 107, 130–3, 169–70
Corc mac Luigdech, progenitor of Eóganachta, 37
Cormac mac Airt, heroic king of Tara, 20, 89, 106–7, 113, 132, 136–9, 140–50, 152, 170, 184–5, 199, 204, 217, 243, 284, 383
Cormac mac Cuilennáin, king of Cashel (d. 908), 93–4
Crimthann mac Fidaig, fosterfather of Conall Corc, 107, 154–6
Cúán úa Lothcháin, poet (d. 1024), 65, 67, 68, 90, 153, 269, 362
Cuanu, abbot of the monastery of Louth (d. 825), 6
Cú Chulainn, hero of the Ulster Cycle, 119–22, 197
Cú Roí mac Dáiri, 120
de Feypo, Adam, Anglo-Norman landowner of Skreen, 374
de Feypo, Richard, Anglo-Norman landowner of Skreen, 74
de la Corner, Richard, bishop of Meath (1230–50), 75, 77
de Lacy, Walter, lord of Meath (d. 1241), 76
de Repenteni, Peter, Anglo-Norman landowner of Tara, 75–6

de Repenteni, Ralph, Anglo-Norman landowner of Tara, 74–6, 376
Diarmait mac Áedo Sláine, king of Tara (d. 665), 107, 161
Diarmait mac Cerbaill, king of Tara (d. ?565), 7, 49, 58–60, 63, 103, 170, 233, 241, 248, 250
Diarmuid 'na gCaisleán' Ó Briain, king of Thomond (d. 1364), 182
Domnall Bán, king of Scotland (d. 1097), 15
Domnall mac Áedo, king of Tara (d. 642), 107, 161, 163–4
Domnall Midi, king of Tara (d. 763), 6
Domnall úa Lochlainn, king of the northern Uí Néill (d. 1121), 165
Donnchad Midi, king of Tara (d. 797), 6
Donnchad mac Flainn, king of Tara (d. 944), 11
Dúnlang, ancestor of the Leinster dynasty, the Uí Dúnlainge, 144
Eithne Thóebfhota, goddess associated with Tara and Cormac mac Airt, 138, 143, 201
Emer, wife of Cú Chulainn, 119, 197
Énna Aircthech, mythical king of Munster, 175
Eochaid Airem, mythical king of Tara, 129
Eochaid Feidlech, mythological king of Tara and father of Medb, 196
Eochaid Finn Fúath nAirt, ancestor of the Déssi, 151
Eochaid Mugmedón, father of Níall Noígíallach, 106, 153–6
Eochaid úa Céirín, poet, 175
Eochaid úa Flainn, poet (d. 1004), 102
Eochu Gunnat, king of Ulster, 138
Erc, son of Cairpre Nia Fer, 122
Érimón mac Míle Espáine, 70
Ériu, goddess, 193
Etaín, goddess associated with Tara, 129
Feradach Finn Fechtnach, mythical king of Tara, 96
Fergus mac Róich, hero of the Ulster Cycle, 118, 124
Fíacc, founder of Sletty, 41
Fiachnae mac Baetáin, king of the Ulaid (Dál nAraide) (d. 626), 234
Finn, bishop of Kildare (d. 1160), 174
Finn mac Cumaill, legendary leader of the Fíanna, 167, 169
Finn mac Rossa, 120
Fínnachta Fledach, king of Tara (d. 695), 10, 234
Fintan mac Bóchrai, 103
Flann Cinach, prophetic king, 81
Flann Mainistrech, *fer léigind* of Monasterboice, poet and historian (d. 1056), 16, 102
Flann Ó Rónáin, poet, 176
Flannacán mac Cellaich, king of Brega (d. 896), 173
Fócortach, dynast of Brega, 57
Garbán Mide, 57
Geoffrey Keating, author of *Foras Feasa ar Éirinn* (d. 1649), 249
Gofraidh Fionn Ó Dálaigh, bardic poet (d. 1387), 181–2
Gregory IV, Pope, 80
Guaire Aidne, 107, 162
Hakon Hakonarson, king of Norway (d. 1263), 87–9
Henrico de Tauerach, 75
Innocent III, Pope, 77
Irgalach úa Conaing, king of Brega and the Cíannachta, 57
John, son of Diarmait mac Gilla Mocholmóc (1230–50), 75
Lóegaire mac Néill, king of Tara (d. ?461), 8, 22, 37–40, 42, 48, 50–4, 157, 158
Loingsech mac Óenguso, king of Tara (d. 704), 57, 173
Lug, 11–12, 110, 112–14, 195, 215–19, 265, 300
Lugaid Coscrach, ancestor of the Cosgrig Temrach, 19

Lugaid Reóderg, mythical king of Tara, 120–1
Lugaid mac Con, mythical king of Tara, 107, 139–42, 145, 147, 217
Lugaid mac Íthae, 93
Lugna Fer Trí, Cormac mac Airt's foster-?brother and ancestor of the Luigne, 137–8, 148, 184–5
Luigne mac Érimóin, 22
Máel Mithig mac Flannacáin, *flaithrí Temrach* (d. 919), 15
Máel Sechnaill mac Domnaill (Mael Sechnaill II), king of Tara (d. 1022), 11, 176–7
Máel Sechnaill mac Maíle Ruanaid, king of Tara (d. 862), 231, 242
Máine mac Néill, dynast of Brega, 57
Medb, goddess of Tara (Medb Chrúachna and Medb Lethderg), 120, 123, 143, 170, 191–3, 196–7, 201, 208, 236
Míl Espáine, 20, 105
Molendinarius, Jordanus, Anglo-Norman tenant at Skreen and Tara, 75
Molendinarius, Robert, 78
Mór, goddess of sovereignty associated with Munster, 194
Morann, the wise judge, 95–6
Mowere, William, son of Richard of Cardomiston, Tara, 77
Mugain, *see* Mór
Muirchertach mac Congalaig, king of Brega (d. 995), 16
Muirchertach mac Erca, king of Tara (d. 536), 8, 159, 203
Muirchú maccu Machtheni, biographer of Patrick, 39, 52–4
Muiris Óg Fitzmaurice, second earl of Desmond (d. 1358), 181
Murchad mac Flainn, king of Mide (d. 1076), 16
Nath Í, 46
Nemed mac Srobcinn, 126
Nia mac Lugna Fer Trí, 137–8, 148
Níall Glúndub, 10, 15
Níall mac Maíl Shechnaill, king of Ailech (d. 1061), 16
Níall Noígíallach, king of Tara and ancestor of the Uí Néill, 21–2, 38, 46, 107, 153–6, 227, 382
Núadu, king of the Túatha Dé Danann at Tara, 112, 114, 173, 219
Óengus Gaíbúaibthech, ancestor of the Déssi, 150
Ogma, 110
Ollam Fótla, 20
Patrick, Saint, 37–56, 77, 168, 284
Patrick, bishop of Dublin (d. 1084), 84–5
Pipard, Alice, sister of Walter de Lacy, 76
Raghnall, king of Man (d. 1229), 178
Rúadán, founder of the monastery of Lorrha, Co. Tipperary, 58–61, 87, 163, 225
Seaán Ó Dubhagáin, poet (d. 1372), 22
Secundinus, 56
Sín, goddess, 159
Tea, wife of Érimón, from whom derives *múr-tea*, an alias for Temair, 70, 93
Temair ingen Áedo Builc, wife of Diarmait mac Áedo Sláine, 161–2
Tigernach Tétbannach mac Luchtai, 120
Tipraite mac Máil, king of Ulster, 132
Tírechán, author of *Collectanea*, 38, 52, 54
Toicthech mac Cinnfáelad, king of the Luigne, 57
Toirdelbach mac Diarmata, king of Thomond (d. 1167), 15
Toirdelbach úa Conchobair, 155
Tréfuilngid Tré-eochair, 103
Túathal Techtmar, grandfather of Conn Cétchathach, 184–5, 383

INDEX OF PLACE-NAMES AND TRIBAL NAMES

Achall, Skreen, Co. Meath, 65, 78–80, 132, 150, 152, 173, 374–6
Airgíalla, 28, 34, 230, 237, 238
Armagh, 41, 48, 50, 51, 52, 54, 64, 231, 238, 250, 252
Banba, 362
Belach Dúin, *see* Castle Kieran, Co. Meath
Bile Tortan, 211
Bile Dathí, 211
Brega, 44, 264, 361, 364, 367, 370
Bréifne, 263
Brug meic inn Óóc, 122
Cabragh, townland of Tara, 311
Caíltrige, 19
Caisel, 92, 236, 254–6, 402
Cardomiston, Co. Meath, 77
Castle Kieran, Co. Meath, 259, 381
Castletown, townland of Tara, 311
Cenél Conaill, 171
Cenél Fiachach, 22
Cermna, 369
Cernae, 166, 172, 176, 369
Cíannachta, 237, 261
Clann Cholmáin, 225
Cleittech, 122
Clogher, Co. Tyrone, 278, 404
Cloonfree, Co. Roscommon, 180
Cnogba, Knowth, Co. Meath, 12, 122, 176, 264
Cnucha, Castleknock, Co. Dublin, 170
Colp, Co. Meath, 79
Connachta, the descendants of Conn Cétchathach, 142, 184, 257
Corco Daulai, 21
Corco Loígde, 19, 21, 142
Corcu Duibne, 126
Cosgrig Temrach, 19
Crúachain, 64, 92, 123, 138, 198, 225, 401, 403
Dail Teamhair, 399–400
Dál Cais, 13
Dál Cuinn, 6
Dál Matti, 126
Déssi, 19, 150, 152, 161–2
Druim Teamhra, 400
Dublin, 89, 237
Duleek, Co. Meath, 79, 82, 368
Dún na nGéd, 163, 165
Dún Ailinne, 64, 225, 243, 340, 402–3
Dún Lethglassa, 41
Dún mac Nechtain Scéne, 122
Dunshaughlin, Co. Meath, 45, 56
Emain Macha, 41, 52, 64, 119, 181, 198, 306, 313, 340, 401, 403, 405
Eóganachta, 19, 21, 37, 142, 229, 254, 257

169

Ess Rúaid, 171
Faughan Hill, Co. Meath, see Ocha
Femen, 370
Féni, 126
Fir Bolg, 108
Fir Chúl, 136
Fir Domnann, 243
Fomoiri, 110, 113
Forach, 173
Gailenga, 96, 261, 263–4
Glencullen, Co. Dublin, 75
Greccraige, 136
Inbir Domnann, 81
Iona, 250, 252–3
Kells, Co. Meath, 73, 122, 143, 160, 169, 253
Knowth, Co. Meath, see Cnogba
Lagore, Co. Meath, 207, 264
Laigin, 8, 126, 143
Leinster, 18, 24–5, 198, 204, 243
Llanthony, Welsh monasteries of, 79
Loch Ainninn (Lough Ennel), 176
Loch nGabor, see Lagore
Loígis, 83
Luigne, 18, 22, 136, 167, 184, 237, 258–66, 363
Mag mBreg, 122, 369
Mag Femen, 370
Mag Rath, 35, 164
Meic Gilli Martain, see Luigne
Mide, 8, 9, 185, 224, 255, 264, 361, 364, 365–7, 369
Mullahow, Co. Dublin, see Odba
Munster, 21, 36–7, 40, 145, 194, 228
Múscraige, 126
Ocha, 377–8
Odba, 379–80
Odor, 143
Osraige, 20
Painestown, Co. Meath, 258
Poll Teamhair, 399
Riverstown townland, near Tara, 312
St Mary's Abbey, Dublin, 75
Saxons, 26, 81
Scone, Scotland, 214, 296, 298
Sentuatha Temrach, 159
Síl nÁedo Sláine, dynasties of, 172, 225
Skreen, Co. Meath, see Achall
Slane, Co. Meath, 39
Tailtiu, 42, 44, 65, 72, 122, 124, 200, 202, 215, 248, 269, 371–3, 401
Temair Érenn, 393–4
Temair Lúachra, 117, 394–6
Temair Singite, 398
Tethba, 382
Tlachtga, 72, 401
Túatha Dé Danann, 109–10, 113

Uí Chonchobair, 154–6
Uí Failgi, 9
Uí Fhorannáin, 62
Uí Gormáin, 6
Uí Néill, 6–13, 16, 18, 22–3, 28, 34, 44, 47–8, 51–3, 96, 115, 153–6, 165–6, 184, 203, 220, 225, 229–30, 232, 234–40, 242–3, 250, 252–3, 257
Ulaid, 35, 166, 234
Uisnech, 72, 103, 212, 248, 383, 403
Vikings, 115, 176–7, 229, 242, 380

INDEX OF MONUMENTS AT TARA

(See texts listed in entries 65–72 for details of monuments)

Adlaic, 285
Blocc, 125, 304
Bluigne, 125, 304
Carcair na ngiall, see Duma na nGiall, 163
Carn in Áenfhir, an alias for Tara, 72
Carthi (coirthi) na nGiall, see Lia Fáil, 62, 138
Cathair Cronidi, an alias for Tara, 105, 111
Cathair Crobinni, Cathair Chrófhind, Cathair Cróuinn, see Cathair Cronidi
Cláenráith Temrach, see Clóenfherta
Clóenfherta, the Sloping Trenches, 51, 62, 87–8, 136, 142, 144, 146, 147
Cnoc Gabála na nGiall, see Duma na nGiall, 108
Cros Adomnáin, 268, 304
Druim C(h)áin, an alias for Tara, 71–2
Duma na mBó, 385
Duma na nGiall, the Mound of the Hostages, 272, 317–22, 324–5, 327–30, 332–4, 336, 340
Forad, 176, 199, 212, 269, 278, 287, 310
Gríanán in én úaitne, 163
In eachrais Ulad, 163
In long Muman, 163
In long Laigen, 163
In chóisir Connacht, 163
Lecht in Abaicc, 84–6, 168
Lia Fáil, 14, 18, 84–5, 98, 109–10, 125, 168, 174, 178, 195, 210, 245, 267–8, 270, 294–304
Liathdhruim, an alias for Tara, 71
Lighi ind Abaic, 84–6
Múr Tea, 93, 269
Múr n-ollaman, 20
Radhruim Dá Thí, an alias for Tara, 178
Ráith Chaelchon, 345
Ráith Ghráinne, 293
Ráith Lóegaire, 157
Ráith Medba, Rath Maeve, 170, 308
Ráith na Senad, the Rath of the Synods, 272, 282, 290, 326, 331, 335, 337–8, 340
Ráith na Ríg, 108, 269, 272, 309–10
Rath Lugh, 307
Rath Miles, 311
Rétla na filed, 163
Sescend Temrach, 283
Slige Asail, 130, 315
Slige Chualand, 130, 315
Slige Dála, 130, 315
Slige Midlúachra, 130, 313, 315
Slige Mór, 130, 315
Slighe na Sochaide, 124
Slige Tola, see Slige Dála
Tech Benén, 39
Tech Cormaic, 278, 287
Tech Midchúarta, 26–34, 112, 116, 119, 149, 157, 163, 196, 269, 305–6

Teg nAirt, 176
Temair Fáil, 139
Temair in trír, 139
Tulach in Trír, an alias for Tara, 72, 133
Tulach techtairechta na tromslúagh, 108